On the Jericho Road

A MEMOIR OF
RACIAL JUSTICE, SOCIAL ACTION
AND PROPHETIC MINISTRY

J. ALFRED SMITH SR.

WITH HARRY LOUIS WILLIAMS II

IVP

InterVarsity Press
Downers Grove, Illinois

InterVarsity Press
P.O. Box 1400, Downers Grove, IL 60515-1426
World Wide Web: www.ivpress.com
E-mail: mail@ivpress.com

InterVarsity Press® is the book-publishing division of InterVarsity Christian Fellowship/USA®, a student movement active on campus at hundreds of universities, colleges and schools of nursing in the United States of America, and a member movement of the International Fellowship of Evangelical Students. For information about local and regional activities, write Public Relations Dept., InterVarsity Christian Fellowship/USA, 6400 Schroeder Rd., P.O. Box 7895, Madison, WI 53707-7895, or visit the IVCF website at <www.intervarsity.org>.

All Scripture quotations, unless otherwise indicated, are taken from the Holy Bible, New King James Version (NKJV). *Copyright © 1982 by Thomas Nelson, Inc. Used by permission. All rights reserved.*

Every effort has been made to obtain permission for cited material. Any omissions or errors brought to the publisher's attention will gladly be corrected in future editions of the book.

Cover design: Cindy Kiple
Front cover photograph courtesy of John "The Commissioner" Williams; back cover photograph courtesy of Chris Duffey. Internal photographs courtesy of J. Alfred Smith Sr. and Allen Temple Baptist Church.

ISBN 0-8308-3200-9

Printed in the United States of America ∞

Library of Congress Cataloging-in-Publication Data

Smith, J. Alfred (James Alfred)
  On the Jericho road: a memoir of racial justice, social action, and
  prophetic ministry/J. Alfred Smith Sr. with Harry Louis Williams
  II.
    p. cm.
  ISBN 0-8308-3200-9 (cloth: alk. paper)
  1. Smith, J. Alfred (James Alfred) 2. African-American
  clergy—Biography. 3. Baptists—Clergy—United States—Biography.
  I. Williams, Harry Louis. II. Title.
  BX6455.S64A3 2004
  286'.1'092—dc22

                                            2004000394

P	19	18	17	16	15	14	13	12	11	10	9	8	7	6	5	4	3	2	1
Y	19	18	17	16	15	14	13	12	11	10	09	08	07	06	05	04			

CONTENTS

FOREWORD

By United States Congresswoman Barbara Lee

We are living in troubled times—times of discord, not of peace—times when the drums of war beat their discordant rhythms in the night of injustice, when the dove falls prey to the hawk. But in the worst of times, the sun yet casts its rays over the horizon. The devastation of the hurricane is really little more than the opening act for the rainbow. The Reverend Dr. J. Alfred Smith Sr., pastor of the Allen Temple Baptist Church, is the rainbow that arches broad and wide over the mean streets of East Oakland.

I was working closely with the Black Panther Party for Self-Defense as a community worker in Oakland, California, when I first met Pastor Smith in the 1970s. He was deeply involved in the struggle for human rights and social justice, and we respected him for that.

In the early 1980s I returned to Oakland from Washington, D.C., to continue my work with a great statesman, Congressman Ronald V. Dellums. It was around that time that I joined Allen Temple Baptist Church. Here I found a church that was committed to making religion real, to making it alive.

Anyone who is committed to economic and social justice has got to understand Pastor Smith's ministry. His life and ministry are based on the Word of God, and he teaches us how to live according to the Scriptures. Pastor Smith is my counselor and spiritual, pastoral adviser. He is the first person I think of when I have extremely difficult decisions to make. He helps me to weigh the facts and sort through the variables. One hundred percent of his advice has turned out to be correct.

My mind goes back to September 2001, following the attacks on the World Trade Center. My colleagues in the U.S. Congress were weighing the option of sending our nation's troops to war. The rush to judgment troubled my conscience. I called Pastor Smith. He prayed with me. He counseled me.

When I decided to cast the lone dissenting vote as the Congress authorized the Bush administration's use of force—a blank check to wage war—Pastor Smith supported my decision. He and I realized that there would be backlash, hate mail, maybe even threats against my life. But in the end, I followed my moral compass and my conscience, and I knew that I must vote "no." Pastor Smith reassured me that I was doing the right thing.

Looking back, I wonder what advice I might have received if I had turned to someone who didn't know the meaning of struggle in such a tumultuous time. Pastor Smith understands it, though. He ministers in East Oakland, which in some ways reminds me of many parts of Africa and the Caribbean where hunger is widespread, people have no access to health care, there is a lack of educational opportunities and job training, and HIV-AIDS rates are among the highest in the world.

East Oakland has its share of hungry children. A great number of its people have no health care. There is a lack of educational opportunities. The HIV rates in Alameda County, where Oakland is situated, are among the highest in the United States. The fabric of the social net has been ripped, leaving havoc and displacement in its wake.

At first glance, the problems of East Oakland may not seem as horrible as those in Africa and the Caribbean, but set in the midst of the richest, most powerful nation in the history of civilization, the inequities in Oakland between the wealthy and the poor are glaring and pronounced. Thank God for men and women like Dr. J. Alfred Smith Sr. who stand in the gap, fighting shoulder to shoulder for social justice. This is an African American of faith who has never forgotten his roots or his culture. Yet people of various nations and languages around the globe clamor to hear the gospel proclaimed from his lips. I'm excited to see his incredible story come to the printed page.

PROLOGUE

By Harry Louis Williams II

The rise of the African American preacher is one of the truly fascinating episodes in American history. For centuries these men and women of the cloth have preached hope and bestowed dignity on the lost and downtrodden in the name of Jesus Christ. Yet more often than not, their own stories are forgotten.

Most of these heroic figures hailed from the South, a great number came from the North, but only a slender handful were found west of the Mississippi River; let alone Northern California. This territory is hard ground, hardly the birthing place of prophets. Church planters agree that Northern California is one of the most unchurched areas in America. And yet, there is the Reverend Dr. J. Alfred Smith Sr.

One author said of him, "Pastor Smith is a powerful preacher. No guest preacher is apt to have the appeal to the Allen Temple Church congregation that he has. They respect him as a man of deep spirituality and unquestioned integrity. He has identified with them. He has walked the streets with them and shared their burdens. He does not hesitate to address any issue of social concern to his people, and like a faithful prophet he is always searching for a 'word from the Lord.' He demonstrates concern and faith, and he preaches redemption, justice, mercy and love."

The Reverend Al Sharpton made his way to the San Francisco Bay Area on the last leg of his presidential campaign. During his Sunday morning address at the Allen Temple Baptist Church, Sharpton referred to Reverend Smith as the "black pope." "You isn't runnin' for the president of nuthin' until you come to Oakland to kiss his ring," Sharpton shouted.

EARNING RESPECT IN THE MEAN STREETS

To understand Reverend Smith's rise to international stature, you must first

understand the city of Oakland, San Francisco's sister city. There are two Oaklands: one you'll find in the tourist books and the other you won't. The first
Oakland has such notable locations as Lake Merritt, the Oakland Zoo and the
Oakland Museum. *Forbes* magazine has called this Oakland the eighth best
American city to live in. The second Oakland is completely cut off from the
fruits of prosperity. If you come looking for America's eighth best city, you are
not likely to find East Oakland—unless you get lost.

Though not as gritty as many of the older inner cities of the East Coast, parts
of East Oakland look like hell with palm trees. Let me introduce you to it. To
get there, we leave downtown on bus 82. Soon after the bus commences, we
notice a small Vietnamese community, and before too long, we pass signs that
say "Taqueria" and "Carniceria." Here, Spanish chatter collides with hardcore
hip-hop music. As the bus passes 61st Avenue, the people become shades
darker. A huge billboard advertises the release of a new album by an imprisoned rapper who calls himself "Ol' Dirty Bastard."

And then we pass the ever popular Cap It Off night spot, whose sign says
"Mature People—Have Your Event Here." The C. P. Bannon Mortuary sits in
the midst of a gaggle of auto body shops, dry cleaners, taco trucks and storefront churches. Easy access to unregistered pistols in East Oakland has forced
Bannon's skyrocketing business to accommodate customers lower and lower
in age. The Havencourt Middle School has these words painted on its side: "As
Long as the Mind Is Enslaved the Body Will Never Be Free."

DEEP EAST OAKLAND

Finally we arrive at the place that some people refer to as "Deep East Oakland" or the "Shady Eighties." The One Stop Liquor store has above its door
a sign that reads "No Loitering, Drinking, Illicit Drugs, Solicitation—Code
647." The bay area is one of the most culturally diverse places on Earth. Yet
very few white people live on this stretch of real estate. Here self-pro-
claimed "thug niggas" and "ballers" war over the lucrative crack cocaine
trade, blasting each others' skulls open for illicit riches and potential penitentiary visits.

The Allen Temple Baptist Church takes up the space of a city block here
in Deep East Oakland. Freshly manicured daisies sprout from the earth in
front of its complex. A caste-iron cross shooting skyward from the roof of
the sanctuary structure causes us to recall the words of Christ: "Upon this

rock I will build my church and the gates of hell shall not prevail against it" (Matthew 16:18 KJV).

The Allen Temple Food and Clothing Pantry sits across the street from the church property. It's a tan building with a fence wrapped around it that reaches almost to its roof. If that were not enough, it's adorned with barred windows and signs that read "No Trespassing" and "Danger, Keep Out."

Two O.G.s sit on the bus-stop bench across the street reminiscing about the good old days and plotting legal strategies. "I got assault charges on me. I broke this dude's arm." The world is passing them by quicker than a meteor streaking through the night sky. And as they sit, their potential rotting in the California springtime sun, a black thundercloud of blood, pain, displacement and hunger looms on the horizon just beyond their sight. The future has been cast, and gentrification might just reassign them to a freeway underpass or a Central Valley tent city.

Welcome to the home of the "drive-by," where the liquor stores open at dawn and hope shatters in the human breast. The newspapers have nick-named it "Cokeland." The Reverend Dr. J. Alfred Smith Sr. calls this place "Elmhurst," its official name, and he is adamant that others respectfully call it the same.

THE PROPHET OF INTERNATIONAL BOULEVARD

J. Alfred Smith Sr. is the pastor of the Allen Temple Baptist Church, and his name is almost synonymous with East Oakland. If your child is arrested, and you live here, you may try to find him. If your children are hungry, and you have no food, odds are that you will find your way to his church. If you fi-nally get tired of running from God, you'll come to hear him proclaim the Word of God.

When the crack plague first began to shake Oakland, Pastor Smith and his minister of evangelism, Donald Miller, took to the streets of the hood under the cover of darkness. Neighborhood residents, some of whom were very afraid of the menace, reached out for his hand. Someone gave Pastor Smith a bullhorn. His voice thundered in the concrete and mortar canyons. Some of the older residents wept, recognizing his voice from the weekly radio broadcasts. The pastor is a symbol of hope here in these killing fields. Many who started the fight to save the inner city have fled or become burned out. Through the grace of God, Reverend Smith has remained.

Reverend Smith and an army of volunteers serve this community. They have waged a fight for its soul for thirty years. And the battle has not been easy: a place known notoriously as the "Shady Eighties" does not draw many missionaries.

Pastor Smith is both loved and hated. He is adored by African American and Latino church members, many of whom have found a way out of the ghetto through his leadership. But often the love stops at the steps of city hall, where this pastor is often viewed as a holy hell-raiser. He is gentle and has eyes that shine when he smiles. Yet he's also passionate, even fiery, about matters of faith, race and justice. He's a fighter, and in Deep East Oakland somebody has to fight. His penchant for candor gets him into trouble in certain circles. Reverend Smith will say out loud what others whisper behind closed doors. And while others have remained passive, Reverend Smith has waged a nonviolent war.

In ancient Palestine, a man of Pastor Smith's character would approach those in power with robes flowing and staff in hand. He would begin his thunderous addresses with the words "Thus saith the Lord." Reverend Smith doesn't sport a robe and staff, but he's no less a prophet than Amos or Elijah.

ACCEPTING A PRESTIGIOUS AWARD

On April 27, 2002, I sat across from Reverend Smith in the back of Brother Earl Nichol's white Lincoln Continental limousine. (Brother Earl is a bearded man with the build of a Detroit Lions linebacker and an easy smile.) He volunteered as the pastor's own personal driver and right-hand man. That afternoon, I sat in the back of the limousine with Reverend Smith as Brother Earl wheeled us away from the badlands. We were on our way to the University of California, Berkeley.

Reverend Smith was his chipper, vibrant self that day. That bright, sunny afternoon he was brimming with joy. He was resplendent in a black tuxedo with kente print hat and tie. A smile as broad as an angel's bow tucked itself underneath his cheeks. I didn't initiate conversation because I thought that the Reverend might have been wrapping his thoughts around the speech that he would have to deliver in the next few minutes. Someone called him on his cell phone. I picked up his side of the conversation. (He was careful not to reveal the name of the caller.)

"Oh my! Well, how did the tests come back?

"Well, I'm glad that you called to let me know something. I was concerned. Nobody had informed me about the progress of the situation, and I was wondering.

"Yes, we will be standing with you and your family in prayer. I believe that God is a healer and he is able."

Reverend Smith tucked the phone back into his pocket.

"Are you excited about the award that you will be receiving today, Reverend?" I asked. It wasn't an abstract question. Awards come often, almost weekly and from all quarters. With this award the outside world was honoring his hard work and the blood he lost as he toiled behind the walls of the ghetto. He tried to hide his emotions, but he's an open book. So I looked into his face and started reading. Reverend Smith was obviously humbled—and overjoyed.

When the limousine pulled up to the building on the Berkeley campus, several members of Allen Temple Baptist Church were waiting for their pastor to appear. He was smothered in smiles, hugs and congratulations.

A TIME FOR PROFOUND WORDS

We were escorted to a room on the third floor where the affair was to take place. The room was packed. People were also crowded in the hallway outside of the door. (Good thing the fire marshal wasn't present!) Several Bay Area religionists received awards, including the Reverend Cecil Williams of the famed Glide Memorial Church of San Francisco. And then the official from the Morehouse College Chapel called out:

"Reverend J. Alfred Smith Sr. of the Allen Temple Baptist Church in Oakland, California, [former] head of a denomination, pastor, preacher, writer, civil and human rights leader. Yours is a commitment to serving the community, the city, the county and the celestial. You are known in Oakland for revitalizing the minority business community, reducing drug trafficking, promoting youth employment, improving educational opportunities, expanding health care, fighting to feed the hungry, house the homeless, organizing boycotts and going to jail.

"You have been named humanitarian of the year, man of the year, one of the most influential blacks in America, doctor of law and doctor of divinity.

"You are on a mission to leave the world better than you found it. Therefore, as the chief usher today in the International House at Berkeley, I am ready to seat you, my dear Reverend, on the same pew with Gandhi, King and Ikeda."

An ocean of applause greeted the Reverend Dr. J. Alfred Smith Sr. as he walked to the podium. He prefaced his speech with the words: "I wish my mother were alive so that she could see me up here with all of these dignitaries."

AN UNLIKELY JOURNEY

Reverend Smith was born the son of an unwed mother and reared in a hard-scrabble outpost of Kansas City. Who knew that one day senators and governors would be knocking at his door, and his sermons would be translated and broadcast in Russia and China? Reverend Smith is one of the most highly respected preachers of the twentieth century. This is the chronicle of his struggle *and* his triumph.

Acknowledgments

I am deeply indebted to the Reverend Harry Louis Williams II for not only his genius as a writer but his patience in working with me in trying to tell the story of my life as accurately as possible. He was kind, sympathetic and understanding, and he worked hard to bring out the many revisions of this manuscript. Without him this book would not exist.

I am deeply grateful to my children, Ms. Amy Olivia Jones, the Reverend Dr. J. Alfred Smith Jr., Mr. Ronald Craig Smith, Mrs. Shari Lynn Rigmaiden and Mr. Anthony Smith for their helpful criticisms, to Mrs. Carlotta Holmes-Herbert for her technical assistance and to Ms. Brenda Walker for her commitment of time and computer expertise.

Many thanks to the staff of the African American Library and Museum, Oakland, California, as well as the Schomburg Center for African Culture and Research, Harlem, New York.

Heartfelt gratitude and love must also be extended to Mrs. Alberta Lastie for her years of faithful service as Allen Temple's publications specialist. Mrs. Lastie maintained an archive room which proved especially helpful in the creation of this book.

J. Alfred Smith Sr.

— 1 —

ON THE JERICHO ROAD

The Howard Thurman Chapel was as hot as a black spot on the sun. I was frying in my loose-fitting black robes, twisting and turning, trying to find a soft spot in a hardwood seat. The spotlights forced me to blink repeatedly.

I thumbed through my notes as a litany of prayers and greetings echoed in the cavernous auditorium. A tall, auburn-complexioned student invited us to stand as she led us in the Negro National Anthem. Her voice danced in the key of C; her range threatened to shatter the stained-glass windows. And then my name was announced. Dr. Lawrence Jones, dean of the school of theology of Howard University, beamed at me from the next seat over. He leaped to his feet, leading hundreds in an exuberant round of applause.

That was my cue. I made my first nervous steps toward the microphone. I gripped each side of the lectern and then peered down into a sea of beige, brown and onyx faces. The bodies leaned forward slightly, like roses anticipating raindrops. I cleared my throat as the clapping subsided. I acknowledged all of the notables present, and then I thanked the students for allowing me the privilege of sharing with them in that historic structure. Next, I announced my sermon title: "The Nigger Did It."

A collective gasp sucked the air out of the room. Black America's intelligentsia, its blue bloods, its talented tenth rocked back and forth startled. And I hadn't even started preaching yet. It was the word *nigger* that rattled them. It conjured up pictures of black men twisting in the dusky light of a Florida swamp, their eyes bulging out of their skulls.

The word *nigger* recalled the image of the backwoods, buck-dancing, watermelon-chomping, gin-swizzling, womanizing caricature that America had created and then hoisted up to the world. *Nigger* was nothingness. It was all that we tried to kill, all that we tried to escape—the dark appellation in our collective closet, the term never said aloud in mixed company by black people. And here comes this slow-talking preacher from California (of all places) to sling our bloodiest nightmare on the stage for public inspection. If looks could kill, I would have been assassinated before I could peel back the black cover of my Bible that morning.

Now that I had their attention, I started preaching. I began with an in-depth exegetical study of Jesus' parable concerning the good Samaritan. According to the story, an itinerant rabbi named Jesus was baited with the question: "Teacher, what is the greatest commandment?" As the two combatants engaged in theological discourse, Jesus raised a telling point that caused the lawyer to retreat with the question "And who is my neighbor?"

Here Jesus tells of a traveler who has wandered down the rocky, winding road that leads from Jericho to Jerusalem. He is surprised by a pack of thieves ("jackers," we call them in East Oakland). They beat the poor wanderer, perhaps even stabbing him with long knives, and then they stripped him of his wallet. As the ever-distant patter of their sandals beat down the dusty road, the man collapsed into a coma, flies buzzing around his bloodied skull.

Two religious figures traversed a blind curve that afternoon and inadvertently laid eyes on the victim. How inconvenient. They tightened their prayer shawls about their shoulders and rushed off, fighting any religious compulsions or feelings of human decency.

But someone else did stop—a Samaritan, an outcast. He was hated by many Jews, so much so that the thought of his shadow falling across a pious Jew's path might require ritual purification. The Samaritan was of mixed Jewish lineage, a bastard. In America he would find direct correlation with the African American. And the Samaritan would have been called, yes, a nigger. But with the hammer of irony, Jesus raises the head of the Samaritan, forging him into a symbol of hope and piety that believers through the ages would look to as an example.

I know the story so well. I had preached it many times and from so many different directions but I always ended up in the same place by the sermon's conclusion. The man or woman who calls God "Father" must wander out to the Jericho Road, the low place, the wasteland, the desert of society. And such people must not embark on their journey empty-handed. The healing and cleansing elements of wine and oil must be in hand. The Christian must intentionally put him- or herself out so that the wounds of the broken might be healed. I was taught this lesson before I was old enough read the Bible, and the truth of it wakes me up from my bed like the glimmer of the rising sun each dawn.

The audience clapped as I brought the sermon to an ecstatic conclusion, and I was relieved. But even if they had bolted the doors and cried for my head, the truth of the Scripture would have remained. It led me from Kansas City, Missouri, to the pulpit of one of the most socially conscious churches in the United States. It has taken me around the world. I want to tell you my story. This is how it began.

— 2 —

FAMILY ORIGINS

Charles Beamon was a field hand on a Jonestown, Mississippi, plantation in the 1920s. He was just another drop in a sea of dark humanity eking out a meager subsistence by wrestling white bolls of cotton from between their thorny cradles. Sometimes his torn and bloody fingers would turn the cotton a brilliant shade of crimson. The oppressive heat caused Beamon's flesh to blister and boil. He was a man of cinnamon complexion, but the summer sun burned his hide to two shades of walnut. This was harsh, mindless labor, the kind that broke the heart and wrenched the spirit from its moorings.

'Water!" Charles Beamon would cry when the swelter became unbearable. At this, a ragged, sad-eyed child would wander down the row of pickers, his bare feet sinking down in the warm, black soil. He would scoop water from a pail and hand Beamon the ladle. All of the workers used the same ladle, sick or well. It wasn't long before the water became frothy with mucous and saliva. The choice was to drink it or pass out from dehydration.

Cotton pickers were the southern poor, damned to the fields until the spine would no longer bend or straighten. They spent their nights in wooden shacks at the periphery of the plantation, and they answered to "nigger," "boy" and "gal." This was to be Charles Beamon's lot—until the incident that would change his destiny.

The plantation was owned by a wealthy southern gentlemen, more than likely a highly respected pillar of the community and a member in good standing at the local Baptist or Methodist church. He was white. He had all the luxuries and accruements due a man of his stature. He also had a daughter.

Now you have to understand that in the South the white woman was considered the flower of society: pure, virtuous and gentle. And a real lady of standing did little more than preen in front of a handheld mirror and ride a pony through the meadow. A southern gentlemen removed his hat in the presence of a such a delicate creature. And a black man could be found in the back bayou with his testicles crudely cut off for merely being accused of staring at her too long. They called this crime "reckless eyeballing."

When the boss's daughter sashayed by, Charles Beamon turned his head away as though she were God; to look her in the face meant death. But that did not stop this southern belle from taking an interest in my uncle. It began with a batting of her long, blond eyelashes. It escalated into a broad, pearly smile. It reached disastrous proportions one afternoon when she cornered him in the barn and suggested that they indulge in a carnal relationship. "This will be our little secret," she whispered intimately.

If young Charles complied with the dainty, feminine flower, she would most assuredly have accused him if the thing were ever found out. If he stormed away and denied her, she might still utter the most dreaded words that a black man could hear from the lips of a white woman in Mississippi: "He tried to rape me."

The sweat coursed down Beamon's brow in the fields that afternoon as he contemplated this cruel turn of events. His heart beat so heavily that he wondered if others could see it through his sweat-drenched shirt.

When the bell at the big house rang, signaling the day's end, Beamon jogged down the red clay path to the wooden shack he shared with his mother, Martha Henry, and his sisters, Amy and Louise Smith. The scent of deep-fried chicken floated through the open windows. Crickets sang a percussive aria as twilight approached. Mother Henry commanded that Charles go out back and rinse his hands before he sat down at the table. And then she noticed that his scarred, calloused hands were trembling.

"Boy, what is the matter with you?" she asked.

"That woman, she wan' me to sleep with her."

The deep-auburn-colored flesh stretched tight across her cheeks. Mother Henry's eyes narrowed.

"Who wan' you to sleep with her, Charlie?"

"Miss, do."

Instantly, Martha Henry's mental screen filled with images of men in white sheets with torches blazing, circling their home in the dead of night. In her mind's eye she could hear broken windows and shouts of "send that nigger out here!"

There was no time to waste. For all they knew, "Miss" was discussing the matter (or her version of it) with her daddy, the plantation owner, at that very moment. Charles Beamon and the two women tossed some framed family photos, a navy blue Sunday-go-to-meetin' suit and some faded dresses into two suitcases. Each member of the family glanced over the two-bedroom flat one last time with tears in their eyes.

"We got to go now, y'all!" Mother shouted.

Generations of the family had come screaming into the world in that little town. Scores of family members had taken their first steps in the grassy fields of Jonestown. The Beamon-Henry family had lived in that small backwoods hamlet since Lincoln freed the slaves, but they would have to escape under the cover of darkness like common thieves, leaving behind everything that they could not carry.

The family hopped a train that night with every intention of heading to the heaven that many had escaped to and wrote home about—Chicago. However, they did not make it that far. The money ran out. At the height of the Great Depression the family settled in a sprawling metropolis: Kansas City, Missouri.

KANSAS CITY

Kansas City was located at the center of the United States. Railroads brought merchandise from all over the county through its city limits. Cattlemen raised huge corn-fed steer, which were housed in pens and sent all over America by rail. But Kansas City was famous for none of those things. In the 1930s, Kansas City was busy earning its reputation as the "Sodom and Gomorrah of the western world."

Prohibition was nothing more than a word in the dictionary to many people in Kansas City. The bustling metropolis was declared an unofficial safe zone for notorious mobsters and wanted felons. Tommy-gun-toting gangsters like the Barker Gang, Baby Face Nelson and Pretty Boy Floyd received the red carpet treatment in Kansas City.

Most of the things that were putting Kansas City on the map took place in an area known to the locals, black and white, as "Nigger Town." The area around 18th Street and Vine played host to whorehouses where the prostitutes doubled as waitresses. Policemen in full uniform could be seen throwing craps as the scent of marijuana filled the air. Heroin was the drug of choice for many.

Nightclubs like Dante's Inferno, the Hey Hey Club, the Paradise, the Sunset Club, the Subway and the Basement offered gin, smoked barbecue and varying degrees of carnal pleasure. Early on, the club owners, many of whom were gangsters, found a draw that filled the satin seat covers in their gin holes. It was called jazz.

Kansas City was the home to the hottest jazz musicians on the planet during my youth. Count Basie's Orchestra featured saxophonist Lester Young. His skills were so enormous that they called him "the president." Cootie Williams, another great saxophone player and the star of Duke Ellington's band, made Kansas City his home. Charlie "Yardbird" Parker, Thelonious Monk and a plethora of the most incredible musicians of the twentieth century came of age in Kansas City.

THE PAUL LAWRENCE DUNBAR DISTRICT

Martha Henry moved the family to the Leeds Addition of Kansas City. The "colored" section of the Leeds Addition was called the Paul Lawrence Dunbar District, named after the great African American poet. The white section of the Leeds Addition had paved streets. But the Paul Lawrence Dunbar District had dirt roads and no sidewalks. Pigs and chickens squawked and grunted across its yards. Its one distinguishable monument was a trash dump with twin brown brick towers that spiraled up into the clouds, belching out black smoke that sometimes blotted out the sun.

— 3 —

Tough Times in a New Land

It was the height of the Great Depression. Hungry men with battered caps, sallow cheeks and stooped backs wandered through the alleys like dried leaves blowing through a graveyard. They tapped on back doors and pleaded, "Can you help me? I'm hungry."

Mother Henry had an Advocate at the right hand of the Father. She sought him for the cornmeal and oil to make biscuits for her children. God was merciful. Her son, Charles, found work in a factory downtown. Soon she and her daughters were also employed.

Eventually Charles Beamon married and struck out on his own. Louise Smith followed in his steps not long afterward, walking down the aisle with a railroad stevedore named Percy Simms. Martha Henry and her remaining daughter, Amy Smith, shared a home together. Together they navigated this new world, spellbound by the shimmer of a snowflake on a bare branch and the whistle of a train on its way to the yards.

In the fall of 1930, Martha Henry noticed a swelling around her daughter's midsection. That "swelling" was me. I was born James Alfred Smith on May 19, 1931. To be born without married parents was shameful and an outrage back in the 1930s. To this very day, I don't know how or where my father and mother met. My father's name was Clyde Anderson. He was a Pullman porter on the Pacific Union Railroad. In those days these workers were considered the black upper echelon. They dressed in white shirts and pants and black billed hats, serving ham-and-cheese sandwiches and carrying bags for American travelers.

My father's shadow never darkened the door of the small house where we lived, and rarely was he spoken of. The only thing that I knew about him was that he was a Pullman porter who worked for the railroad. Life went on in our corner of the Leeds Addition without his active involvement.

LIVING IN LEEDS

I had a good life in Leeds. We were surrounded by a loving community of warm, generous people. If my grandmother ever ran out of sugar, she would send me to a neighbor to borrow a cup. When we left our house, we could leave our front door unlocked. We knew that no thief would enter our home. The people of the Paul Lawrence Dunbar District helped each other. The older people kept watch over the boys and girls who skipped rope and played hopscotch in the streets.

In the cool of autumn, our neighbors—maids, farmhands, factory workers and bricklayers—would stroll outside of their homes, stretch their limbs and then roost beneath the starry expanse of the heavens. I can still see them: the Singletons, the Whites and the Williams. They would light fires in their front yards to chase away the chill and sit in rocking chairs, playing checkers or discussing the happenings of the day.

Surrounded by friends and family, I felt safe in the Paul Lawrence Dunbar District. However, the world outside of our little grove of towering oak trees and dirt roads was not as friendly. When Mama would take me to the stores downtown, I would see doors emblazoned with signs that read "White" and "Colored." I don't remember anyone ever explaining the meaning of these strange postings to me. Somehow, I knew intuitively that ours was a restricted universe. It seemed that we were hated just by virtue of our chocolate-colored flesh. I could not fathom the reason for this, nor was it ever explained sufficiently to me.

MAMA

Mama worked in the white world beyond Leeds. Domestic work was virtually the only opportunity for a black woman without formal education in those days. My mother's work uniform was a black dress with a white apron. The job required Mama to drop down to her knees and scrub the crevices and corners of the employer's kitchen. The smooth, supple hands that held my face as she kissed my forehead scoured the toilets and baked the bread for well-to-do white folks. Mama was at the beck and call of her employers; she had to live at the big house so that she could respond to their demands day and night.

One day I went to see Mama at the big, white house jutting up from the expansive green lawn like one of heaven's mansions. I pushed the doorbell and waited for what seemed like an eternity as the ring echoed through the great structure. The lady of the house answered the door. She was a stout, matronly woman; her green eyes sized me up. "What are you doing here?" she growled.

"I'm here to see my mother."

The hatred in her emerald eyes scorched the back of my young mind. She stared at me as though I were canine excrement that she had just scraped off the bottom of her shoe. I shifted from my left foot to my right uncomfortably. She seemed to be looking through me.

"Go to the back," she growled.

My head dropped below my shoulders as I complied with her orders. Trudging through the back door of the house, I felt a piece of my humanity dissolving. Someone sent for my mother. I fell into her soft, ebony arms, emotionally spent.

As I stood there in that dark kitchen, alone with Mama, she explained to me as best she could the world that I had been born into. A world where blacks are relegated to the balcony of the movies and the back of the bus is also one where African American people have to knock humbly at the back door of a white person's house. The darkness of the truth overwhelmed me.

"Mama, do you have to go the back door?

"Yes, son," she answered.

"Mama, how can you tell me that I'm as good as anyone else when we have to go through the back door?"

"Son, I have to support you," she answered. "I go around to the back door so that one day, you can go through the front door." Those were her exact words. What she believed was that if she could support me while I obtained an education, my destiny would be different from those who went before me.

MY BABY BROTHER

In 1935 my mother's belly began to swell again. She pulled me close to her one day and said, "James, soon we're going to have a little visitor." And sure enough, my little brother and future best friend, Joseph Harold Smith, appeared not too long after that. He and I had different fathers. I met his dad when I was young, but I don't remember much about him.

GOING TO SCHOOL

In September 1937 I entered the first grade at the Paul Lawrence Dunbar Elementary School. Like the rest of our world, the school was segregated. The white students went to a freshly painted, well-maintained building directed by teachers who earned generous salaries at the top of the state's pay scale. The black students inherited the books the white students would have thrown out when they received new ones. These books had broken spines and missing pages. Crude graffiti etched in blue magic marker covered key sentences, making it difficult to read.

But our teachers were up for the challenge. They strolled into the classroom with lightning in their eyes. Learning was turned into an adventure. We were passengers on a ride through the worlds of history and imagination. These instructors made the educational process exciting. Our teachers nurtured the human spirit. They spoke our names with love. These men and women set high standards for their pupils and would settle for nothing less than excellence.

Failure was considered completely unacceptable at the Paul Lawrence Dunbar Elementary School. And in the African American community in Kansas City, the teachers enlisted formidable help in their efforts to prepare us. If a student failed a math test, his or her parents were as likely to be visited by the pastor of the local church as the teacher. The teachers, pastors and parents worked in concert to make sure that no child was left behind.

Each morning when the rooster screamed at daylight, I would rise from bed to meet the day. Our house didn't have running water, so we heated water from a tea kettle and poured it into a wash pan to clean ourselves up. I made my bed, chopped firewood in the backyard and threw feed down for the chickens—all before I touched my Raisin Bran and milk.

Grandmother barred my path to school each morning. I wasn't going anywhere without a rigid inspection. First, she would say, "Stick out your hands, boy!" Then Grandma would bend down to make sure that there was no dirt beneath my fingernails. Next, she would twirl me around, making sure that my hair was combed and my shirttail was tucked in. This done, she would watch as I grabbed my books. And then she sent me off to school with a tender kiss, a hug and the daily admonition: "Boy, you behave yourself today. Don't make me have to come out to that school!" Grandmother was a firm believer in the old saying "spare the rod and spoil the child." I certainly didn't want her coming up to the school to investigate behavior problems!

Education was the only tool left for the black person to free him- or herself from the bondage of serfdom and near slavery. It wasn't long after I learned how to spell my name that I realized that book knowledge may have been the only difference between the alcoholic swaying down the street in a drunken stupor and the sharp, black lawyer who rode around Leeds in a brand new Chrysler and a gray fedora.

I ran into a problem, however, in the first grade. I couldn't master the printed word. My teacher decided that it would be best for me to repeat the first grade. Though Grandma had not been blessed with a free education— such luxuries were not afforded an African American lady who grew up in Mississippi not long after the dark night of chattel slavery had been abolished—she knew that the miracle of the printed word would be my salvation. The stigma of repeating a grade might have tainted my view of education. If the teacher allowed me to fail at such a crucial period in life, perhaps I would never recover. Grandma decided that we would have to fight. "Please don't fail my grandson," she begged the teacher. "Let me work with him over the summer." The teacher relented.

And so each day during that summer, after the breakfast dishes had been cleared away and the chores completed, Grandma would take me out to the front porch. There, she would sit me down on her knees. She opened the huge family Bible, and together she and I would strain to pronounce the "thees," "thous" and "begats."

Finally, September rolled around again. On the first day of school, the teacher commanded the class to take out their reading books. She called on student after student to read the ever-continuing adventures of Dick and Jane. I stretched my hand toward heaven, causing my shirttail to pop out. I wanted to participate, but the teacher, remembering my woeful attempts of the previous year, wouldn't give me the opportunity.

I found a way to counter this small setback. Whenever one of my classmates stumbled over a word, I would pronounce it for him or her. After everyone had read, the teacher, peering over the top of her bifocals, prepared for the worst. "Read, James," she commanded.

I took a deep breath and began to read where the last child had left off. I raced from sentence to sentence as though I had written the text. The teacher's jaw fell open. She jumped up from her seat and rushed out of the classroom. A hush fell over the room. Moments later, she returned with the principal in tow. "Start reading again, child," she commanded. The principal stood behind the teacher, his hands folded in front of him. He raised his open palm in the direction of the open book.

Once again, my reading was flawless. I didn't miss a word. The teacher snatched the book away from me. She dropped a copy of *Time* magazine in front of me and opened to an article about Winston Churchill. "Read this," she said. Unshaken, I began to read, my voice tempered with inflections at the proper times. She snatched away the magazine and opened the geography book to a paragraph about the Amazon rain forests. Again, I read. The teacher stared as though I had just walked on water or turned fish into bread; I guess, in a sense, through the blessings of God and Grandma, I had.

The teacher's eyes squeezed tight as a smile enveloped her whole face. She couldn't believe that I was the same child who, just months earlier, had stumbled over single-syllable words. The principal led the class in a round of applause. I was so filled with joy and pride that I almost cried. I couldn't wait to go home and tell Grandma.

For my grandmother, education equaled freedom for black people. Thanks to her foresight and wisdom, I was developing a lifelong love affair with the printed word. From that day on, I couldn't wait to get into the classroom. (Eventually, I would go on to author or edit close to sixteen books.)

— 4 —

GRANDMA'S GREATEST LESSON

A s a child I learned enough life lessons from Grandma to fill two or three books the size of the one in your hands. For example, one summer at the height of the Great Depression when I was nine and my brother was six, we watched a horse and carriage with a rakelike instrument attached to it clean a nearby field of its broken bottles and other assorted debris. The next day, Grandma told us, "Boys, we're going across the street to work that field." We toiled like indentured servants, bending at the waist to plant crops under the hot, hot sun. Grandma gave us specific instructions: dig a hole, drop three seeds inside and then water. Months later, when the crops came up, we pulled the corn stalks from the ground and canned the corn kernels.

The labors of summer were the bounty of winter. The food we harvested in the summer kept us from being hungry in the winter. Grandma taught me the blessing of hard work. Through her I learned the truth of the proverb: "Go to the ant, you sluggard! Consider her ways and be wise" (Proverbs 6:6).

THE TORNADO AND PRAYER

One afternoon, an announcement roared over the school's public address system: "Children, get home as fast you can." A stampede of scuffed Buster Brown shoes poured down the front steps of the building and onto the sidewalks. Torrential rain cascaded down my face, making it difficult to tell the sidewalk from the street. Wild claps of thunder left me disoriented. Streaks of blue lighting landed beyond the city limits like crooked exclamation points. The tree tops waved and shuddered as the wind gathered velocity. Cars were skidding. People were shouting things that I couldn't understand. I knew that I had to get home. I was soaked through to the bone by the time I reached our front porch. My chest heaved in and out violently. My grandmother and brother sat huddled together on the living room couch. This was the only time that I'd ever seen fear in her eyes.

A gust of wind landed against the side of the house like a giant fist. The storm became so powerful that it sounded like a freight train roaring right past our house. When the winds reached a crescendo, it was blowing trees, lawn chairs and squawking chickens past our house. The lights went out; the radio was silenced; shards of glass flew from a window that just gave way. I felt our small house rise up off of its foundations and then settle back down seconds later. It rose up again. I thought the wind was going to blow the house away. If that happened, I knew that we'd all be killed.

"Get under the table, boys," Grandma hollered.

Grandma didn't have to tell us twice. As we trembled in the face of the unknowable future, Grandmother commanded, "Pray, boys."

My brother and I nodded and prayed like rabbis before the great temple wall in Jerusalem. As the house shook on its foundations, Grandmother hollered, "Pray harder, boys!"

The wind lifted the house up one more time. This time we thought that the house wasn't going to settle back down. It felt like something was trying to twist the base of the building away from its concrete underpinnings. We could hear something trying to rip away from the earth beneath the floorboards. I could hear my grandmother say, "Please, Lord!"

As our last moments on earth threatened to ebb away, my brother cried out: "Lord, Grandma said, 'Please.' Didn't you hear her?" I busted out laughing.

The wind continued to blow, but the house no longer shook in its fury. After a few minutes it completely died down. When we were sure that the danger had passed, we scrambled to our feet and raced outside to assess the damage. We were astounded. All around us, our neighbors' homes lay as flat as pancakes. One of my classmates had lost his father.

We were still terrified, wondering whether my mother had found safe harbor in the storm. That afternoon she was on the street when the storm arrived.

But some kind person saw her and picked her up in a car, saving her from sure disaster. When it was all over, people all over the Paul Lawrence Dunbar District fell to their knees and gave thanks to God.

GOD AND COMMUNITY

God was the unseen member of our community and our family. When a warehouse worker received an unexpected bonus, he would say, "Thank the Lord." When our next-door neighbor came over to talk about a child she had counseled not to marry a "no 'count man," she said, "It's in the Lord's hands now." When a loved one passed on, Mama would say, "The Lord knows best." When the bills mounted up higher than the bank account, Mama would bow her head at the kitchen table and say, "Lord, help us." And when the white folks at work humiliated Mama, she would wander through the door and say with a teary smile, "God will make everything turn out alright."

They called him "God," "Jesus," "Lord," "Father" and a host of other names and titles, usually in soft tones with head bowed. Who was this powerful person who had such a broad number of names?

As a small child I remember sitting beneath an elm tree and staring up at the wispy clouds as they circled around the heavens. I thought of God in anthropomorphic terms. I tried to see him in my mind. I wondered how big his hands were. I was amazed at God's creation—the animal life, the bird life, the plant life—and life itself.

On those hot, lazy summer days, I was communing not so much with nature as with God. My young mind was filled with the exquisite poetry of the King James Bible. My mother was a master storyteller who could make the stories of Exodus live. I sat at her knee with my face cupped in my hands as I pictured Moses standing before the burning bush. I could see mean, old Pharaoh, his eyes blazing and his face as red as an unripe plum.

In my mind's eye, I could hear the children of Israel screaming as the whip cracked and fell in the shadow of the pyramids. And then I saw Moses, a child born in extraordinary times to unusual circumstances. I pictured myself as Moses, facing down the wicked Rameses in his own palace, with nothing but God's Word and my brother to back me up. And as Mama told the story for the thousandth time, I saw myself praying as Pharaoh's army approached at the Red Sea, believing for a miracle.

I also loved the stories of Jesus. The Christ child was born in a neighborhood not unlike the Paul Lawrence Dunbar District. The people whispered about his heavily questioned parentage. Nevertheless, Jesus loved everyone and he treated everyone with kindness.

INSIDE THE CHURCH

In the Paul Lawrence Dunbar District, there was only one thing that was held in higher esteem than education. That, of course, was religion. A large percentage of Kansas City's black residents were migrants from the deep South, where coffles of slaves once trudged through the marsh country, singing sorrow songs.

In the church, everyone was accepted. The lawyer and the school janitor might both serve together on the deacon board. African American people who were relegated to the bottom rungs of society in Kansas City made all of the major decisions affecting the church. Of course, the church was beset by the problems that trouble any other church, however, there were no "niggers" at the Pilgrim Rest Baptist Church. Everyone was treated as a brother or sister in the Christian faith.

What other organization in a segregated society could boast of a love ethic that could tear down class lines? As a youngster, I didn't have all of the theological pieces lined in a row, but I knew what love looked like, and I knew that I felt love as soon as I walked through the doors of the church. I could feel it when the elderly women glanced at me through the corners of their eyes during the service. I could feel it when my Sunday school teacher hugged me as I walked through the door. I could feel it when the Cub Scout master patted me on the back for exhibiting good sportsmanship.

Our West African kinfolks might have been proud of us had they been able to peek inside of the Pilgrim Rest Baptist Church in Kansas City. The smacking of rough calloused hands and the stomping of spiked heels and Buster Brown shoes gave a heavy percussive bottom to the organ and piano. The choir danced in place at the direction of the choir master. They looked like mahogany angels bedecked in crystal blue robes. Eventually, some woman in the choir would be overcome by the Spirit. She would grab the back of the pew in front of her, bow her head and then begin to shout and cry. One of the other sisters would grab a cardboard fan by its wooden stick handle and wave it in her direction. (The name and photograph of some local funeral director was always displayed prominently on both sides of the fan.)

The shouting and singing were the royal prelude to the message that the pastor would bring to us from the throne of God. The highest object in an African American Baptist church is the pulpit. This is symbolic of the importance placed on both the message and the messenger. The highlight of my week was shaking the pastor's hand at the end of the service. It was like touching God himself. In our world the pastor was our black-robed shaman-poet. He was God's mouthpiece, and it seemed as though he knew something about everything: from parsing ancient Greek terms to the late model car with the lowest gas mileage.

I loved the Christian religion. I also feared it. The thought of a Christless eternity in a burning hell gave me the night sweats. Early in my life I realized that I wanted to be a part of God's church forever. At age nine, I walked into the house and announced that I desired to be baptized. Now in the black church, salvation, baptism and membership into a community of faith often occur as simultaneous parts of one complete experience. It was nothing that anyone took lightly.

My grandmother was less than impressed with the idea of my making this eternity-changing decision. I could not explain my belief in the virgin birth, the crucifixion and the resurrection to her satisfaction. When I stumbled over these basic concepts, she said, "James, Jesus did not stand up in the temple and tell his parents, 'I must be about my Father's business' until he was twelve years old. That sounds like a good age to me."

I was disappointed, but that didn't extinguish my thirst for the things of God. I couldn't get enough of the church. I loved the smell of cologne as it collided with pomade and hair grease in the sanctuary on Sunday morning. I loved to sing the hymns. I knew all of the answers in Sunday school.

From time to time I also attended the Gilbert Memorial African Methodist Episcopal Church in Kansas City. The pastor there saw something in me. I was quiet and shy, but he took to me and encouraged me. He said kind things that boosted my self-confidence. The other A.M.E. preachers knew me and liked me. I felt drawn to these men of God, and they felt drawn to me even though I was only a child. Sometimes there would be a knock on the door at home. One of the A.M.E. preachers would be standing there and would ask my mother for permission to lay hands on me and to pray.

On Sunday afternoons, Mrs. Grimes, our neighbor from across the street, took her daughter and me to the Metropolitan Spiritual Church. The services were very different from the Baptist and A.M.E. services that I attended. They burned a lot candles in that church, and Bishop Taylor had a closet full of expensive gold, blue and red clerical robes. The choir dressed in white.

The Metropolitan Spiritual Church was quite mystical. Church members and visitors would come up to the altar at the given time and the bishop would give them what people in Pentecostal circles call a "word of knowledge." He would say things like "You're going to marry this person" or "You're going to come into some money," "You're having trouble in your home and the person giving you trouble is your uncle. Here is what you should do . . ."

The thunder of clapping hands, the banging of tambourines, the high-pitched shout of a woman as the Holy Spirit stirred within her captivated me. Even today, I can remember Bishop Taylor preaching the sermon "Jesus Is the Light of the World."

I would come home from church waving my hands, stomping my feet and throwing up my arms just as Bishop Taylor had when the sermon reached its crescendo. I would stand in the yard beneath the spreading arms of our massive elm tree and preach "Jesus Is the Light!" to the roosters—and to the four corners of the earth.

— 5 —

LIFE WITH MY EXTENDED FAMILY

Uncle Charles Beamon had moved to the Westport area of Kansas City. There, he sang bass in the Westport Baptist Church. I would sit at his knee and listen as he rattled off tales of the old country, Mississippi. I found him a fascinating man. But there was no real male influence in my home.

Back home things were tough. Each month my grandmother and mother scrimped and sacrificed to pay the rent on our little cottage home in Leeds. It seemed that there was never enough money. I remember waiting for my grandmother to come home with food donated to us by the Works Project Administration (WPA) at the height of the Great Depression. Eventually, we had to give up our home.

We moved into a wood-frame house with my Aunt Louise Simms and her husband Percy. Finally, there was a steady male presence in my home. Uncle Percy was a tall, slender man who wore bib overalls every day of the week. He laughed easily and entertained us with stories about the world "down home."

It seemed that Uncle Percy was always on his way to work. His railroad job required him to lay down heavy iron bars and hammer big metal spikes into the ground. Sometimes he would have to put in twelve straight hours of stooping, grunting, hammering and lifting. The railroad sometimes required him to work weekends. When Uncle Percy stumbled through the front door at the edge of night, his back would be tender and sore, his lanky, carefree walk a stagger.

Uncle Percy had no formal education, but he had earned a Ph.D. in common sense with a major emphasis on family. Uncle Percy was a wonderful provider. At the end of the summer before school was ready to commence, he would walk my brother and me all over town to shop for shoes and clothes.

Aunt Louise Simms was a tremendously gifted gospel singer. She had a voice that must have made the seraphim around heaven's throne stand back in open-mouthed awe. Whenever someone from the African American community made the transition to the next world, some grieving relative would ask Aunt Louise to sing at the funeral.

However, Auntie was a moody lady. For example, one New Year's Day, Uncle Percy, my brother and I were huddled in front of the radio. We listened to the play-by-play as the Illinois half-back Buddy Young gave the opposition fits. As we sat mesmerized by this young African American's explosive play, my aunt stormed into the room and snapped the radio off. Just that quickly and without a word or reason the game was over, at least for us. This was the same lady who turned the church out with her solo rendition of "Precious Lord."

A THWARTED TRIP

When I was six years old, my family was preparing to visit our relatives back in Louisiana. Mama, Grandma, Uncle Percy and Aunt Louise had filled my ears with wonderful stories about "back home." I wanted to see what a blood-red moon looked like rising huge and luminous over the bayou. I wanted to taste pecans straight from the tree. I wanted to see black men with gold teeth and wide brim hats sitting beneath the floating branches of the wisteria tree and hear them pick the Mississippi Delta blues. Most of all, I wanted to ride on the big train that would leave from Union Station and take us down to Jonestown, Mississippi. As the day grew nearer, I could hardly sleep at night, so filled was I with excitement.

Finally, the school year drew to a merciful and abrupt end. My brother and I were packed and ready to go. The afternoon before departure time, Uncle Percy, Mama, Grandma and Aunt Louise were gathered out in the back yard holding adult conversation. In those days all conversation was adult conversation; it mattered not whether that conversation centered around the price that string beans were bearing at the market, a neighbor's cheating wife or Joe Louis's latest conquest in the boxing ring. It was considered disrespectful for a child to "jump in grown folks' conversation."

The adults converged in an area between our house and the outhouse. I had to go to that outdoor toilet, but I was afraid. My uncle had recently purchased a rooster that would peck us boys if we came in the yard. As I hesitated, my bladder began swelling. Hot tears began to run down my cheeks. I was paralyzed by my fear of this ferocious bird. I couldn't move. I called out to Uncle Percy.

He hollered back, "Boy, go on to that toilet."

"I'm afraid," I said.

"Well, pick up a stick. Don't you know better than to interrupt when grown folks is talkin'?"

The red-topped rooster seemed almost human. He was a stalker. The evil beast would run up behind me, and when I stopped walking, he would stop. When I started walking, he would start walking. If he sensed fear in me, he would dispense with the rigmarole and attack. I once saw him peck at my aunt's leg until the blood ran. In my fear and trepidation, my bowels and bladder released. I messed on myself.

Not an hour later, Mrs. Grimes came walking through the yard. She took one look at me and began to giggle. There I was, a six-year-old boy standing around in a dress. You see, we had no washing machine and dryer. After I had my accident, someone had to wash my clothes out in the washtub and hang them up on a line.

I don't know why they put a dress on me, perhaps to punish me. But it hurt me that Mrs. Grimes had seen me in a dress. Yet her words stung even harder than the embarrassment. She said, "Hello, Mary." In my shame and anger, I lashed out, "My name is James Smith. Don't call me no Mary!" Of course, I laced that sentence with two words of raw profanity. Looking back, I can appreciate the absolute absurdity of what Mrs. Grimes saw that day. There I was, a six-year old boy in a woman's dress, cussing out one of the grown ups like a drunken sailor. It must have been a bizarre sight to behold.

Mrs. Grimes went to the back yard and told my aunt what I had done. Aunt Louise called, "James Smith, come here!" Tears began to run as I tucked my head down and slowly walked over to her. "Hurry up, boy! I ain't got all day! Boy, did you cuss Mrs. Grimes?"

The water works had turned into a river by now. There was no need in denying anything. The question and answer portion of the proceedings was just a formality. My immediate future had already been decided.

Aunt Louise held both of my hands together with one of her hands. She gritted her teeth as she used her free hand to slap my rump again and again and again. My grandmother walked in the house and received the news of what I had done. She repeated Aunt Louise's time-proven remedy. Man, what a day this was turning out to be!

My backside was good and sore by the time Mama got home. She got the news before she could walk in the door. Mama was completely mortified by what I had said to Mrs. Grimes, our respected neighbor. It didn't bother her that I had already been spanked twice. Mama wore my tail out again! But nothing hurt worse than the final punishment that I received for cursing Mrs. Grimes. It was decided that I wouldn't be allowed ride the big train to Mississippi the next day. I would stay with one of the neighbors while my family went on their vacation.

I had disrespected an elder. The outer community had no respect for our elders. Black senior citizens leaning on wooden canes had to wait until white teenagers were served milkshakes before they could purchase their medicine at the local Woolworth department store. The most respected of our elders could be called "gal" or "uncle" by a white child and nothing was made of it.

Yet the social order of our African American community was built on our reverence for those who had paved the way for us—our seniors. Respect for elders was one of the things that had held our fragile community together. I had broken the code. Trust me, I only broke it once.

FINALLY MAKING A TRIP TO MISSISSIPPI

The next summer Mama packed a suitcase for my brother Joseph and me. We were being sent "down home" for the entire summer. This summer the adults were not going with us. Mama had arranged for our relatives to meet us at the Clarksdale, Mississippi, train station. Part of our vacation was to be spent with family in Memphis, Tennessee, as well. I kept my mouth shut this time. Nothing was going to stop me from getting on the train. Joseph and I couldn't have been more excited if we had been presented with toys at Christmas.

Grandma stuffed a huge cardboard box with fried chicken, marble chocolate cake and sweet potato pie, enough to last for the whole train ride. It had to last. African Americans were barred from the dining car. Like everything else in our America, the train was segregated. African Americans were sequestered in a separate car, often directly behind the train's engine. Smoking was not allowed in the "Whites Only" cars. Therefore, unsmiling white men with tweed suits and two-tone shoes would come to the "Negro car"; here they could feel free to blow pungent cigar smoke into that tight enclosure. They choked us senseless, and soon our clothes wreaked of smoke.

Even though I had heard stories about the South, nothing prepared me for my visit. Sixty years after the abolition of slavery, little had changed in the closed society. When the train pulled into a small-town station, I would hold my breath in terror. Young white kids from those small backwoods towns invariably ran up to meet the train, crowding around the "colored" car as though it were a traveling zoo. They pressed their faces against the window glass, twisting their visages into contorted masks of hate. I can still hear them hollering "nigger, nigger" at us over and over again.

On lawns all over Mississippi, coal-black lawn-jockey statues with fire-red lips held lanterns on the lawns of well-to-do whites. I fantasized about going around one night and stealing them all. I hated racial stereotypes. I wouldn't eat fried chicken or watermelon around white people because it was said that African American people had an unnatural craving for such things.

AN EYE-OPENING RUN-IN

Soon after we landed in Jonestown, Mississippi, my brother, who was four years younger than me, ran up and down the street making friends. He racked-up breakfast invitations with the neighbor families in no time flat. He was a lovable, gregarious person. I have always considered myself a friendly person, but I wasn't always as fortunate as Joseph in the friends department.

One day, while walking down the street in Jonestown, I walked past an elderly white fellow rocking in a chair on the porch of his shotgun home. His blue bib overalls were stretched over his protruding belly, and his straw hat was pulled down over his silver hair. The gentleman leaned forward to spit tobacco juice into a copper-colored spittoon.

"Hello," I called to him.

"Hello, little nigger."

The man said it with a gentle smile as though he were talking to his pet poodle.

"My name is not 'nigger.' It is James Smith," I quickly snapped.

The old man frowned and reared back as though I had just slapped him.

"You're not from around here, are you?" he asked in shock. (It was more of an observation than a question.)

"No, I'm not," I answered quickly. And then I stomped off.

When I got back to the house, I related what had happened. My great uncle's eyes stretched as wide as two silver dollars. His mouth gaped open. He was too startled for words. I could see black spaces where he was missing his back teeth.

"Boy, is you crazy?" he asked as soon as he could form the words. "This is Mississippi!"

The other family members carried on as though I had committed some heinous crime. I apologized for speaking back to the white man. But in my heart, I wasn't sorry. Mother had taught me that I was a human, not a "nigger." It was hard to turn that off and on.

My relatives were not cowards. On the contrary, it took incredible bravery not only to survive but to raise a family in a world were the police may or may not be Klansmen and lynching was a way of life. In their world blacks who spoke up for themselves were considered "uppity," and an "uppity nigger" could end up with a bullet in his or her head quicker than a sparrow could whistle "good morning" at sunrise. God only knows the atrocities that they had seen in Mississippi.

The rest of the summer went without a hitch. My brother and I had the time of our lives. We fished along the banks of the big, muddy river. Perch and trout jumped on our lines. We clapped our hands as an old blues man twanged out the down-home blues. Fried catfish and French fries were our supper. We almost hated to go home.

— 6 —

Wrestling with My Religion

—⚉—

Upon our return to Kansas City, tragedy struck. Uncle Percy lost an eye while working for Missouri Pacific Railroad. My uncle had given blood, sweat and tears for that company. He never missed a day of work. He was never late. He gave them the best years of his life *and* his right eye. In the end they awarded a disgracefully inadequate disability settlement to a black man who could hardly read.

Did God care about what had happened to Uncle Percy? Of course he did. Any African American preacher worth his or her weight in salt would have told you that. You see, there is no line of demarcation separating the sacred from the secular in black religion. I realized that back when I was twelve years old.

I began to think of it this way—what would have happened to Moses if he had gone back to Egypt with this message: "Friends, God has come to deliver you but only in a religious sense. You see he's not concerned about your slavery. He doesn't care that you are marginalized in a crumbling, crime-infested quarter of society with an infant mortality rate triple that of most industrialized nations. Ultimately, it's some unseen part of you that is solely important to God. So God has sent me to see that you experience freedom—purely in a religious sense, mind you. I'll show you the correct way to worship, yet you will remain slaves."

If Moses had gone to the Hebrews with that message, the story of Exodus would have had a different ending. Pharaoh and Moses would have become great friends. You see, the great monarch of Egypt would have supported this kind of religion, one that kept people peering into the clouds and talking solely about the afterlife and would have allowed him to burn their backs with the bullwhip without regard for retribution. When they complained about the terrifyingly high infant-mortality rate or the brutality of the Egyptian police, Pharaoh would simply have said, "One day, you'll be in heaven, so take it and shut up." And as they walked away, he would be laughing his head off.

On the other hand, the people of Israel might not have embraced a religion that asked them to accept slavery and segregation in exchange for eternal considerations. It would have been difficult for them to conceptualize a religious freedom that did not address the injustice of their situation. More than likely, they would have stoned Moses.

In junior high school I first realized that black people could not afford a completely other-worldly religion that was oriented toward the "sweet by and by" but silent on the nasty now and now. These were the thoughts that I wrestled with when I went to visit the house where Mama worked. The good Christian white folks that she worked for thoroughly disrespected her even though she was on her hands and knees, sweating great drops of perspiration for them. The lady of the house would often refuse to pay my mother the courtesy of using her name. She called my mother "gal." She told Mama that she would get rid of her if she didn't straighten up. I was standing right there!

I reasoned, if the cries of the children of Israel reached the ears of God and caused him to wage war against Pharaoh, surely the Lord must be outraged that a woman could call herself a Christian and treat my mother that way right in front of me. And if God was indignant with the woman, surely he was furious with the Christians who knew about the evil that was perpetrated against us but chose to say or do nothing about it.

BAPTIZED

On Easter Sunday in 1943, my mother, my brother, my grandmother and the whole Paul Lawrence Dunbar community assembled at a baptismal pool located behind the church. My day had come. My pastor, the Reverend Harley Akers, was the brother of the famous gospel singer Dorothy Akers. He was a tall, stately man with flowing black locks. He could have easily passed for white.

Reverend Akers squinted when he peered into my eyes and said, "Do you believe that Jesus Christ is the Son of God, that he died on the cross for your sins and then rose again on the third day? Have you repented of your sins? Have you accepted Jesus into your heart as your personal savior?"

"Yes, I have." I said.

Without another word, Reverend Akers dipped me head first into the ice-cold pool. My life would never be the same. Water filled my nostrils and blinded my eyes. A loud shriek, like the ripping of the temple curtain came from the back of the crowd. With their bony, brown hands stretched toward the heavens, women shouted, "Praise him. Praise him." An usher in a plain, navy blue suit sang the first four bars of "Leaning on the Everlasting Arms." The entire congregation joined him. It was as though I could feel God embracing me, clothing me for the journey ahead.

THE FAITH I FOUND AT HOME

As a boy I was mesmerized by the story of a good Samaritan who loved a mugging victim enough to tend to his wounds. The Samaritan dipped into his own pocket to make sure someone of another ethnic group could be made whole. I found myself appalled by the behavior of the two religious professionals who crossed the street to avoid any contact with the man who might have been near death.

The good Samaritan caused also me to wonder how white Christians could shed tears when talking about the lowly Jesus yet be unmoved by the plight of their black Christian brothers and sisters trapped in the squalor of the ghetto. They said, "We must focus on the things of the spirit. Heaven is the land flowing with milk and honey. We may have ours now, but someday on the other side of the chilly Jordan we will all have our bellies filled." My mother and grandmother had a different take on the application of that Scripture.

EXAMPLES OF SERVICE

My mother was a missionary worker in the Pilgrim Baptist Church. She was the chairperson of the church's youth department. Grandmother Henry was president of the Mother's Board of the Church. (Today, we would call her a deaconess.) Yet their relationship to God and his church went much further than the titles they bore in church.

My grandmother and mother showed me the importance of service to humanity. Mama's life was hard and her days long. She had been abandoned with two boys who ate everything in sight and were growing out of their clothes almost as fast as they could put them on. Many nights her joints ached from scrubbing floors. It would have been easy for Mama to simply give up, to wallow in self pity, to spend her time swilling down cheap liquor at the corner juke joint. But Mama took another course. She internalized the words of Christ who said, "Thou shalt love the Lord thy God with all thy heart, and with all thy soul, and with all thy strength, and with all thy mind; and thy neighbor as thyself" (Luke 10:27). Mama poured much of her soul and a great deal of her spare time into the lives of others.

Mama was a block captain in the Paul Lawrence Dunbar District. When the neighbors heard her loud rap on the front door, they knew she was there to insist that they work to keep the neighborhood free of litter and debris. She petitioned absentee landlords to paint their properties and clean up in front of their tenements. Mama kept pressure on the city officials to create a livable environment for the children of our community.

If that were not enough, Mama also served as a den mother for my Cub Scout troop. Even after my brother and I had grown up and moved away to California, Mama maintained her position as a Cub Scout den mother. Some of the Cub Scouts who passed through her den grew up to contribute to society in a mighty way; among them were Kansas City's vice mayor Alvin Brooks, noted Baptist pastor Kenneth Ray, and Jacob Armstrong, a prominent newspaper man.

THE MESSAGE OF HOPE

My mother and grandmother had one sermon between them. They preached it often. The title was "Boy, You Can Make It." They told me that the possibilities for my life were as limitless as the stars in the sky. One afternoon, Mama brought home a paperback copy of Booker T. Washington's groundbreaking autobiography, *Up from Slavery*. She demanded that I read it and the autobiography of Dr. George Washington Carver too.

Today, a young African American can turn on the evening news and open a newspaper to see black people of power and influence. In my youth, when segregation was a way of American life, there were few people of color that society held up as role models. Whenever the NAACP called a mass meeting, Grandma grabbed me by hand and took me across town. The great "race men" of our time would be the featured speakers. The appellation was one of great honor. These were the defenders, the protectors of our people. Race men sought the elevation of black people. Often they were lawyers, civil rights workers, educators or ministers of the gospel.

Grandma reasoned, and correctly so, that exposure to these gallant warriors of the world would expand my boundaries and inspire me to higher heights. On these special evenings the municipal auditorium would be packed with black men and women dressed in their Sunday-go-to-meeting best. You didn't have to beg African American people to join the NAACP back in those days. It was the preeminent organization fighting against the oppression of the black man and woman in America.

I recall the electricity that flowed through the air the night that Walter Francis White, the executive secretary of the NAACP, held court. Walter White was the NAACP's man without fear. As a boy White had picked up a shotgun and held off a sea of armed Klansman who were going door to door seeking black men to harass. Later, his light skin and blue eyes allowed him to infiltrate lynchings, posing as a white man.

In 1946 White helped create the National Emergency Committee against mob violence. He fought for enfranchisement for southern blacks long before Dr. Martin Luther King had been ordained to the Christian ministry. White successfully lobbied President Roosevelt to promote Colonel Benjamin O. Davis, the highest-ranking African American in the armed forces, to the rank of brigadier general. He also served as a foreign correspondent for mainstream newspapers.

Grandma took me to see other noteworthy men of color who came to Kansas City during the days of my youth. A. Philip Randolph, the son of a Jacksonville, Florida, preacher, founded the Brotherhood of Sleeping Car Porters, a union organized to protect black railroad employees. Randolph under threat of death, organized the first African American union ever to be recognized by the AFL-CIO.

Grandma Henry and I were there when Mordecai Johnson, the president of Howard University, came to Kansas City. Benjamin Mays, the president of Morehouse College, inspired me as he said, "Every man and woman is born into the world to do something unique and something distinctive, and if he or she does not do it, it will never be done."

Grandma would tell me that there was nothing to stop me from rising to the clouds where these great men walked. It was Grandma's dream that one day I too would be in a position to help our people. Personally, I didn't have any idea how that would happen. I had no clue what I was supposed to do with my life. I had seen neither visions in the night nor handwriting emblazoned on the dining room wall. And still there was one tremendous obstacle in front of me, blocking out the sun. I had no father to help me.

FATHERLESS IN KANSAS CITY

At age twelve I wondered how a child could contribute to the world without the support of a father. Even though I had never known my father, I felt the impact of his absence every day of my life.

One of my best friends was Clyde Williams. Occasionally when I would visit Clyde, our roughhousing and wrestling would turn to real fighting. When this happened, Clyde's grandmother would rush into the bedroom and holler out, *"Go home, James Smith, you little bastard!"* She couldn't have wounded any deeper had she taken a sword and thrust it through my skinny ribs.

THE BARBERSHOP RITUAL

On Saturday mornings my mother would send my brother and me to Papa Slim's barbershop. It was the hub of the African American community. This is where the gardeners and the butlers could feel free to remove the masks that they were forced to strap on in the other world. Here they were free to express opinions that would have shocked their employers, had they been able to press an ear to the wall.

The barbershop had its protocol. Those under twenty-one did not speak unless spoken to. We listened to the elders talk about sports, women, the church and politics. The barber would sometimes pull away from someone's head and then use the clippers like a lecturer's point, leaving me to wonder if he could talk and cut hair at the same time. Each man who entered the shop added another dimension to the discussion.

One of the things that turned a trip to the barbershop into an important ritual was that fathers brought their sons with them. My classmates would sit in the waiting room under the lanky arms of their fathers. My brother and I had no man to take us. While my world was being forged in the furnace of life experience, my father was in some other state fornicating his way through the pages of the telephone book.

Who would teach me the things that a boy should learn from his father? Who would guide me and discipline me? Who would take me to the church's father-and-son picnic? Sometimes I would watch the other boys play catch with their dads. Their fathers would come to the sporting events to cheer them on. My father hadn't seen fit to be a presence in my life. Why?

Could it have been that Daddy's sole responsibilities were to his sexual appetites alone and that they did not extend beyond the four corners of his bed? After all, he did create children with different women all over the United States. I wondered, when he gorged himself on Oysters Rockefeller and Chablis at a four-star eatery, was he ever curious about his offspring whose bellies growled from want? As he stuck his fork into the chives and sour cream that simmered on his baked potato, did he think of his young children who lay awake at night in some back-water town, their teeth chattering as the cold winds swept through their clapboard hovels, their fingers turning red and blue like popsicles in a supermarket freezer? As he flashed his pearly teeth at an unsuspecting date, did he ever wonder about me or what I was like?

I was angry with God. Had he decided to punish me for my sins by teasing me with an invisible father? Why had God not seen fit to insulate my life with the love, protection and guidance that comes from a faithful father's heart?

DADDY'S LYING LETTER

Occasionally a letter would arrive in the mail with my name on it. The letters were from Daddy. I would write back, rarely asking for anything, just happy to know that somewhere out in a world beyond my own was a man whose blood flowed through my own veins.

When I reached the fifth grade, an announcement was made that caused me to sit down at the dining room table and write to Daddy. The school system was going to offer musical instruction. We lived in the jazz mecca of the universe, and like every child in the Paul Lawrence Dunbar area, I wanted to blow saxophone like local-born bebop originator Charlie "Yardbird" Parker. The instruction was free, but students were required to supply their own instruments. So I wrote to California where Daddy was living at the time. He was working at a defense plant and making good money.

It wasn't long before my father wrote back to me. He said: "Son, keep an eye on the mailbox; soon the saxophone that you requested will be coming your way." Each afternoon I practically tackled the mailman as he neared our front porch. But one day it dawned on me. Daddy was never going to send that saxophone.

If he initially had written a note saying that he could not afford to help me, I would have understood. However, Daddy had promised to come through for me, and he failed. He didn't even make an excuse. By doing so, he unwittingly dropped some destructive seeds in the soil of my unformed soul. My eyes became dark, my mood sullen. To this very day, Daddy's failure to keep his word to me about the saxophone has been the greatest disappointment of my life. I hated him for it.

WRESTLING WITH RESENTMENT

Grandma saw the bitterness lodged behind my pupils. She fell to her knees, taking my case straight to God. One afternoon she called me over to herself. She slipped her arm around my shoulders pulling me close to her. "James," she said, "your father didn't do right by you. You know it, I know it, and most of all God knows. But God is also looking at you son. You see, Jesus forgave you. He carried your sins on that cross. He forgave your sins and now he's looking to see what you will do. Can you forgive your daddy, or will you spit on Jesus by holding on to that hate for your father you hold in your heart?"

I lay in bed that night staring at the ceiling, hot, salty tears dripping from the corners of my eyes onto the pillow. "Lord, help me to let it go," I prayed. And eventually he did. Sometimes feelings of resentment toward my father would still resurface. However, when they did, I quickly confessed them to the Lord. Looking back, my decision to forgive my father for his parental neglect was one of the greatest choices I ever have made. My father's failure to keep his word had brought my life to a crossroads. In the midst of my pain I saw the mercy of God. Unforgiveness has destroyed many a wounded soul, and it almost short-circuited my future.

Many of the young men walking the streets of America's ghettoes with guns in their waistbands were children abandoned by the males who sired them. When they pick up that pistol and aim it at another person, I am convinced that they are trying to pay daddy back for the anguish and misery that he has put them through. I know what I'm talking about—I've lived their pain.

One afternoon, with tears flowing Grandma hugged me and whispered, "James, go empty your piggy bank and tell me how much you have saved." Grandmother was working in the kitchen of all-white Central High School.

She had salted away a modest savings. She took what I had saved and sup-
plemented it with the blood money that she had pieced together from her
harsh work. The next day while I was in school, she went down to the pawn
shop and purchased my first saxophone, a C-Melody. When I began to develop as a musician, my grandmother traded that C-Melody in for an E-flat
alto saxophone.

You see, God had blessed me with two wonderful parents: a mother and a
grandmother. Their sacrifices, their commitment to raising my brother and me
was a fantastic gift from God. I would come to see that in later years and appreciate it with all of my heart.

— 7 —

SEARCHING FOR
A MALE ROLE MODEL

In the absence of my father I looked at the black Baptist church deacons and got an idea of what it looked like to be a man. Deacon Carter, my Sunday school teacher set the bar high for me. When I fell short, I heard about it in no uncertain terms. He expected me to have studied the Sunday school lesson thoroughly before I walked into the classroom. Deacon Carter asked me hard questions and pushed me to go deeper as a student of the Word of God. And then there was Deacon Moseley, our Sunday school superintendent, who was something of a prophet. He once pointed at Kenneth Ray and me and said, "You young boys are going to be preachers." We smiled at him curiously. Years later it happened just as he said it would.

I will never forget those men who treated me like a son. They gave me a chance.

UNCLE JAMES STEPS IN

I would be remiss if I didn't write of the mentor who was dearest to my heart. My father's brother, James Smith, after whom I was named, was a Pullman porter like Daddy. It was a stressful job. Often, the smiling face that picked up a white person's bag at the train station belonged to a medical student or an engineer whose skin color held them back. Pullman porters often made an adequate living, but they were by no means rich. Men like Uncle James would sometimes have to dance the buck-and-wing on the train platform to pick up tip money to supplement their incomes.

When Uncle James made his runs through Kansas City on his way to Chicago, he would call me. At his summons, I would take a streetcar down to Union Station, a magnificent architectural structure, and would march through the marble pillars of the station. And there I would find him, standing as stately as a black president in that starched and pressed white suit and black-billed hat. I became weightless in his grasp as he hoisted me off my feet. Uncle James's voice was like pecan ice cream when he would say, "James, you get bigger every time I see you."

I wondered if Uncle James looked like my Daddy, if he sounded like my Daddy. Why could Uncle James care so much and Daddy not care at all? Uncle James would take me to the luncheonette, where we would sit down over hamburgers and milkshakes and talk about school, girls and church. He would regale me with stories of ports unknown, distant worlds known to me only as words in a geography book.

Ultimately, he would snatch out his gold pocket watch and glance at it with a frown. There never seemed to be enough time to visit. My heart always sank as the time of his departure grew nigh. I talked faster, hoping perhaps to stretch a few extra moments into our time together. Eventually, he would rise from his seat and give me the oft-heard admonition, "Be a good boy, James. I'll be back soon." Then, I watched Uncle James turn and walk away—until the next time.

Uncle James was steering my life. He didn't have to spend great sums of money on me. His financial investment in my life was rarely more than a coke, a hamburger and a few dollars in spending money. But his time was invaluable. His smile, his words of affirmation to a fatherless boy with a fractured ego couldn't be measured in money. Until my last day, I will thank God that Uncle James took the time to be with me.

COMING OF AGE

As a teenager entering high school, I read everything that I could get my hands on. Black newspapers like the *Kansas City Call*, New York City's *Amsterdam News* and the *Pittsburgh Courier* kept us informed of the issues that confronted African American people. The pages of these publications brought us news about people like the great dancer Josephine Baker and Father Divine, a black man back East whom many thought was God in the flesh. We followed the trial of the Scottsboro Boys, teenagers who hopped a freight car that happened to contain two white female stowaways. The two transient women claimed that the Mississippi youths raped them. The African Americans were convicted and strapped with long sentences.

We read about Paul Robeson, the athlete, actor, singer, activist who was being hounded by the U.S. government for favorable comments made about Russia. The papers carried the stories of the Harlem Renaissance and the writers, poets and artists who were bringing black creativity and expression to the world: people like Countée Cullen, Claude McKay, Langston Hughes and Zora Neale Hurston. Boxing heroes like Joe Louis and Sugar Ray Robinson were featured. And from the black newspapers I learned about the famous African American opera singer Marian Anderson and United Nations diplomat and Nobel Peace Prize winner Ralph Bunche.

We also were kept abreast of what was happening in the world through the newsreels shown between films at the local theater. However, when I was growing up there was only one movie theater for "colored" in Kansas City: the Lincoln Theatre on 20th and Vine. We would ride public transportation there, passing many "white only" theaters on the way.

BLACK BASEBALL

Like most everything else, baseball was segregated. Professional baseball teams had a silent agreement that they would not allow a black man to don a uniform. On February 20, 1920, Rube Foster, a noted African American businessman, called several of his colleagues together for a meeting at the YMCA in Kansas City. The end result of this gathering was the inauguration of the Negro National League.

I loved to watch baseball as a teenager. My memory is still fresh with the fun that we had in those early years. As a teenager, my brother and I went to the Blues Stadium where the Negro baseball teams played at the height of the summer. The stadium was packed with African American humanity dressed in wide-brimmed hats, frilly dresses, suits and ties.

I recall our local team, the Kansas City Monarchs, playing Birmingham's Black Barons, the Newark Eagles and Pennsylvania's Homestead Grays. At Blues Stadium I saw the some of the greatest players of any color ever to touch a baseball. Number 25 for the Kansas City Monarchs was a tall, lanky fellow named Satchel Paige. My brother and I would howl as Paige would call in his outfield and have them sit down while he gave a pitching exhibition. Paige was the biggest draw in black baseball. Paige faced down sluggers like Josh Gibson and Buck Henry, who had been nicknamed the "thunder twins"; the newspapers called them the black Babe Ruth and Lou Gehrig.

In 1947 black America experienced one of its greatest victories of the day. Branch Rickey, owner of the Brooklyn Dodgers, broke the color line by drafting a member of the Kansas City Monarchs. His name was Jackie Robinson. The world was changing.

BLACK IN HIGH SCHOOL

When I was growing up, Kansas City boasted several high schools, but God's dark children could attend only two: Lincoln High School and R. T. Coles High School, a vocational high school. In September of 1944 I entered the latter as a freshman. The black teachers within that terrible, segregated system loved us. They were like a second group of parents for the students. They repeatedly told us, "They aim too low, who aim beneath the stars."

My English teacher, Mrs. Mila Banks, would ask us to stand up and read from the works of Langston Hughes, Gwendolyn Books and Countée Cullen. It was she who put Richard Wright's books *Native Son* and *Black Boy* into my hands. I was fascinated by them because his books mirrored real life. Jeremiah Cameron, a literary genius who had studied at the University of Chicago, required us to read the works of a black Russian named Alexander Pushkin. Mrs. Ferguson, another English teacher, introduced me to the Shakespearean tragedies. Mrs. Gertrude Bardwell made history come alive. She painted vivid pictures of historical figures ranging from Joan of Arc to Kaiser Wilhelm. I owe my passion for world history to her.

At the end of a particularly rousing session in history, Mrs. Bardwell dismissed the class. "James, I want you to stay behind a moment," she hollered as I hit the door. I took a deep breath and retraced my steps. Hadn't I been well behaved? My assignments were caught up to speed. Why would Mrs. Bardwell ask me to stay after class?

When the last student entered the hallway and closed the door, Mrs. Bardwell said, "James, you should run for class president." Like every boy, I dreamed of rising to such a height, but I hardly thought it possible. These positions belonged to people who were well known and idolized—the athletes and cheerleaders. Yet Mrs. Bardwell thought that I could win. She believed in me so heavily that she met with me on several subsequent occasions to help draft my campaign speeches.

On the election day I joined a panel of school presidential hopefuls in the high school auditorium. When my name was announced, a warm wave of applause went up. I glanced back at Mrs. Bardwell, who nodded proudly. I took a deep breath . . . and then it was over. People were clapping again.

Mrs. Bardwell was right. I won the election! Not only did I win the presidency of my freshman class, I also won that office every year until I graduated. I was not only the class president but the president of the entire student body. In my senior year, I was also named to the all-city student council.

In my senior year Mrs. Bardwell looked at this poor son of Leeds and showed him a peculiar kindness, which has never been forgotten. Mrs. Bardwell gave me a gift I hadn't even dreamed of possessing. She purchased my senior class ring. My mother, who worked as a domestic, would never have been able to afford such an extravagance. It might as well have been the Hope Diamond.

Coach Isaiah Banks was my football coach. He too took a special interest in me. He mentored and encouraged me. He once gave me a bag of socks that he no longer needed. I was overcome by his generosity. At Mr. Banks's suggestion, I stepped up my involvement in the local YMCA. I became a staunch supporter of the Hi-Y program, which was committed to helping African American people understand domestic and international events. Forums were held on Sunday afternoon. I was fervently committed to the YMCA philosophy of physical fitness and social uplift.

Ralph Brady, the secretary of our local YMCA branch, was a great encouragement in my quest to make something of my life. His intelligence, integrity and civic-mindedness were a beacon of light. At one time I wanted to attend the George Williams College in Illinois, where people were trained for careers in the YMCA. But there was another profession calling me.

BETWEEN THE FLESH AND THE SPIRIT

Kansas City was the jazz capital of the United States. Nobody loved the improvisation and melody of that music more than I did. I loved to hear the great musicians play intricate scales to the rhythm of the trap drums. On Sunday evenings I joined all the local jazz buffs to hear the big bands at the municipal auditorium. Count Basie, Duke Ellington and Jay McShann led a hit parade that included all of the great vocalists and instrumentalists of our day.

I played E-flat alto saxophone in high school and had developed quite an aptitude for the instrument. My musical gift earned me a spot as a union musician. I paid dues to Local #627, along with Cootie Williams, Count Basie and others. I was often called to perform at local venues. Each summer, I played in the park with Kansas City's concert band. But my elders saw jazz as the Kansas City curse. They considered jazz music an elixir brewed by the devil himself, and they did not look favorably on his patrons. I was trapped between the music I loved and my immortal soul.

Not only music, but questions of faith and race filled my mind during my teenage years. As a high school student I hungered to know Jesus in a deeper, more intimate way. I felt my prayers had been answered when I saw an advertisement in the newspaper for a rally sponsored by a well-known evangelical parachurch organization. This highly respected youth ministry was bringing a noted Caucasian preacher to the city. The newspaper said that everyone was welcome, so I put my suit on and went to the hall alone. I was anxious to hear what the preacher might say to encourage my faith.

I sang "A Mighty Fortress Is Our God" along with the audience. This service was much different than any that I had attended at the Pilgrim Rest Baptist Church. No one shouted or clapped. There wasn't a tambourine in sight. As the organist began to belt out the introductory notes for the next hymn, a slender white fellow in a drab olive suit and horn-rimmed glasses came to where I was sitting and slipped a note into my hand. Why was he passing me a note? I didn't know this gentleman.

Quickly I unraveled the tiny piece of paper. It said in print that looked as though it had been typed: "If you want me to arrange for you to have your own youth crusade rally please let me know." My white brother was trying to wrap his bigotry in a cloak of civility, but what he was really saying was something like, "Nigger, don't you know that we don't even want to pray next to you and your kind. You are not welcome at gatherings such as this."

I looked back at him, but he never acknowledged me with his eyes. He was singing with fervor and gusto as though God Almighty himself were standing in the front of the room listening to his voice alone. It was hard for me to concentrate on the message that night. That man hurt me. Occasionally I would risk a glance back at him. He was a picture-perfect postcard of piety and holiness. The fellow jotted down notes in the margins of his Bible as the famous preacher orated. Tears formed at the corners of his eyes when the preacher spoke about the virgin birth.

I was seething inside. I wanted to walk back there and punch him dead in the eye. Of course, then the evening would have ended with a lynching instead of an altar call. Rather than singing "I Surrender All," they would have been shouting "Where can we string this nigger up?"

You see there were some givens in that auditorium. The organizers had been very ethnocentric in their choice of music. Although they had run an ad that said "Everyone Is Welcome," they chose a speaker from their culture who was prepared to speak to it alone. True to form, I may have been the only person of color in the entire room.

I thought to myself, *What if that preacher had looked out at the lone black-eyed pea in the bowl of white rice and asked, "Where are the rest of our black brethren?" What if he had addressed the issue of Jim Crow? Surely those Christians would have listened to one of their own.* Instead, he reinforced their evil with a silence on the matter that stank to heaven like rotted fish. By his silence the preacher was telling these people that as long as they didn't cuss, smoke or dip snuff, they could righteously belong to a society that mistreated people based on the color of their skin. He should have been ashamed of himself. I would have been.

Wasn't there any Christian who had the courage to finally use that pulpit to denounce racism and segregation? Wasn't there a preacher anywhere who would call the powers that be into question in the name of Jesus Christ? Oh, how I prayed and wondered.

ON THE ROAD WITH THE BAND

Until I could find the answer to those questions, I went back to playing jazz. In fact, I joined a band at the close of my junior year, and against the wishes of my grandmother I went on the road.

The band was filled with older jazz musicians who were serious about their craft. We barnstormed through the Midwest, playing one-nighters in small, cold-water towns where young people would come to dance the Lindy Hop and hear us race through the hottest dance hits on the Top 100 charts. Some of us were young. Most of us had never been very far from home. But we were having good time. The audiences loved our music, and we loved entertaining them.

Breakfast, lunch and dinner were always a problem for us. The nationally known restaurant chains generally adhered to a strict backdoor policy when it came to their African American patrons. We entered through the door marked "Employees Only." And in the dim back rooms someone would bring us a hamburger. (In such instances, it was best not to check to see if your plate had been washed clean.) At some places, "White Only" meant no "coloreds" in the front door or the back!

When I was on the road with the band, we couldn't stay in the major hotels. When we hit town, the driver would pull the bus over at the first corner populated by idle African American men. "Say Jack," he would holler, "Where do the colored people stay in this town?" Directions received, he would steer the bus past bars, funeral parlors and barbershops until we located the transient rooming house. Barbecue smoke floated through the air. Pimps and whores lounged on the front porch, their eyes scoping the block for marks and suckers. They nodded as wide-eyed, blue-suited men from the big city disembarked from the bus with hard-shell instrument cases in hand. "Where y'all from?" they'd invariably ask. "KC," we'd respond.

The band's manager was not particular about where he booked us to play. Once we went out to western Kansas to play for hillbillies with blue denim overalls and cowboy hats. They entered the hall grinning and laughing. They were jovial and agreeable—until we struck the first chord. We played Kansas City jazz. They were looking for the Grand Old Opry. The men stumbled over their pointy-toed cowboy boots as they tried to swing their sweethearts to our brand of hard-bop music.

"What are you doing, nigger?" a hostile voice resonated over my saxophone solo. I kept playing. "You niggers have got some nerve!"

I put the saxophone down. "My name is not . . ."

Heavy wooden chairs started flying. Big, steer-fed ranch hands started racing toward the bandstand. It was time to make a run for it.

BROKE ON THE ROAD

The manager hired us out to play in support of a traveling carnival. The carnival was run by a rough-and-tumble crowd, some of whom had just fallen out of the penitentiary. Our job was to sit down in an orchestra pit and play background music for what were politely called "burlesque" dancers. Today, they call them "strippers." I had come a long way from the Pilgrim Rest Baptist Church.

Some nights, as I lay on my back staring up at the plaster peeling from the ceiling above, a faint voice would begin to call in the nether regions of my mind. It was God. He was calling me to Christian service. I quickly turned over and tried to go to sleep. I was having too much fun.

One Friday, payday came and the boss didn't show up with our money. He sent word back that we shouldn't worry. He would have our cash in a few days. This was a catastrophe for me. I was living hand-to-mouth already. By the end of the week, my stomach was empty. My trousers were beginning to fit loosely at the waistline. In my despair I prayed, "Lord, if you just help me now, I will answer the call to the ministry."

One night after the carnival had closed for the evening, one of the carnie ladies took a look at me and said, "The kid's got to eat." That night God moved the heart of a stripper to purchase my dinner. I was greatly moved. That simple kindness tenderized my heart for ministry. I don't remember that woman's name, but her sacrifice remained with me even after the carnival was history. That one selfless act affected how I treat any individual who walks up to me with the words, "I'm hungry; can you help me?"

God can take all of your experiences and use them to bless someone else. If you've ever been hungry or denied a job, that experience might be a blessing in disguise from God. You can't really minister until you've had some hardships. You can't really counsel someone whose heart is broken unless your own heart has been broken.

ANSWERING THE CALL

One night I followed my band mates to the band shell, placed my horn to my lips and began to play. What happened next is difficult to explain. The presence of the Divine impressed itself on my soul. A strong call of God to ministry was on my heart. There were no audible words. I saw no burning bush. Yet I felt something so real that I had trouble keeping my mind on "Take the A Train." Somewhere deep down inside, the voice of God asked, "Do you want to play one-night stands all of your life?"

Before dawn the next morning, I rose from my bed and dressed quietly. My friends were all asleep. I grabbed my horn and then walked down to the Greyhound bus station. I purchased a one-way bus ticket back to Kansas City, Missouri.

As I watched the dust curl in the skies above the interstate, I wondered just what I would do now. I was relying on my music to earn my college tuition. Where else in the world could a black man earn the kind of money that I was making with my saxophone? Would I end up like so many other poor but honest black men—washing dishes at the Woolworth luncheon counter or working as some rich, white person's chauffeur? I had done well so far in school. Would I now have to forget all of that and take a job setting pins in the bowling alley or grinning and scraping and bowing to keep the rent paid?

On the way back to Kansas City, the voice of God continued to summon me to his work. At one point I attempted to bargain with the Holy Spirit. I said, "Okay Lord, you don't want me to be a musician, let me be a social worker. Let me be a YMCA secretary." I told God, "If you get me a job like that, I could save a lot of boys, save a lot of families." But God said no.

Finally, I was home. Mama threw her arms around me and squeezed my neck tightly. Grandma kissed my cheek and pulled my head close to hers. Joseph, who had grown almost as tall as I, squeezed my hand with a silly grin and punched my right shoulder. I breathed a sigh of relief. No one laughed at me or gave the speech about why I shouldn't have gone with those bad jazz men. I had crossed that great hurdle. The larger one ahead of me was crossing the threshold of the Pilgrim Rest Baptist Church.

On Sunday morning I wasn't in any hurry to get to Sunday school. The Paul Lawrence Dunbar District of Leeds was not a big place. By this time everybody knew that I had left the church to play what the preachers called the "devil's music."

I tightened the knot on my tie that Sunday morning with some trepidation. I was somewhat embarrassed as I tucked my Bible beneath my arm and walked down the street with Mama at my side. We nodded at a full-figured woman in a broad straw hat who was dragging two pressed and perfumed girls behind her. Car horns beeped, and we waved at neighbors.

Even though I had strayed far from my faith and upbringing, the church didn't turn its back on me. The pastor inspired me that morning; the choir lifted me. When I left the church, my suit was wrinkled from all of the hugs that had smothered me. The elderly mothers of the church left ruby-red lipstick prints on my cheeks.

Deacon Joseph Page, a tall, stately man in a neatly pressed black suit, grabbed my shoulders and pulled me to the side of the narthex. "James, you looking for a job?" he asked. "Why yes, sir," I answered. "Be dressed for work tomorrow afternoon. I'll put you to work on my paint crew." I nodded exuberantly. My heart was so full that I didn't trust myself to speak.

Working as a house painter gave me a lot of time to think. I was preparing to enter my senior year in high school, a crucial time. In a matter of months I would be graduating. What would become of me? I desperately wanted to attend college, but my folks were poor people. It was a struggle for Mama to keep clothes on our backs and bread on the table. Grandmother, who was getting up in years now, worked only sporadically. How could she meet tuition bills? I had planned to earn money for college by playing jazz, but now the Lord had silenced my horn. As I painted strokes on the side of small houses in Leeds, I tried to figure a path that would lead to the doors of higher education. Occasionally, the whisper of God's voice would stir inside of my bones. I tried to ignore it, but eventually the call of God had me surrounded. The Holy Spirit said, "You made some promises to me in Oklahoma. You've got to announce your call to the ministry."

One afternoon I was brushing blue paint on the side of a building when the Voice filled my spirit again. I was tired; I couldn't run any longer. I did the only thing that I knew how to do. God's divine providence had engineered the circumstances of my life so that my employer was also my deacon and spiritual guide. I didn't have to go far to find direction. When the break was called, I pulled Deacon Joseph Page to the side and I told him what I had been fighting inside of myself. That day after work he took me to speak with our new pastor, the Reverend F. D. Robinson. We found him at home in his personal study. He smiled broadly as I entered the room. The Holy Spirit had broken me down. I was his.

OFF TO COLLEGE

During my senior year I was called to the podium of Pilgrim Rest Baptist Church. My palms were sweaty. My heart was beating wildly. I made a short speech. "God has called me to preach. Please pray for me." A chorus of "amens" from all over the church rushed to meet my ears. After the service my friends pounded me on the back. "You'll be alright, Smith," they said. I wasn't so sure. I wasn't sure of anything.

Around that time one of my good friends made the announcement that he too was called to preach. His fortunes looked much brighter than mine. His parents announced that they were sending him to Grace Bible College in Omaha, Nebraska.

The black community put a high premium on "trained" preachers, which is understandable. If a Christian sister announced that God had called her to dentistry but she did not go through the grueling preparation and testing in dentistry school, would you let her reach into your mouth with a high-speed drill to perform a root canal? If a Christian brother said that God had called him to defend the innocent through the legal system but he had not studied in law school, would you let him represent you at your tax trial?

An African American pastor does so much more than preach sermons. The pastor is the community representative and a civil rights advocate. Church members seek the pastor's counsel on matters of life, death and beyond. I wanted to be ready when I donned the clerical collar, but that took something that I had precious little of—money.

I didn't have a dime for education. My mother had no money. And by this time I knew that Daddy would be of no help. I got on my knees and asked the Lord to help me. My elders told me that God would not fail me, but doubt crowded my mind as my high school career came to completion.

I graduated from high school in June of 1948. It was a proud day. Tears welled up in Mother's eyes. I had done what neither she nor my grandmother had been able to do: I walked the stage. I was the class valedictorian. My speech drew whistles and applause. Grandma and Mama looked at each other and smiled. But they weren't the only family present. Aunt Louise and Uncle Percy and Reverend Robinson were there. Uncle Charles Beamon, who had caused our family to have to flee to Kansas City under cover of night, nodded silently as he slipped an envelope into my hands. There was money inside. I appreciated his gift, but I needed thousands of dollars to think about going further in school. I began to see myself at age forty in a white T-shirt and a paper hat scrubbing old cheese and saliva from soiled dishes at the bus station cafe.

A popular saying among Christians these days is "Pray until something happens." That is just what I did. And one day a letter fell through the mail slot. I had been granted admission to a humble National Baptist college called Western Baptist College. I stood there in the center of the living room, tears of joy streaming down my cheeks. I was on the way.

On July 4, 1948, I preached my trial sermon, which is the initiation into the ministry. It's sort of like your birthday and college graduation all wrapped into one. Uncle Percy and Aunt Louise were there in their Sunday finery. Uncle Charles sat next to Grandma and Mama. All of the people that I had grown up with, my high school teachers and the entire Leeds community embraced my entrance into Christian ministry. I barely remember the sermon, but I do remember the shivering, the jitters and the cracking of my voice. When it was all over Reverend Robinson handed me a certificate. It was my license to preach the gospel of Jesus Christ.

— 8 —

COLLEGE DAYS

The heat of summer gave way to the cool winds that blew across the Missouri River and past our front door. Golden leaves began to appear on the trees as summer began to show her age. The days grew shorter. Soon it was September and a time for goodbyes. Mama wrapped her arms around me as though I were going to Mars and not just across town. I punched my brother in the shoulder. He was growing into a man in his own right. A mustache was beginning to push its way through the line above his top lip. I would miss being around him, offering him guidance and protection.

Grandma hollered, "Do good at that school. Make us proud, boy!" I promised my best as I opened the door and ran down the street dragging my suitcase and praying that that the bus had not left me behind. I was off to chase the voice of God that had whispered to me from a burning bush on a jazz bandstand. As I ran, I had no idea that my life was flipping a page. I was the first in my family to be able to go college.

My community was proud. The Paul Lawrence Dunbar District was nothing but fistfuls of dirt, clapboard houses and unpaved streets. But it was home. I would never be the same person nor see things in quite the same light. I remembered Grandma helping me to read. I remembered the prompting of my elders. I reflected on the great race leaders who had come to Kansas City, I remembered the Voice in Venita. Butterflies filled my stomach. I didn't know what life would hold for me.

NEW CHALLENGES

Western Baptist College was an all-black school located at 2119 Tracey Avenue in the heart of the African American community. Well-trimmed hedges framed its buildings. Some of the students were from big cities in other states. Would I be able to cut it here? In high school I had been a big fish in a small pond. But this? This was something different. Although I had the love and encouragement of my mom and grandmother, here I felt I was in a vacuum with no support. But there were expectations back home, people who never had the opportunity to go to college were counting on me to finish the race. Everything in life had taught me the importance of education, and I was ready to scratch and claw my way to a diploma if need be.

I was assigned to a private room in Goings Hall. The room was comfortable but the food was bad, even for institutional fare. On any given night mystery meat, sticky mashed potatoes and a noncarbonated sweet drink might serve as dinner. On the weekends, the meals were composed of bread, lunch meat and mustard. Nevertheless, the education that I was receiving was taking my mind to places it had never been.

QUESTIONING THE UNQUESTIONABLE

I was brought up in a fundamentalist Christian household. We were taught to never ask questions. Our mantra went something like this: God said it. The preacher interpreted it. I believe it. And that settles it. In college, professors confronted us with questions that I would never have dared to think, let alone ask.

Was the world made in seven literal days, or is Genesis an allegory explaining God's creation of the world to illiterate people in the first century? Did God really tell the Israelites to murder babies, or did the Hebrew people put that into the record to justify the mass slaughter of innocent people? Was David truly a "man after God's own heart" or a usurper to the throne who exercised sovereign control over how scribes would have him remembered? It didn't stop there.

For as long as I could spell the word *God,* I wondered why he was so silent about black men twisting from ropes or my Mama on her knees scrubbing the floors in a white man's house. Why was "wait for the descent of the Son of Man" the only offer of liberation from the pulpit? At Western Baptist College I was introduced to *A Theology for the Social Awakening* by Walter Rauschen-

busch. Rauschenbusch had a theology that was much different from anything
I had learned in Sunday school. (I still read his work.) I had no trouble with
liberal theologians because they at least gave lip service to freedom and democracy. The fire and brimstone preachers of conservative theology had nothing to say about racism and the reality of the black experience in America.

In college I encountered professors who had a profound effect on the way I
see the world. W. R. Howell discussed history as though he had been living for
centuries. He had never earned a doctorate, but he was more learned than
many educators with a Ph.D. And despite his great span of knowledge, he was
an incredibly modest man. Dr. Maynard Turner was the first African American
that I met with a Th.D. in Old Testament. He encouraged me to be a critical
thinker.

Dr. C. A. Pugh, a short man with a big, booming voice, taught the fundamen-
tals of preaching. (He also served as the pastor of Stranger's Rest Baptist
Church in Kansas City.) Walking down a hallway, you could hear him preaching with exuberance. Teaching us how to preach with burning passion, Dr.
Pugh electrified the classroom. He made preaching seem so vital and important, I couldn't wait to get there. Dr. Pugh also taught me how to use logic when
arguing a biblical point. Through his teaching I learned to take the Scripture
text seriously, seeking out the implied meanings as well as the obvious.

When I went home on weekends, I would visit my pastor, Reverend Robinson, whom I continued to love. However, I began to see my faith was expanding. Seeds of change were being planted in my mind.

THE WOMAN OF MY DREAMS

One afternoon when I was visiting my mother, I saw the woman of my
dreams. She stepped out of a magazine—literally. My mother had opened up
a magazine to a picture of a high school student who had just been awarded a
scholarship to Western Baptist College. My heart skipped a beat.

The next September I was mystified when I saw her walk through the halls.
Here she was in the flesh. When the pecan-complexioned, young girl with al-
mond-shaped eyes sashayed past me, I saw the heavens open and the clouds
momentarily stop their path through the sky. I could almost see angels step
aside to let her pass. I loved her the first time that my eyes rested on her. She
could have turned a purebred atheist into a tongues-speaking saint. She was
that gorgeous.

I tried to speak, but I could only stare at my feet until she made her way past me. James Hunter, a big offensive tackle from Chicago, knew that I had a crush on JoAnna Goodwin. He also saw that I was too afraid to ask her out for a date. He said, "Little Smith (which is what everyone called me) if you won't ask her, I'll ask her for you." One afternoon Big James came into the dining hall with a toothy grin spread across his round, brown cheeks. "Little Smith, she says that she'll go out with you."

I had dated off and on in high school, but never seriously. My dates were escorts that I accompanied to a prom or a church social. JoAnna was different. Before I exchanged the first sentence with JoAnna, I said to myself, *Boy, this is somebody that I would like to spend the rest of my life with.* On the first date we dressed almost identically. She wore a gray and white pinstriped two-piece suit and so did I. We went to the movies, but our evening was interrupted by a theater page who requested that I come to the cinema manager's desk. I received the message that my grandmother was near death, and I had to rush back home. (James Hunter escorted JoAnna home for me.)

I dreamed of JoAnna. I doodled her name on the corner of my notebook pages during class lectures. I grinned at the oddest times. I wrote poetry promising her my undying love. Still, I wasn't sure how she felt about me until one cold day in the fall of 1950.

Back in the 1950s a 5' 7" man could not only play college football, he could start on both the defensive and offensive line. I was such a man. It was the fourth quarter of a football game. The play was a sweep, which called for the offensive guard to lead a charge over the left side of the line. I sprinted head-first toward the first-down marker, and out of nowhere a Mack truck of a football player laid me out with a forearm.

I was trying to collect my thoughts while lying on the turf, but my mind was twirling within in my skull. I thought I heard a woman scream. JoAnna apparently leaped down the bleachers and began to run onto the field. The coach tried to restrain her, crying, "Get back, Ms. Goodwin." She would hear none of it. Her high heels caught in the mud, causing her to slow down as she fought to get to my side. Hundreds of necks craned in our direction.

By that time I could have risen. My head had cleared, and I was fine. I just wanted to see how this thing would play out. When JoAnna ran out to where I lay on the field, I knew that she loved me!

When my attention to JoAnna Goodwin became public, I received a repri-

mand from the president of the school. He informed me that the faculty had
great plans for Ms. JoAnna Goodwin. She was not only their beautiful belle,
she was an academic standout. He obviously saw me as a young fellow born
out of wedlock who hailed from a very rural community where the people still
had outhouses and where chickens and hogs ran freely. My grades were aver-
age at best. Where was I going in life? Where could I take her? But that did not
deter me. Instead, I improved academically.

MEETING THE PARENTS

I met JoAnna's parents at a Sunday afternoon country-basket dinner. The
Goodwins had invited me to preach at their church. Small churches in the rural
areas would host a special church service that featured six or seven young
preachers, each of them delivering ten-minute sermonettes. After the sermons
were completed, the church members and guests would enjoy an outdoor picnic of soul food that had been prepared by the women of the church. I
preached my sermon from the depths of my soul, hardly taking my eyes off of
Mr. Goodwin, who nodded when I quoted from the Bible.

Jodie Goodwin was an ebony-complexioned farmer from just outside War-
rensburg, Missouri, about fifty miles from Kansas City. He owned eighty acres
of farmland. Mr. Goodwin was a Baptist deacon and a man of prayer. He
would start the day by gathering his wife and eight children for prayer and
meditation. In the evenings you could hear his supplications to God a full
quarter mile from the farm.

His wife, Olivia, was a very fair-complexioned woman. She loved to laugh
and tease people. Because our personalities were so similar, we hit it off immediately. Mrs. Goodwin was a great cook. I have never tasted collard greens as
wonderful as those she used to make.

That summer the Southern Baptist Convention funded a program that sent
missionaries across Missouri. JoAnna and I were both accepted into the program. We were sent across the state as a missionary team. At the invitation of
a local pastor, JoAnna would teach the children hymns of the faith and I would
share from the Word of God. We developed arts and crafts for the younger children. It was fun and inspiring. Young people came to faith in Jesus Christ
through our two-week programs, and this ministry drew JoAnna and I closer
together. Prayer became a major part of our relationship. The Scriptures tell us
that the man who finds a good wife has found favor with God. When I looked

into JoAnna's bright brown eyes, I realized that heaven had indeed smiled upon me.

There was a precious intangible about JoAnna Goodwin that I had never seen in another woman. I saw us working together for God as a team. I needed a woman who could "get a prayer through" as the older saints back at the Pilgrim Rest Baptist Church would say. I needed this woman by my side, so that I could serve God with all of my senses. But there was a small problem: JoAnna's family nickname was "Mish." Her dream was to go to Africa, and her family always assumed that she would achieve her dream of being a missionary. Undaunted, I shared my vision with her.

Aunt Louise, Mama and my classmate, the Reverend Charles Briscoe, came out to the Goodwin family farm with me in my sophomore year. Following an afternoon of dinner and fellowship with JoAnna's family, Charles voiced the family consensus. "Boy, you better marry that girl."

Thank God, I was able to persuade JoAnna to cast her lot with me. My grandmother went with me to city hall to get my license. She had to sign for me because I was nineteen, too young to marry without permission in that time.

Three years after our first date, JoAnna and I were married. We were married on September 5, 1951, at JoAnna's aunt's house in Kansas City. Reverend Robinson performed the ceremony. We've been together ever since.

— 9 —

THE BITTER AND THE SWEET

God had revealed much of his will for my life. I had married a wonderful woman who would be my partner in God's work. I was learning much about Scripture and preaching. Yet I still needed practical advice and spiritual counsel. I wanted to lift my people up, and I wanted to fight against prejudice and racism. How would a preacher accomplish these things?

I began to study preachers like an aspiring prize fighter studies tapes of Muhammad Ali. I sought opportunities to sit down for coffee with the preaching giants of my day. I understood that I needed mentors, and I was constantly searching for Elijahs and Deborahs to deposit their wisdom into my life. My life was full of black pearls and diamonds—men and women who invested in me. College was a gold mine full of wise elders who gave precious advice and direction. These mentors also opened ministry doors for me. It is difficult to succeed in the work without them. Three of my mentors were

- Dr. Elder B. Hicks: a black minister working for the American Baptist Home Mission Societies. He was the former executive minister of the Kansas Baptist Convention. Dr. Hicks was a gifted administrator and was considered a giant in our denomination. Like a million other aspiring preachers, I met him when I was a freshman at Western Baptist College. But somehow Dr. Hicks must have seen something in me because he took me under this wing. He gave me some advice that changed my destiny.

- Dr. E. A. Freeman: the first black man to earn a doctorate in theology from Central Baptist Seminary. He served as the president of the Kansas Baptist Convention and also was one of the leaders of the National Baptist Convention. He regularly preached about justice and righteousness. I met him in college and held on to his friendship and guidance for decades to follow.

- Dr. I. H. Henderson Jr.: the pastor of the Friendship Baptist Church in Kansas City and the state president of the Missouri Baptist Convention. He delivered his sermons like a lawyer arguing before a jury. He always had a word of counsel for me as we discussed the nuts and bolts of church leadership. From time to time he would sit down with me and show me his sermon preparation process. He was such a busy man, but he always made time for me.

GRANDMA PASSES AWAY

Life is both bitter and sweet. During my first year of marriage, I tasted life's most bitter fruit. My wife and I were living in Kansas City with my mother and grandmother when Grandmother became very ill.

This was the woman who had raised us, fed us, fought all the hellish forces that transpired to take us under and loved us. This was our hero and our sunshine. And now Grandma lay dying. She was desperately ill and had no desire to live. She said, "All of my friends are on the other side of the chilly Jordan. I have more people over there than here. I am ready to go and join them."

Her eyes seemed warm but unfocused. A blue blanket stretched from her toes to her chin; silver blue hair peeked from beneath her rimless sleeping cap. She stretched her right hand out in my direction. When I squeezed it, she began to pray. Much of what she prayed is lost to the years, but I do remember her final words: "Lord, please send James friends who will help him in his journey as a preacher of this great gospel."

MY BROTHER'S PAIN

My family from Mississippi flew into town for the funeral services. Uncle Percy and Aunt Louise helped Mom and Uncle Charles plan the funeral service. This left my brother and me with some time to share. Even in this dreadful season, I was thankful for the opportunity to see how things were going with my baby brother.

It seemed as though Joseph had come of age overnight. One day he was the little kid in short pants tagging along as I went to the football field with my peers. And now he was sixteen and had hair on his chin, almost a grown man. Joseph liked boxing, and he was a pretty good middleweight. He could take a punch. Yet something had happened the last summer that really knocked the wind out of him. I'm not sure that he ever completely recovered from it.

One day that summer, Joseph was sitting on a milk crate in front of the corner store when a red Ford pickup truck came speeding up the road. Dust particles swirled around as the vehicle came to a stop. A white man with Dickies overalls and a straw hat leaped down from the running board. "Which a you boys lookin' for work?" he asked.

There were four young men sitting with my brother. "Take me, Mister! Take me!" they hollered, each waving his hand frantically.

The fellow put his hands on his hips and gave out a deep belly laugh. "I see I got me some strong bucks here!" His eyes narrowed. His voice dropped down a register, "Won't be easy, ya know. Come out to my place and y'all gonna hafta work!"

The boys needed little convincing. My brother was desperate for work. We'd been taught that a man earns his own way and pays his own keep. There was shame in unemployment. Joseph needed more than money; work was tied to self-esteem. He would have marched down to the gates of hell in a gasoline soaked T-shirt for the opportunity to do an honest day's labor. But there were no jobs in Leeds for a young black man. In those days, when you opened up the newspaper you'd find an ad that might read something like: "Counter Help Wanted—Woolworth's Department Store. Must be hard worker. Competitive wages. Whites only need apply."

The white farmer arrived at the corner store before dawn the next morning. Sure enough, Joseph and his friends were there waiting. They piled into the back of the pickup truck as the sun peeled back the layers of darkness. The dampness of the morning dew chilled their bones as the pickup shook and bounced on the red clay roads. Finally, the Ford took a turn down a winding country road, perhaps twenty miles away from Leeds. Then they saw it: amidst waist-high weeds was a five-bedroom home that had not seen a paint brush in fifty years. There were holes in the roof, and the windows were broken out.

"Y'all get down!" the farmer commanded. He pointed at the shell of a house and said, "Now boys, we got five days to put this house back together!" The farmer said "we," but he never picked up a paintbrush or a hammer.

The project seemed impossible. Joseph knew that they would need a plan if they were going to complete such a difficult job. My brother took on the role of foreman. He handed out tasks and then went to work like John Henry, his hammer flashing in the sun.

Each morning the farmer would pick them up at the store and take them the twenty miles to his farm. He never provided lunch and balked at water breaks. Despite the farmer's inhospitable ways, my brother kept the building program on track. By Friday the last coat of paint was being applied to the exterior. Joseph's chest swelled with pride. "I tell you what, guys. Let's not take lunch today. Let's get this thing finished before quitting time!"

The windows had been replaced. The house was now a pretty sky-blue color. My brother and his friends had even planted flowers around the entrance way. By quitting time it was finished. Joseph and his friends looked at each other and cheered. They felt a tremendous surge of pride. They had virtually raised this beautiful house from the dust. Their muscles ached. Their sinews had been stretched. Flecks of paint speckled their flesh. There was dirt caked beneath their fingernails. They slapped each other on the back. The project was finished. It was quitting time and pay day. So they walked up to the farmer's door with grins of anticipation on their faces. My brother rubbed his palms.

"Man, I'm-a take my girl to the movies tonight!" said one young fellow with a bald head.

"The first thing I'm-a do is pay my tithes and buy my mama a whole cabinet full-a groceries," another fellow announced.

My brother knocked on the door. There was no answer. He knocked a second time. The farmer couldn't have left the house—they were in the middle of nowhere. Even if he had left the house, he couldn't get anywhere without that pickup truck. Finally, the door flung open like the spring on a mouse trap. The farmer burst through the door with a double-barreled shotgun aimed at eye level. His face was made of stone. He pointed the barrel at one young fellow and then another.

"You stinkin' niggas get off my land now. I'm-a givin' ya till the count of three! One, two . . ." He cocked the hammer.

The young men turned and raced up the lane, high-tailing it for the highway. The farmer's ghastly cackle rang in their ears as they ran for their lives. The boys cried with anger and shame most of the way home. It was dark before Joseph walked through the door at home. His feet were blistered and sore. But it was his heart that was damaged worst of all. He wondered to himself how that man could be so cruel as to mistreat high school kids. Even his faith could not overcome the blow.

After Grandma's funeral, I stayed at Joseph's side for a few days, encouraging him.

That wasn't the last time Joseph would walk through the fires of racism, but it was the worst—and it left him wounded. Even as a man in his sixties he would interrupt a conversation about Shaq and the L.A. Lakers with, "J, you remember what that white man did to me back in Missouri?"

JOANNA'S BIG SURPRISE

Yes, life is bitter *and* sweet. Here is the sweet. Five months after our wedding, JoAnna gave me the greatest news that a man could ever receive. Over breakfast one morning, she said, "Honey, we are going to have a child." I was ecstatic—but I was also afraid.

"O God, you've given us a child," I mused in my prayer closet. The blessed announcement made me think of my own father and his neglect, how the absence of his love made it feel at times as though I were growing up on the dark side of the moon.

Any male with working parts can sire a child, but will he be there when the child is screaming like the flaming chariots of God racing through heavens? Will he be there when the child needs love and understanding, care and tenderness? Will he be there for his toddler after his whole world explodes at work? Will he work that second job or take that night-school class to make that child's life better? Will he be a model of godliness, sacrifice and civic duty for eyes that see and measure truth through his actions?

My father would still write letters from time to time. Yet he had never been "there" for me. My prayer and fervent hope was that I could be those things for the infant in my young wife's womb.

FIRST-TIME FATHER

Is any first-time father ever really prepared for the birth of his child? I had done everything on the checklist to prepare for this sacred occasion. We had purchased a bassinet and a lifetime supply of diapers. Since I had no car, one of our neighbors, a friend named Walter Phillips, had agreed to drive us to the hospital whenever he got "the" call. I was all set. But when JoAnna tapped me on the shoulder, I went to pieces. It was like the television newscaster had just announced the Battle of Armageddon.

I called Walter with the same edge that would have filled my voice had the whole world been burning down. Our neighbor was pounding at the door within milliseconds. "Come on, Baby, we got to get out of here," I shouted to JoAnna. Looking back on it, I must have seemed like a crazy person to her. The truth is, I was afraid that I was going to lose her.

I stuffed JoAnna into the back of Walter's car. I prayed all the way to the hospital. I begged God to save her. (At the time it didn't occur to me that babies are born every day, all day, all over the earth.) When we arrived at the all-black Phyllis Wheatley hospital, I grabbed JoAnna's bag. She rested on my arm, moaning softly. What had I done to put my wife through all of this? My heart shuddered within my chest.

The hot lights in the maternity ward shined down on us like the penetrating eyes of God. A nurse took one look at JoAnna and ushered us into the delivery room. I had done my part; now it was up to the good Lord and the doctors. I was handed a hospital gown. The smell of alcohol, the screaming, the crying, the machines with their beeps and dashes, the nurses in white, the doctors' hushed whispers: it was all too much for me. I fainted and fell to the floor. A nurse with narrow eyes and a square jaw shook me awake. Her voice had no mercy in it. "You should have thought about this nine months ago," she thundered.

My first child, Amy Smith, was born in a segregated facility in Kansas City, Missouri. Amy was the most perfect thing that I had ever held in my hands. It was September 26, 1951. James Alfred Smith Jr. came into the world the following year on September 9.

GOD'S GIFT

People see me as a tough man. (I can roar like a lion.) And if the poor and disinherited are threatened, I will wade into battle like Spartacus with the sword of the Lord in my hand. However, in reality I am fragile man. God gave me somebody who could protect me—JoAnna. She became my rock of Gibraltar. She is steady as could be in a storm. She has been intensely loyal to me. There hasn't been much that could move her.

— 10 —

PRESIDENT OF THE MISSOURI NAACP

In 1951 I was elected to the presidency of the Missouri NAACP while still a college student. I helped to engineer voter registration drives in churches all over the state. One of the most heated discussions on the table was desegregation. I argued for integration, which is like a church potluck dinner where everyone brings a favorite dish to share. Desegregation meant that only one group would contribute to the dinner. But black people had so much to share with the world that they should not be excluded.

The presidency of the NAACP was rewarding because I became a spokesman for my people. I was finally allowed opportunities to speak out for justice.

NEXT STEPS

From the time I was a child, the dream that shaped the landscape of my life cast me as a "race man": a Walter White, a Mordecai Johnson, an A. Philip Randolph. My heart burned to speak on a full-time basis against the evils of segregation that choked the soul of the black community. I dreamed of speaking hope to my downtrodden brethren. I wanted to be God's Trombone, as depicted in James Weldon Johnson's epic poem. But as my college education came screeching to an end, I saw no way to carry on the crusade to the extent I desired.

There wasn't much call for a full-time race man in 1952, the year I graduated from college. So I set about the business of making a living for my family
and myself. An opportunity opened up for me in Keytesville, Missouri. I became the principal of the Lincoln Elementary School. There the music of my
world became the sound of size-four feet tramping through the front door of
a two-room school. I taught grades 5-8 in one room. Alice Tolson, a former college classmate, taught grades 1-4.

We had our work cut out for us. The public school system had a policy
never to buy new books for the students in the hovels and lean-tos that housed
its African American students. As I stood in front of that room on the first day
of class, I remembered the highly motivated, poorly paid educators who gave
me hope in the future even though a segregated society told me that I was
nothing. And as I faced that river of hair bows and rows of pearly white teeth,
I wondered, *Am I worthy?* As I poured my soul into those young minds, I
prayed for wisdom and strength from on high.

I approached the classroom with the care and precision a brain surgeon
might bring to the operating room. I was working with the delicate part of the
human anatomy—the mind. As I watched my young charges labor with pro-
nunciation and the rules of grammar, I remembered Grandma. Her picture in
my heart gave me immeasurable patience. I felt as though we were building
the future, but not everyone saw it that way.

One day my superintendent cornered me with the fires of hell burning in
her eyes. "James, what are doing here? Why are you teaching these children
art, music and science? All they are going to be is field hands and maids, and
all they need to know is how to read, write and count." She had strict rules
against the teaching of African American history. Both the black and white
schools were under orders to skip the Civil War period of American history—
we wouldn't want to inflame passions, would we? Like my ancestors on the
plantation, I found a way to squeeze the message of our African past between
reading and arithmetic studies. How can a child have any sense of self-esteem
without some knowledge of his or her cultural roots?

The superintendent would squint her eyes in my direction as though she
were attempting to read the ingredients on my soul. I learned quickly how to
assuage her fear by telling the woman what she needed to believe. Once her
soul was soothed with the knowledge that she would always have a dark domestic labor pool, I was able to teach those young people about every black

person of note that I could think of, from Mansa Musa to Marcus Garvey. I told them that it was their right and responsibility to resist oppression.

I also learned that my work at the school was a ministry. I was not serving the Lord any less when I stood in front of a classroom with a pointer in hand than I was when I was slamming down my hand on the pulpit and exegeting the finer points of a text. God's calling on a person is often multifaceted. God had called me not only to be a preacher but an educator and a staunch advocate for equal public education. And as my career continued, the thirst to see poor children receive a good education continued to burn within me.

In 1954 the groundbreaking case *Brown v. Board of Education* was settled. In Missouri, African Americans accepted the news with mixed emotions. We knew that it would not mean integration but desegregation. Black teachers with masters degrees from accredited white institutions were fired from their teaching positions because when black children were finally brought into white public schools, thus desegregating the classroom, black educators were not permitted to teach white children. *Brown v. Board of Education* closed up black institutions and black teachers were driven away and disenfranchised.

THE PASTORATE

In 1951, while I was a junior in college, I was called to pastor the Mount Washington Baptist Church, a small church in Parkville, Missouri. JoAnna served as the pianist. An iron stove stood in a corner of the tiny building. When we arrived on Sunday morning, we had to fill the stove with firewood and then light it to warm the place up. After this was done, I would hop in my car and drive around the community to pick up my members. Later, during the sermon, I would be starting on my third point when I realized that the fire was going out, so I had to leap down from the pulpit and throw a few more logs in the fire. At first this was a major disruption, but eventually I learned to do this without interrupting the flow of the message.

That congregation gathered my family into their hearts. Memories of their warmth and kindness lived with me long after we left them. The church had six members when I started there and thirty-three when I left.

A WOMAN IN THE PULPIT

While teaching school in Keytesville, Missouri, the Ebenezer Baptist Church in Armstrong, Missouri, opened its arms to my family and me. In this close-knit, rural community, the Baptist and Methodist denominations shared one church building, using the building on alternate Sundays. In Armstrong I was exposed to something that I had never seen before—a woman preacher! The Methodists sent a female to fill the pulpit. She was a highly anointed woman. The people loved her. She could preach as well as any man that I had ever seen.

When I was growing up, women sang in the choir, taught Sunday school, served as members of the usher board and kept the church's mission work going. They cooked fried chicken and fed the church. They prepared the Lord's Supper for the pastor and male deacons to serve, and they cleaned up after the service. Women also prepared the baptismal garments. Women raised the money, and the men told them how to spend it. The women made the church run, but they dared not set foot in the pulpit. The sacred platform was set aside only for God's all-male clergy. I never questioned it. That was the way it was, so I assumed this was the way it was supposed to be.

In college I had begun to question the role of women in the church. Thank God for college professors who taught us to think critically. I took a course called "Introduction to the Bible." In the Old Testament portion of that class, I read about a woman prophet named Huldah, who interpreted for young Josiah the meaning of the scrolls that the workmen had found in the temple. This was the book of Deuteronomy, the second law. We owe the book of Deuteronomy to this woman. If you don't believe in women's ministry, you have to chop that book out of the Bible, because a woman helped interpret it.

SEMINARY AND THE PASTORATE

While I was teaching in Keytesville, I was called from the pastorate of the Ebenezer Baptist Church to serve the Second Baptist Church of Huntsville. JoAnna and I accepted their offer with joy. The people of this church did not have much in the way of financial resources, but they helped us in other ways. In the winter I was escorted to their smoke houses, where I helped myself to fresh bacon and venison. In the summer, baskets of fresh apples, tomatoes, lettuce and blueberries appeared at our parsonage door. The folks didn't have much, but they shared with us. Between 1953 and 1957 these gifts came in handy, and we loved these generous people. We still communicate with them.

My family had expanded. Shari Lynn Smith was born on January 14, 1955. God sent Ronald Craig Smith to us on March 7, 1956. Things were tough. I barely had money to purchase diapers. My family lived in a house with no plumbing. The bathroom was an outhouse in a field beyond the house itself. Many was the night when I forced myself to "hold it" rather than to risk battle with the rattlesnakes and field mice that might be roaming around the outhouse in the dark.

My wife was an excellent household budgeter, but we couldn't make ends meet on the $25.00 a week that the church was paying. I had left my teaching position behind in Keytesville, so I had to get another job to supplement my income. One of the members told me about a man who was hiring on a farm not far from the church. I went to check on it and was awarded a position laboring in the fields, hauling hay. Every sinew and nerve stretched as I picked up the heavy bundles and tossed them on the back of the truck. Strands of hay lodged in my hair. It itched when it fell down the back of my shirt. I left the plantation at the end of each day weary, soiled and somewhat angry. Had I fought my way through college for this?

There were other jobs, all of which required a broom and a dust pan. JoAnna rubbed my back on those dark nights when I dreaded the sunrise. "Don't worry, James. God is good. He will bless us." And what she said was right. However, I also remembered the words of a college professor who had advised, "I think that you should consider furthering your education beyond the B.A. level. The opportunities for service will be far greater."

With the professor's words ringing in my ears, I enrolled in a graduate studies program at the University of Missouri. It was like someone had handed me the owner's manual to life in the twentieth century. Sociology class provided a guided tour through the fabric of cities and civilization, the network of relationships and the nature of societal inequity that grants group status or corporate disfavor. I found out why places like the Paul Laurence Dunbar District of Leeds existed on the edge of a prosperous metropolis.

I also sought theological training at the Missouri School of Religion, the religious arm of the university. The Missouri School of Religion was founded by the Disciples of Christ, but the education offered was interdenominational. Baptists, Methodists and members of the United Church of Christ attended this school.

The seed of education that Grandma had planted so many years ago in that kitchen in Leeds had grown to full bloom. I didn't go to seminary seeking the prestige of more letters behind my name. I went seeking a reasoned faith. I was a disciple sitting at the feet of the learned men of the land.

I had a thirst for learning and a love for books. I was seeking answers. Why did God allow black men to be tested and challenged by oppression that choked their lives and dreams? Why did Christian preachers, both black and white, evade the issues of freedom and segregation in favor of the safety of heaven? And why did this cause people of color to shout praise instead of outrage? And how could I be part of the solution instead of part of the problem?

As I drove to the campus each day, I looked around and wondered. Every African American community in America had a liquor store, a barbershop, a funeral parlor and a barbecue joint. Always sitting in the middle of them was a church. I wondered, *If my church disappeared one night and a delicatessen opened in its place, would the neighborhood be any different?* And if the answer was no, I had to find out why. My sociology studies taught me the results of evil while my theology classes taught me the roots of it.

One of my professors was a Reformed Jew named Isadore Keyfitz. I learned to look at the Old Testament through his lenses. He called it the "Hebrew Bible." I studied the Hebrew language under his tutelage. For the first time I studied in-depth the eighth-century prophets, firebrands and revolutionaries who raged against the excesses enjoyed by the upper class at the expense of the poor and despised.

My fingers trembled as I turned the pages. I was Amos as he cried out:

Hear this word, you cows of Bashan, who are on the mountain
   of Samaria,
who oppress the poor,
who crush the needy." (Amos 4:1)

I was Micah at the city gates hollering:

Now hear this,
You heads of the house of Jacob
And the rulers of the house of Israel,
Who abhor justice
And pervert all equity. (Micah 3:9)

I was walking through the streets of ancient Palestine with Isaiah as he cried:

The Spirit of the Lord GOD *is* upon Me
Because the LORD has anointed Me
To preach good tidings to the poor;

He has sent Me to heal the brokenhearted,

To proclaim liberty to the captives,

And the opening of the prison to *those who are* bound;

To proclaim the acceptable year of the LORD,

And the day of vengeance of our God;

To comfort all who mourn,

To console those who mourn in Zion,

To give men beauty for ashes. (Isaiah 61:1-3).

At the Pilgrim Rest Baptist Church, I had been raised to view my faith as a fire insurance policy that protected me from the eternal ravages of hell. The Missouri School of Religion helped me see not only my horizontal relationship with God but my vertical relationship with humanity. I also learned how to tolerate the viewpoints of people who think differently than I do.

Since I was child marching through the muddy streets of Leeds, I had been taught that sin was an individual matter. For us, sin was theft, lying, adultery and a long list of other missteps. Seminary taught me that along with the aforementioned list, there were societal sins, institutional sins. These were the wrongs that countries perpetrated, making each citizen bear a portion of the responsibility. The prophets spoke the word of the Lord not only to individuals but to nations and political systems. All of God's people suffered or prospered because of decisions made by the people in power.

As I studied, I realized that in America we inherit social status and transferable wealth. To live and to profit in a system that has bankrupted whole portions of its citizenry so that some might have much is to participate in its sin. This type of sin is in the genetic coding of a nation conceived in and built on slavery. As long as Christians approached social inequity in silence it would continue to grow and spread like mold spores in the bottom of a petri dish.

TAKING THE MESSAGE TO THE CHURCH

I never went home to talk to Reverend F. D. Robinson about the things that I was learning. He never would have understood. I knew that he was to the right of me theologically. However, that did not stop me from trying to share my newfound knowledge with the good people of Second Baptist Church. After all, why shouldn't they share in these newfound truths? I served them communion; I taught them the precepts of our most holy faith; I counseled their marriages; I baptized their children; I extended the right hand of fellowship to them; and I ate fried chicken dinners in many of their homes. They had been receptive to the messages of sin, the sacrifice of Christ, resurrection and redemption. That's why I was surprised at their reaction when I tried to incorporate into my sermons what I'd learned in seminary. Even the gray-headed deacon in the second pew, whom I could always count on for an "amen," shook his head as if I had just gone mad. I raised points that I expected to be greeted with shouts and affirmations, but I got nothing. I could hear icicles melting on the South Pole.

After the closing hymn had been sung, I took my post in the church narthex. JoAnna stood at my side. Some of the members were polite. "Nice sermon, Pastor. God bless you." But their faces did not match their words. Eventually, some lay member with less etiquette spoke the collective mind: "God doesn't care if Negroes can vote or not. We want to hear more sermons about heaven."

The reluctance of the people to accept the fact that God was outraged at our plight puzzled me. You see, we were living in dangerous times. Just months earlier Emmett Till, a smooth-faced man-child with shining eyes, was ripped from his family's home in the middle of a muggy Mississippi night. His body was found weeks later—bloated, disfigured, butchered. The black newspapers printed his crushed visage at the insistence of his mother. Everyone thought, though no one said (at least out loud), *That could be my son.*

Till's killers sat in the courtroom chomping on wads of tobacco and day dreaming of fly-fishing on the bayou. In his closing arguments the defense counsel called for a not guilty verdict from the jury, addressing them as "every Anglo-Saxon one of you." Of course, the killers went home free that day, back-slapping and grinning all the way.

But now my members grew angry as I raised a Christian view to the race crisis. Looking back I understand their reluctance. Black people in that church had been taught for generations that it was wrong to make waves. Every pastor who had ascended that pulpit before me had probably said, "Injustice is best left in the hands of the Lord. He will deal with it on the last day." I should have realized that God had not just clicked on the lights in the pitch-black room of my mind. No, first he had immersed me in the marketplace of ideas. Revelation concerning the social aspects of the Word of God came to me over a long period of time. I should have realized that this kind of teaching should be fed to congregations in teaspoons. It would take time for my church to grab onto these concepts. I can see all of this in hindsight. At the time, however, the gospel's drive toward social change was *so* obvious to me, and I naively believed that it likewise should have been just as obvious to everyone.

FAMILY SACRIFICES

Meanwhile, things grew steadily more difficult financially. JoAnna took a job teaching grades 1-8 at the one-room, all-black school where she had come of age. In order for her to do this, she and the children had to move back to her father's house. I missed my wife and children during the week, but I would pick them up every Friday night, and we would stay together in the parsonage until Sunday evening. It wasn't an easy time.

— 11 —

HARD TIMES ON A NEW JOB

During the week I lived in the men's dormitory at the Missouri School of Religion. I attended my classes and then studied until it was time to go to work. I worked on a cleaning crew that maintained a State Farm Insurance Company office. For the first time I worked with college students from India and Egypt. In this society that practiced apartheid, the hue of their flesh dictated that they would serve beside me, qualified only to scrub floors and scour toilets.

The company's mistrust of its employees of color was so complete that it hired Mr. Griffin, a pink beachball of a man with an cigarette dangling eternally between his thumb and forefinger, as our supervisor. Where else but in America could a man who could barely write his own name be hired to supervise astrophysicists and biochemists? The absurdity of racial politics had apparently been lost on someone at management level. Mint jelly stains decorated the drab white shirt that hung over Mr. Griffin's potbelly. He made snorting noses as he walked the floor, hands clasped behind his back, scrutinizing our every move as though he were General Patton reviewing the troops at Anzio.

My job there was to wipe mirrors, sweep floors and mop. Mr. Griffin's job was to keep an accurate record of the cleaning supplies. The trouble was that for all of his posing and posturing, Mr. Griffin couldn't read words of more than one syllable. When we got low on supplies, he ordered me to put down my broom and follow him into the stockroom. Beyond the sight of the other employees, he handed me a pencil and the appropriate forms, and then he gave me orders to update the inventory records.

I was being paid as a janitor. I received no compensation or official recognition for my duties as Mr. Griffin's bookkeeper. In fact, as soon as I finished the bookkeeping, Mr. Griffin would snatch the forms from my hands and scratch out his own illegible signature at the bottom as though he had done the record keeping himself. "Okay, James, you can go now," he would say after this ritual was done.

What could I do? I was a black man in a white man's world, and I had a family to feed. Mr. Griffin would chuckle as I turned my back and walked out of the room. *Oh God, please help me,* I prayed. *Lord, give me a chance to speak the truth to this humiliating injustice.*

Every few months Mr. Griffin would summon me with the curl of his index finger. There, lying on top of the Sunday comics and a stack of gun catalogues, would be the employee evaluation forms. "Sit down heah, James, and work wid me on dese." Mr. Griffin would drawl.

I would call out a name from the stack of forms. Mr. Griffin would squeeze his eyes together and then thoughtfully touch his chin. Then he would snort and say, "Write this down: 'Lazy, shiftless; must be watched alla time.' " It was as though he were commenting on the habits of runaway slaves in the eighteenth century.

Inevitably, my own evaluation would come up. And I would invariably have to write it out just as he dictated it. Each report period I was forced to write some variation of the same words: "Jim is learning. He is making some progress on this job." And then I had to sign my name, signifying that I had read the evaluation and agreed with it.

Famed eighteenth-century abolitionist Frederick Douglass recorded the words of his master concerning the subject of slaves and education. He said, "Learning will spoil the best nigger." And in his crude way, he was right. Once Douglass found the skill to match words with syllables, he had a greater grasp on the injustice of his plight. After he had perused some of the literary classics, he became outraged at slavery, and he wondered how other slaves could be almost oblivious to their plight.

At the State Farm office, I was like the young Frederick Douglass. I emerged from the back room seething with anger. I pushed my broom feeling as though Mr. Griffin had violated me intellectually. He was using my skills to bring down a salary that was four or five times what I was making. And then he'd force me to write "James is making some progress on this job." It was almost too much to bear.

On those harsh, lonely nights at work, I brought along a stack of index cards with class notes written on them, and as I swept the floors I would hold them out in front of me, studying for my classes. I also kept a textbook hidden in the bathroom, and I would go into the stall to read a page every now and then. And during those long nights, I would pray, *Oh God, please make things better for your dark children.*

In 1957 I was called to pastor the Second Baptist Church of Columbia, Missouri. Even though I had yet to graduate, they were offering a full-time position at a larger church. After some prayer we decided to take the offer. I moved my family into the parsonage.

MY AFRICAN FRIEND

Thank God for friends who helped bear my burdens. I found a kindred spirit in Abel Muzorewa. He was a Methodist seminarian at the Missouri School of Religion who'd come to us from Rhodesia (now Zimbabwe). Abel shared his first Thanksgiving dinner with my family. It was the first time he had tasted turkey. I purchased his first overcoat so that he would be able to withstand the brutal winters.

I saw something in Abel. I knew that he was destined to help humanity in a fantastic way. Upon graduation Abel returned to Zimbabwe, where he was one day appointed bishop of the Methodist Church. He founded the African National Congress and became the most powerful black man in Rhodesia-Zimbabwe. Under his leadership the white minority government was dismantled. After generations of rule, black people finally came to power.

INCIDENT AT A SEGREGATED CAFE

During my senior year in seminary, Dean Thomas Shrout escorted a number of students to a seminarian conference in Merom, Indiana. The white folks that I was traveling with were ignorant of the racial customs that ruled our world. On the return trip they stopped at a roadside diner hoping to grab some hamburgers and cokes.

The rail-thin black man who was mopping the floors said nothing when we walked through the door of the restaurant, but when he looked at me an expression fell across his face that said, *Negro, are you crazy?* The white folks who were with me didn't notice, but I read the look clearly. I turned around to leave but my classmates insisted on staying. They were completely oblivious to his cue.

The owner had no problem serving my fellow seminarians. However, he looked at me and barked, "We don't serve colored people in here. But if you want, I'll have his food brought out to the car." The dean looked at the proprietor and then back at the students and said, "Well, if Jim can't eat here, we aren't going to eat here."

Some of the white seminary students were quite angry. They could hear the sizzle of cheeseburgers and fried onions on the grill, a thick cloud rising up toward heaven. One of the most popular students looked at the burgers and then back to Dr. Shrout. He said, "*We* are hungry!" The dean upbraided them all in a harsh tone. He said, "We are a *Christian* school. We can't go ahead and eat and not let one of our students eat." The dean prevailed and we moved on. We were able to eat in the St. Louis Airport diner because federal law had already desegregated that place. But my hamburger tasted like wood chips.

It was hard for me to look my classmates in the eye after that night. As far as I was concerned, there wasn't a bit of difference between them and the square-jawed proprietor of that restaurant. The only difference was that they had the honorific title "Reverend" in front of their names. I started picturing them with white cone-shaped hoods over their heads.

TIME FOR A CHANGE

I felt like a juggler on a tightrope; balancing seminary, the pastorate and my roles as both a father and a husband. On top of all of that, I was elected president of the student body in my senior year. There were evenings when I should have been studying that I chose to play with my children. There were times when I was huddled in front of a textbook instead of my plate at the dinner table. Sleep was something that people did in novels. I survived on catnaps—a stolen fifteen minutes here and a borrowed ten there.

In the spring of 1962 I was looking at daylight. My days at the University of Missouri School of Religion were just about completed. JoAnna and I began to seek God's leading for our next steps.

Second Baptist Church was growing and thriving. I was learning much about ministry to God's people through each encounter with a sick member and through preparing each Sunday sermon. Yet there was a vacuum in the pit of my stomach, a gnawing that pronounced itself at the oddest times. It overwhelmed me as I drove past fields where haggard, unsmiling men dragged heavy hoes through unyielding soil, their toes poking through the tops of their black plastic shoes. Sun, wind and age wrinkled the pores of their brown flesh. Every once in a while, one of them would look up to holler, "Hello, Pastor!"

I felt that gnawing sensation when I drove past a crumbling hut with a sign atop that said, "Colored Elementary School." I thought of the dark, airless classrooms with their leaky roofs and the flies that circled the children's heads.

A MENTOR OPENS A DOOR

Some Sunday evenings after having preached my guts out, I would call mentors like Dr. Elder B. Hicks and cry about my frustration. I would weep over the plight of our people and say things like; "Dr. Hicks, it seems like my feet are stuck in cement. I can't get people here to listen to what I really feel the Lord is saying and yet he is not releasing me to go."

And like the wise, old sage that he was, he would say, "Be still and wait on the Lord, James. The time will come, my son. The time will come." And when Dr. Hicks found a way to help me, he rang my phone. That's the difference between a well-wisher and a mentor. A mentor not only shares invaluable advice, he or she uses personal influence whenever possible to open doors for pupils, which is what Dr. Hicks did.

He called one day and said, "James, go get a pencil and write this telephone number down. The General Baptist Association is looking for a field secretary to cover the northern California region. I've already put your name in. Just call that number and make the arrangements to meet the interview team at the denomination convention in Des Moines, Iowa." When I hung up the phone, I realized that the old axiom is true: "It's not *what* you know. It's *who* you know."

I landed in Des Moines bewildered. What was God doing in my life? Could I be a blessing to my people as a "suit" in denomination headquarters? I also had some trepidation about going to California. I had no family ties in the Golden State. What if things didn't work out? I would be so far away from home.

These questions troubled my mind as I drifted through the halls of the convention center where the American Baptist Convention gathering was being held. Thousands of people drifted past me, each going in a different direction. I glanced at my watch. I was late and lost. Fortunately, in the midst of the crush

I spotted a smiling, caramel-colored visage that I thought I recognized. The fellow extended his hand toward me, and when he spoke, I recognized his voice from the radio. Perhaps he could tell that I needed direction. He said, "Hello, my name is Reverend Gardner C. Taylor." "Hello, Reverend Taylor," I responded. "I seem to be a little turned around. Can you help me find my way?"

He'd been at the convention site for two days, so he knew exactly where I needed to go. He led me to a room where seven men and women sat around a table that had one empty chair. The eighth chair was the hot seat. It was just for me.

I loosened the knot on my tie as questions came shooting at me from all corners of the table. "Explain your soul salvation." "What is your take on the doctrine of eternal security?" "What did Martin Luther mean by the term 'priesthood of all believers?' At the end of what seemed like an eternity, they rose one by one to shake my hand. It was impossible to read the expressions on their faces. I called JoAnna and said, "Honey, I don't know what to make of it all. Perhaps Reverend Hicks was wrong this time. It happens, you know. He is human like you or I."

Two weeks later the phone rang. They offered me the job.

I graduated from the Missouri School of Religion with a bachelor of divinity degree. It was time to go. I had mixed feelings about leaving Missouri. But many people were leaving Missouri in a great migration west. They were calling California "God's country." Certainly the educational opportunities would be better for our children. Still, I was afraid to leave the slow pace of Missouri to go to a fast-paced, multicultural world. It was JoAnna who saw it as providence. She said, "James, this is the hand of God."

LEAVING THE LAND OF MY BIRTH

Although I worked at Second Baptist Church full time as a pastor, I still made little money. My five little children were always in need of new shoes or notebooks. Sometimes there just wasn't enough paycheck left to keep us going. On these painful occasions I would walk to the corner grocery store and make arrangements to carry groceries home on credit. I became so indebted to the grocer that I had to sign my entire paycheck over to him the day before we left for California.

On the morning that we drove away, snowflakes as big as stones fell from the skies. There were seven of us crammed into my 1957 Chevrolet. It was a tight squeeze: two-year old Tony nestled between JoAnna and me. Amy, Jim and Shari shared the back seat. Craig stood on the hump. The car shimmied and slid on the icy roads beneath us.

"Baby, hand me a piece of that fried chicken!," I cried out to my JoAnna. The kids sat quietly, peering at the windows for a last look at the school where they had met their lifelong friends and the swings and slides in the park playground. Even JoAnna sighed. Leaving Columbia, Missouri, in 1962 was a difficult thing to do.

The cold wind whipped around the car causing us to fishtail. I fought to keep the car in the middle of the road. Snow drifts piled up like white mountains by the roadside. I put on a jolly exterior, but my heart was torn. I thought of the members of Second Baptist Church whom I'd come to know and to love. We had shared our lives in a journey that spanned four years, and now that had all come to an end.

I had mapped out a journey that would have taken us through Denver. I looked forward to pointing out the majesty of the Rocky Mountains to my children. But the radio broadcast told us that the mountain passes were closed because of a snowstorm. I knew of only one other route that led to northern California. This course would lead us south. I found the thought of lodging my family in a backwater, "colored-only" motel repugnant. So before we headed south, I pulled into an Esso gas station to seek counsel.

The gas station attendant handed me two AAA publications. One was a standard map of the United States; the second was called "Go." I had seen "Go" advertised in *Ebony* magazine. "Go" contained a list of motels where African Americans would be boarded in the segregated South. A white fellow in line behind me complained to the attendant, "You only gave me one thing. You gave him two. Don't I need the other?" The attendant explained, "Well, no. It's because he can't stay in every place that you can."

I frowned at both of them. Its funny how we took segregation for granted, even perpetuated it by creating publications that listed safe accommodations for people with brown flesh. As I walked out of that service station, I thought: *At least my children will not have to grow up in a world so deeply scarred by racism. I'm going to work for Christian people in an enlightened place.* I looked forward to working with the American Baptists in California. I assumed that they would be bastions of social justice because they had given Martin Luther King Jr. and Dr. Walter Rauschenbusch to the world.

— 12 —

California Dreaming

Northern California was filled with rolling hills, gigantic palm trees, cool Pacific breezes, mauve twilight and the gentle perfume of eucalyptus trees. The winters were warm. Smiles came freely. The San Francisco Bay region was a harmonious land of Asians, African Americans, Anglos, Hispanics and Pacific Islanders. We were a mixed salad of colors, shapes and sizes.

The American Baptists lodged us in a temporary home in Oakland. We later relocated to Berkeley. My children attended multiethnic schools equipped with highly motivated staff and state-of-the-art classroom equipment. I was sent to work in the San Joaquin Valley, where the sun of summer seldom sets and the frosts of winter seldom come. My predecessor was the famed African American preacher and writer Dr. Henry H. Mitchell. He gave up the general secretary job and went to pastor at Second Baptist Church in Fresno. I came in behind him to fill some very big shoes.

My exact job title was field secretary of the General Baptist Association. The Association consisted of ninety black Baptist churches from Weed, California (the northernmost point of the state where Mount Shasta stands in glory, capped with a diadem of snow) to Tulare, below Fresno. These black churches were affiliated with the American Baptist Churches, but they were not meeting with the larger denomination in their geographical area. The black and white churches practiced an informal apartheid. Strangely enough, they insisted on living under a common umbrella. My work was cut out for me.

LATIN AMERICAN OPPRESSION

As I drove up the highway, I saw hundreds of Latino men and women stooped beneath the midday summer sun as it rained down heat from the heavens. Low flying, single-engine planes were dropping gallons of chemicals on their heads. The owners thought so little of the migrant workers that they didn't even ask the workers to vacate the fields when pesticides were dropped on the crops. In those same fields a Catholic Christian named Caesar Chavez was fighting to organize the largely Mexican masses. It seemed like the type of fight that the church should have thrown all of its weight behind. In California the plight of these migrant workers was the social justice issue of the day.

The growers were paying slave wages, denying the people who did this soul-crushing labor any kind of healthcare benefits. These arrogant despots were housing their employees in the most wretched shacks in the northern hemisphere. Unbelievably, the white pastors that I was sent to work with had taken the side of the wealthy and the powerful against the beleaguered migrant workers.

You see, many of the planters were tithe-paying members of their churches, which meant that the churches were financially dependent on the fruit growers and farmers. And the fruit growers and farmers depended on the pastors to keep their mouths shut about the planters' unjust working conditions. It was a convenient little arrangement for both sides.

The writer of Ecclesiastes put it most eloquently, "Money answereth all things" (Ecclesiastes 10:19 KJV). These believers soothed their consciences by throwing gospel tracts at their beleaguered Mexican brothers. And the church hid from the issue.

If I hadn't grown up in an openly segregated society, the hypocrisy of my white brothers and sisters might have shaken my faith. Whenever such hypocrisy became overwhelming, I tried to remember that it was *religious* people who killed Jesus. The religious right is often wrong. History has proven this many times.

SHOT DOWN

I woke up one morning burning with inspiration. I had an idea whose time had come. At work that morning, in a regular staff meeting with the Northern California American Baptists, I proposed that we should invite Dr. Martin Luther King Jr. to come out to address our annual meeting. After all, he was a member of our denomination. Could we arrange this?

One of the denominational leaders, a white man, stared at me like the captain of a sinking ocean liner weighing a request to cut the lifeboats loose. Deep red lines cut into his forehead. "Martin Luther King! Our strongest givers to our mission budget are growers of grapes in the San Joaquin Valley. This will cause trouble."

"But we've got that kind of trouble. Look at how they're treating our Latino brothers and sisters in the fields," I retorted. Now the flesh was in the frying pan. I was supposed to know better than to bring up the migrant worker issue. His worst fears about me had just been confirmed. I wasn't the smiling accommodationist that he thought he'd hired but an uppity darky, a Nat Turner who spoke the Queen's English.

Before he asked me to close the door on my way out, he reiterated the denomination's position. I was told that the church should not concern itself with the blood of the innocents on the grapevines of northern California but the blood of Christ shed on Calvary.

Could one truly be divorced from the other? That was my question. But the white folks who controlled the denomination did not want it raised. They felt that they had already done their part by bringing me on staff. I was the only person of color on staff, a fact that they reminded me of at every conceivable opportunity.

At the quarterly meetings these men of power and religious influence would stare across the table at me as though I were Moses representing the entire nation of newly liberated slaves. "Your people are not pitching in their fair share to the mission budget, James. Why don't you go out and raise some interest in *that*?" I sat there steaming as they tweaked the numbers on the budget, a grim look on my face. There was no arguing with these people. They had all the truth that they were willing to embrace.

For them I was the unnamed character in Ralph Ellison's seminal work *Invisible Man*. So as they suggested, I went unto my own.

SITTING DOWN WITH THE BLACK PREACHERS

Not long after I started work, I answered an invitation to address the denomination's black clergy. I arrived five minutes early but was surprised to find the meeting already in session. Heads turned as I walked into the room, my arms filled with mimeographed copies of the evening's agenda.

The African American preachers were even less cordial than the white ones.

A short, bald-headed preacher threw his hand over his mouth and snickered when my turn came to address the gathering.

"Howya doin' brother?" he drawled, placing a heavy exaggeration on "brother."

I read the facial expressions and body language around the room. I measured the guarded comments and spontaneous giggling. They had done some talking about me before I had ever walked into the room. The consensus was that I was an Uncle Tom; a white man's lackey sent to keep the field Negroes on the evangelical plantation in line.

When one of the preachers would drop his guard and say something like "Those folk back at headquarters don't care anything about us," the others would raise their hands to hush him, fearful that I would carry intelligence reports back to Oakland. It took exactly two closed-door sessions for these men of the cloth to figure out that this was absolutely the last thing that they would have to worry about concerning me.

Once I gained their confidence, the rest was easy. I said, "If your churches are paying dues to the denomination, you might as well get the full benefit of your money."

Jesus tore the temple veil that separated humans from God. When are we going to tear down the veil that separates us from each other? My, that was a hard sell. Many pastors, black and white, couldn't understand that the race issue had to do with religion. They thought that I was talking apples and oranges. The same issue still stalks the church today. We may talk across the aisle, but rarely are we genuine friends.

RUN IN PORTLAND

In the spring of 1962 I took my family to the annual American Baptist meeting in Portland, Oregon. We drove the twelve-hour journey past raging waterfalls, mahogany colored redwood trees and lavender sunsets. At nightfall we arrived at the parsonage of a church made available to us by the denomination.

The next day we dressed the kids and headed for a riding tour of the sights. Amy, James Jr. and Shari traced the flight of red cardinals with their tiny fingers as the birds glided overhead. Occasionally one of my babies would break out into a song or a nursery rhyme. We would all sing along like a little choir. The perfume of pine trees left their intoxicating aroma everywhere. We were bathing in the sunlight and reflecting on the goodness of God.

It was a perfectly idyllic day—until a white fellow in a shiny black Buick sedan pulled up beside us. He sneered and then began to use the most vulgar of profanities and racial epithets as though the very presence of black people on his highway was revolting.

I shouted out of my window, "Sir, please watch your language. My children are in this car with me." But that seemed to enrage him all the more. His jaws drew tight, his face grew blood red. His stream of profanity became a waterfall, and then he sped off.

We were cruising through downtown Portland when the black Buick pulled up beside us at a red light. My wife hollered, "James, James, don't do it!" I unbuckled my seatbelt and then gently closed the car door behind me. I strolled calmly over to the Buick, my Florsheims clicking on the hot, black asphalt.

The man still had his window down. A sneer of contempt curled his lips. He leered at me as though I were any black man who had ever serviced his car or shined his shoes or freshened his drink. In my face he saw every person of color he had ever abused or insulted without reprisal.

That's why he was so surprised when I bent down, reached inside his car and snatched him up by the starched collar of his sky-blue sports shirt. He gasped in terror; his head jerked backward. I slapped him hard across the face. It was loud like a firecracker echoing in an empty room. His natty straw hat went flying out of the passenger window like a Frisbee. The print of my open palm glowed on his white cheek like a red tattoo. His slate gray pupils stretched wide like pool balls. He stared at me as though I were Lazarus walking out of the tomb.

The high pitch of screaming children brought me out of my trance. My eyes met the young man's, but I said nothing. I merely dropped him back into his seat like a plastic bag of overripe grapefruit. Then I tipped my hat and said, "Have a nice day."

He gaped at me with his lips parted in shock. Calmly I opened my car door, buckled my seat belt and took off at a reasonable speed, never once looking back in his direction. My knuckles throbbed and ached as I grabbed the steering wheel and pulled into the fast lane. I'm not a man of violence. In fact, I abhor it. My children had never seen that side of me before. And they peppered me with questions: "Ooooh, Daddy, why you hit that man?" They couldn't understand what made Daddy snap like that. You see, we were flesh and blood humans made of sinews and bone, soul and intellect, no more or less than that gentleman. That man's words were a violation of the necessary social contract that human beings make to coexist in a free society.

What I did was wrong. My wife reminded me of that over and over again. "James, I thought you were a Christian! That was what you told me when I married you!" she said. I have since repented of my actions. Yet I can't help but wonder what that foul-mouthed fool went home and told his family that night. I imagine dinner time conversation started off with something like, "Daddy, some crazy nigger slapped the spit out of me at the red light."

And just on the off-chance that the fellow has picked up this book, I would like to say to him: Sir, my name is not "nigger." It is James Smith.

— 13 —

BACK TO COLLEGE

I grew frustrated with the slow progress of racial reconciliation within the church. And to tell you the truth, I was slightly disillusioned. Maybe I had been an idyllic dreamer hoping for utopia on earth. I never realized that Christ's admonition that Christians should be "one" as a witness to the world would be so difficult to achieve.

When I saw the utter hypocrisy of a church that accommodated racism, I wanted to leave. And it just so happened that around that time an offer came from Bishop College in Dallas, Texas. So in 1963 I accepted a position at Bishop College to become the director of development and assistant to the president. My mission was to obtain funds, friends and freshman. I saw this as an opportunity for my children to grow up around black scholars in an academic setting. There were fantastic black role models for them there. It would also give JoAnna the long-awaited opportunity to complete her undergraduate education.

Leaving the San Francisco Bay Area was hard on my children. They had experienced multiculturalism in California. (Amy's best friend was a young Asian girl.) They had grown accustomed to the cosmopolitan lifestyle of the San Francisco Bay Area: Thai food one night, barbecue spare ribs the next.

Texas didn't offer the same kind of diversity. In fact, in Dallas the superintendent of public schools didn't allow black teachers in that city to belong to the NAACP. Eyebrows went up when it was heard that I was to be hired at

Bishop College. I was measured in some quarters as an outsider, and they feared that I was going to cause racial unrest in the student body.

REVISITING SEGREGATION—FOR THE FIRST TIME

Right outside of Marshall, Texas, we stopped at a gas station with three restrooms. They were marked, "White Men," "White Women" and "Colored." My children piled out of the car, dancing from one foot to the other. I warned them, *"Do not go into the restrooms marked for whites!"*

They dutifully responded in unison, "Yes, Daddy." And with my eldest daughter Amy leading the way, they headed right for the whites-only restroom. My wife was aghast. She hollered, "James, you brought us down here to get us killed!"

I straightened them out good when we got in the car. Again, they said in chorus, "Yes, Daddy!" But they were defiant. I painted the picture of our reality as best as I could, but they said, "We're not afraid to die." (I'm still trying to figure out where they got that from.) But they soon learned about the evils of racism.

We arrived in Dallas late that night. Bishop College was locked up tight; there wasn't a soul in sight. There was nothing left to do but get a hotel room for the night. The trouble was that no one would break the color barrier to let us rent a room overnight. We ended up driving to the ghetto, where there is always space in some rundown motel.

After we were settled in Dallas, my boys were playing football with some young friends on a field on the outskirts of the campus when a pickup truck slowed on the road adjacent to the college property. A white man stuck a pistol out of the driver's window and started popping off shots at my boys. Was he trying to kill them or just scare them? That's a question that remains unanswered. Thank God no one was hurt.

My children now had to face an indignity that I had grown up with: white and colored water fountains. They hated segregation beyond what mere words might convey.

THE BLESSINGS OF LIFE AT BISHOP COLLEGE

Dallas was a difficult place to live, but it also had its blessings. Seminary had almost deconstructed my faith. It left me with a heart full of doubts. In Dallas I joined the Good Street Baptist Church, which was pastored by the Reverend C. A. W. Clark.

Reverend Clark's preaching put it all back together for me. He exhibited the genius of the black pulpit that refused to dichotomize reason and faith. Reverend Clark preached with a synthesis of head and heart. For the first twenty minutes his messages would be very scholarly, but then he would bring it home with an explosion of spiritual ecstasy. Back on campus the president brought in the giants of the black church: Reverend Dr. Samuel DeWitt Proctor, Reverend Sandy Ray and Reverend Fred Sampson. Under the inspired preaching of these men, I rediscovered myself *and* my faith.

MY WIFE ON THE HONOR ROLL

JoAnna became a model student. Her grades were always at the top of the class. Sometimes she would look at me and say, "James, listen to this." And then from memory she would rattle off a long passage from Longfellow, Wadsworth or Hughes. We shared a love for literature. I enjoyed discussing great books with her.

Though JoAnna loved college, one day juggling home life and eighteen credits a semester became too much for her. She walked into the house to find dishes piled high in the sink and children tussling on the floor. Distraught, she said, "James, I just can't do it anymore. I'm going to drop out of school." A tear slipped from her eye.

My heart began to palpitate. For a moment I forgot to breathe. JoAnna had sacrificed so much for the family and for my ministry. I really wanted her to achieve her goal. She had to get that Bachelor of Arts diploma. "Baby, you keep on doing what you're doing. I'll fix everything," I told her. I went into the bedroom and then called Amy because she was the oldest.

"Come in here and close that door behind you!" Dutifully, she obeyed. "You let your mother study or else! Do you understand?" I was red with anger, but I have always allowed my children to speak their minds. So when Amy said that she had something to say, I didn't interrupt her.

"Daddy, I hate Texas. Can't we go back to California?" I made her a promise. I said, "Daughter, if you stick it out and help out more around here, we will move the day after graduation." One by one I called each child into the bedroom and made the same series of threats and promises.

FITTING IN

To tell you the truth, the kids weren't the only ones who were ready to leave

Texas. I too felt frustrated. The struggle for civil rights was in full swing all over America. It was 1963, the year of the great March on Washington and the "I Have a Dream" speech. Dr. Martin Luther King was fighting to desegregate places like Albany, Georgia. The Student Nonviolent Coordinating Committee was organizing freedom rides, matching integrated teams on Greyhound journeys through the South. People like Reverend Adam Clayton Powell Jr. were fighting to desegregate Woolworth's and place blacks in the halls of Congress. Black people were rising up, their voices heard at a louder pitch than ever before. But Bishop College president M. K. Curry sent me out on a different mission.

He sent me to speak at a large United Methodist Church adjacent to the Southern Methodist University. A young white university student stood up to challenge me during the question and answer portion of my presentation. He asked, "Is it true that the president of your school will not allow the students at Bishop to participate in Civil Rights demonstrations?"

"Yes," I said. "Our president feels that if students want to demonstrate, the best place for them to demonstrate is in the library by studying and producing academic excellence." The words tasted like Elmer's Glue on my tongue. But it was true. The school's supporters would have cut Bishop's economic throat if they believed it might raise up another Dr. Martin Luther King Jr.

I began to resent what I was doing. I was in a straightjacket. I wanted to tell the school's supporters "Business as usual is over." I wanted to sing the words of the old spiritual "Ain' Goin' Let Nobody Turn Me 'Round." But that would never have worked for the president of Bishop College. No matter what he thought inside, he was a pragmatist in the tradition of Booker T. Washington.

Bishop was an institution founded by ex-slaves and the American Baptist Home Mission Societies. And not once since the great Reconstruction had black people ever had the money to support Bishop College outright. White people owned stocks and bonds, and rich white trustees were pumping millions of dollars into Bishop. They had access to financial capital that blacks could only dream about.

The president had no choice but to say to himself, *The teachers must be paid and black students must learn.* He wasn't an evil man. He was a defender of Bishop College. He taught me many lessons that still help me on my Jericho Road journey.

ASSASSINATION IN THE CITY

On November 22, 1963, I was in the office of a large black Baptist church in Dallas making a pitch to Dr. L. Butler Nelson. I was trying to coax him into signing a pledge card to support Bishop College. He was ready to sign on the dotted line when his phone rang. He answered it, gasped and jumped up from his chair. He said, "President Kennedy was assassinated across town." It was a great catastrophe for African American people because he represented hope for us in America. I can remember picking up all of my pledge cards and stacking them in my attaché case. I walked back to my car and then drove slowly on the freeway back to Bishop College on Simpson Steward Street.

I saw a big, black Cadillac that had pulled over to the side of the road. The driver, a white man, sat there with his head bowed. He was crying like a baby. When I arrived at the campus the school had closed down. It was like a morgue. It was one of those days that you never forget.

— 14 —

MEETING DADDY
FACE TO FACE

⟨ornament⟩

There were benefits to working at Bishop College. One of them was that my father lived in the South. Through the years Daddy and I had continued to correspond. I was now the father of five children. I had finished college and seminary, pastored several churches and held an important position at a historically black college. I would write to him of my victories and my trials. His letters were often brief and impersonal, but I treasured each of them like a gambler treasures a winning lottery ticket. Yet I had never seen Daddy face to face.

One day I worked up enough nerve to write these words: "Daddy, I am going to bring my wife and children out to meet you in person." A letter with a Shreveport, Louisiana, postmark soon followed. Daddy welcomed us.

We loaded up the station wagon with our five children, who were ecstatic at the thought of a long road trip. JoAnna seemed to be looking forward to this journey from Texas to Louisiana. Butterflies fought for wing space in my stomach. JoAnna placed her hand on top of mine and smiled sweetly. Her face said, "Baby, I'm with you. God is with us, and we will see this through together."

Wooden shacks. Barefoot children playing kick-the-can on rocky roads. The sunset dimming on the treetops. Crickets singing in the distant pasture. Houses with no numbers. These were the sights as we trekked down red clay roads and across railroad tracks that separated communities. Finally, I pulled the car over to talk with a family that was sitting on their front porch. "Good evening!" I hollered, "I'm trying to find out where Clyde Anderson lives!" A bony finger pointed at a house, 1640 Murphy Street.

Dust surrounded us like a gray cloud when we pulled to the curb. I told my family to stay put as I climbed the rickety wooden steps. I felt like I was knocking on the door of eternity. It swung back filling the air with cologne and cigarette smoke. "James? James Smith?" a voice inquired. It was like looking into the mirror.

"Clyde Anderson . . . Daddy?" He laughed. I grasped his hands in both of mine. By this time JoAnna and the children had unfolded themselves from the car and stood smiling and stretching at the base of the porch.

A NEW GRANDMOTHER

"Daddy, this is my wife, JoAnna. This is my family." My children stared tentatively into the grinning face of the stranger who stood before them with outstretched arms. Daddy reached down and scooped them up in his arms, smothering them with hugs and Budweiser kisses.

The aroma of fried chicken beckoned us inside. Daddy's mother, my grandmother, had prepared a veritable feast for us. I found her a fascinating woman. She and I got into a conversation about race relations in America. Her views were interesting. She felt that young blacks of my generation were pushing things too fast—things should be left to the gradual train of progress. She couldn't understand our impatience with Jim Crow, and I think that I know why.

Grandmother Anderson had a very fair complexion. In fact, she could have easily passed for white. There must have been times when people saw her outside of the African American community and didn't know that she was black. Her light complexion allowed her access to areas that darker blacks would never see. She had a cushy job down at the Greyhound station. These things tempered her accommodationist philosophies.

I didn't agree with her politics, but Granny sure could cook! Her butter beans and gravy were out of sight! After the last chicken back had been stripped clean, we put the children to bed. I kissed JoAnna, and then I went to meet Daddy on the porch. The moon stared down at me like God's winking eye. Daddy sat back in a woven rocking chair, a can of Pepsi-Cola dangling from his left hand. The radio played softly. Lightning Hopkins sang the blues as his acoustic guitar accompanied him.

I took the seat next to Daddy and together we searched the heavens for shooting stars. There weren't many questions about the past. Looking back, I wish that I had broached that subject. I wish that I had said, "Daddy, where have you been all of these years? Why didn't you send that saxophone? Why didn't you show up at my high school graduation? Why didn't you send any money to help with my tuition?" I had come to Louisiana full of questions, but to tell you the truth, many of them escaped me. I was just so glad to see my father face to face, my flesh and blood. I remembered how old Mrs. Williams from Leeds used to holler, "James Smith, you little bastard!" How I wished that she was here. I felt like Adam looking into the face of his Creator. I felt whole.

By the time we left, however, many of the questions that I had asked God concerning my family were answered. My grandmother had spoiled my father. She waited on him hand and foot. Nothing he did or said was ever wrong.

God had not cursed me by the absence of my father. No, in fact God had highly favored and blessed me.

During my stay, cousins that I had never met dropped in at Daddy's. They wanted to see Clyde's boy, the preacher. I drew a joy from watching them trying to match his eyes and nose with mine. Satisfied, they would observe, "Yep, that's Clyde's boy alright."

After a few days we said our goodbyes and headed back to Texas. The doors had been open for my dad and me to finally get to know each other.

A year later President Curry called me into his office. "Reverend, I want you to do me a favor," he said. "My secretary made a mistake. She's got me scheduled to speak at two different places on the same day. Would you go out to Shreveport and give a high school commencement address for me?"

I was more than happy to comply with his request. You see, Daddy lived in Shreveport. This would be his first opportunity to hear me preach.

Upon arriving home I telephoned my dad. "Daddy, will you be free on May 24th?" I queried. After I explained, his response was, "Yes, James. I'll be waiting for your visit."

I drove to Shreveport, Louisiana, in a Bishop College station wagon. Daddy was standing on the porch in a stylish camel-colored suit with a matching straw hat. When I arrived his face seemed gaunt, hollow. He looked a bit thinner than the last time that I had seen him. A smile spread across my face as I pumped his hand. He was a man short of stature like me. I saw my own eyes peering back from his face. Daddy, I'm parked just outside." He said, "Well, let's go, boy!"

We were late. I heated up the back streets of Shreveport taking the corners on two wheels. The school was a hulking, four-story, brown brick building that looked like a section of the Pentagon. After hunting for an empty parking space, we made our way inside. Daddy said, "I think I'll just set with the folks in the audience. I'll meet up with you after it's all over." I nodded and then asked a young student for directions to the principal's office.

I barged in and said, "Good afternoon, my name is Reverend James Alfred Smith Sr. I am here from Bishop College."

The principal expelled a breath of relief. "Thought you weren't going to make it there for a minute."

"I'm sorry," I said. "I had an important stop to make on the way."

I don't remember if the choir sang well that day. I don't remember if the boys and girls were excellent in their recitations. But I do remember two things about that afternoon. First, the place was packed to the rafters. Second, my father was there.

The principal introduced me by reading all of the minutia on my resumé. Then I stood up to speak. I opened with prayer, and then I reached for all of the preaching skills that I had been able to amass during my years in ministry. My voice rose and fell at the proper places. I prophesied of doors that would one day open up for people of color and told the young people of the attitude of excellence that the future would demand of them. I dared them to dream, to hope, to pray.

At one point of my oratorical flight, I happened to glance at Daddy. A flood of tears was streaming down his face as he rocked back and forth. (To this day I wonder what was going through his mind.)

When it was over, Daddy and I went out for fried catfish sandwiches and Coca-Cola. The time for my departure arrived too soon. With tears in my own eyes, I shook Daddy's hand, still staring into his eyes, searching for my own image. Little did I know that this was the last time that I would see Daddy face to face.

— 15 —

CALIFORNIA ONCE AGAIN

The year 1965 was bloody. Dr. King led a group of marchers across the Edmund Pettus Bridge in Selma, Alabama. A horrified America looked on as they were brutally beaten by police clubs and doused with tear gas. That same summer the streets of Watts in Los Angeles exploded with fire as the angry children of disinherited ghetto blacks took to the streets, overturning cars and tossing Molotov cocktails through store windows.

Christian people were looking for an answer to the looting and mayhem that was shaking America's cities. And as America burned, the American Baptist Churches of the West searched its own soul and created a position for a "minister of community witness." This person would represent the denomination on social justice issues. The board was expressing the view that God created humanity to live in community. If God was in Christ reconciling the world to himself, why should humans, and particularly Christians, be estranged from one another?

This new minister would be hired full-time to promote healing and restoration. I was hired for the position. Finally, I had found a pair of spiritual shoes that fit my feet. And just as I promised my family, we moved from Texas back to California the day after JoAnna graduated from Bishop College.

My installation service was held in San Francisco on October 3, 1965. Some of the most powerful figures in Bay Area religion were there for the inauguration of the position. The Honorable Judge Joseph Kennedy of the Municipal Court of San Francisco represented the San Francisco Religion and Race Conference. Reverend John P. Hestter of the Social Justice Commission of the Roman Catholic Archdiocese of San Francisco and Rabbi Herbert Morris of San Francisco were also there. James Chuck of the First Chinese Baptist Church of San Francisco was one of those who gave a "Message of Challenge." (Years later, he and I would be colleagues and great friends at the American Baptist Seminary of the West in Berkeley.)

The litany we shared that afternoon gives insight into the new direction that we were heading.

Leader: These are the things that you shall do: Speak the truth to one another, rendering at your gates judgments that are true and make for peace.

Response: Let justice roll down like waters, and righteousness like an overflowing stream.

Leader: Learn to do good, seek justice, correct oppression, defend the fatherless, plead for the widow.

Unison: Thus says the Lord, "Keep justice, and do righteousness, for soon my salvation shall come, and my deliverance be revealed."

I wrote in the bulletin:

The position of Minister of Community Witness is a challenging opportunity to serve with other dedicated people in responsible action for reducing man's inhumanity to man. A shot in Asia affects the world. Substandard living conditions in a city slum bring disease and disorder to the entire community.

Though the church may lack the necessary technical knowledge to solve every social and economic problem, the Christian message serves as the conscience of the society wherever human welfare is concerned. Since Jesus Christ is Lord of all, man's individual and collective life is subject to his message and will.

Believing in the Lord's concern for the whole man, the Department of Community Witness pledges commitment and service.

My time had come. God was using me to speak to issues of social justice. I sponsored conferences that dealt with job discrimination. I promoted career days for the folks of the inner city and camps for the children who had already run afoul of the law. I worked on a program called HOP (Homes Open, Please). It was a project aimed at getting Native American children from the reservation invited into Bay Area homes.

DINING WITH DR. KING SR.

In the spring of 1967 I was booked as a speaker by the American Baptist Convention for their Christian education conference. I looked forward to the serenity of Green Lake, Wisconsin, the American Baptist conference center. It seemed that the lush oak tree groves and swirling lake were a natural place to seek the face of the Lord. I was blessed more than I could have imagined.

Some of our denomination's most famous preachers flew in for the conference; the pastor of Atlanta's Ebenezer Baptist Church was among them. Martin Luther King Sr. and Alberta King (fondly known as Daddy and Mama King) took an instant liking to me. The Kings sat in the front row as I preached my heart out at the vesper services. We shared every meal together that week, and we sought each other out during informational workshops.

One morning Daddy King, a dignified man with graying temples, called to me from the back of the auditorium before service began. "Little Smith," he said, "I want you to meet another young preacher who is also very brilliant. This is Reverend Dr. Charles Adams from Detroit, Michigan." Reverend Adams and I thus began a friendship that has lasted for four decades.

The Kings were cordial, down-home folks who didn't seem at all moved by the notoriety that they were receiving due to the brave leadership of their son, Martin Luther King Jr. Grinning shutterbugs thought little of snapping unauthorized pictures of the vacationing Kings. Daddy King had a sweet way about him, but his smile would flip over at such intrusions. Sometimes the camera buffs would have the decency to ask before they took aim. However, they didn't want me in the picture since I wasn't part of the family. Reverend King would say, "If you want the picture, Reverend Smith is going to be in it."

Among my many memories of our time together, I recall one thing that Reverend King had said about his famous son: "They gave my son a lot of money when he won the Nobel Peace prize. I told him that he should have put that money into a college fund for his children. He didn't listen to me. He gave that money away." For Dr. King Sr., family came before ministry. I will never forget his wise counsel in that area.

I hated to say goodbye to the Kings at the end of the week.

A STRANGER AT THE GATES

I was filling out some reports in the American Baptist Churches of the West headquarters one afternoon when a tall, brown-haired man in a black, tapered suit strode through the door of my office. He introduced himself as Dr. Erik Rudin. As it turns out, he was the general secretary of the Baptist Union in Sweden. He was here on business.

It was lunchtime, and except for me the entire staff had gone out. He was a friendly man, full of questions. "What do you think of Dr. Martin Luther King?" "Why are blacks following his leadership?" He was very interested in King's love ethic.

No white person had ever before been interested about my perspective on the issues of race in America. If they allowed me an opinion on the subject at all, they wanted to formulate it and hand it to me in advance. They seemed to be saying, "If we want your opinion, we'll give it you."

But Dr. Rudin seemed to care. He wanted to hear how I felt, what I thought. That fact alone caused me to be as fascinated by Dr. Rudin as he was by me. It took all of fifteen minutes for this Swedish clergyman to make a lifelong impression on me.

Eventually, the person with whom Dr. Rudin had made his appointment came through the door. Dr. Rudin rose to leave but not before saying, "James, I want you to come to Sweden and speak to our young people about the American race problem. Will you do it?" I swallowed hard, not believing my ears, and nodded.

Dr. Eric Rudin wrote a formal letter to Dr. Russell Orr of the American Baptist Churches of the West and to Dr. Atha Baugh of the American Baptist Home Mission Societies in Valley Forge, Pennsylvania, requesting my services in Sweden, Norway and Denmark. The Scandinavian Baptists agreed to pay travel and housing in Scandinavia if American Baptists would pay for my air travel expenses. The American Baptist Home Mission Societies agreed to pay them if I would do missionary deputation in New York City prior to flying abroad.

I was assigned to preach a week in the Bronx at an all-white church pastored by Dr. Keith Russell. Through the years our friendship has grown tremendously. Today he serves as the president of the American Baptist Seminary of the West in Berkeley, California.

16

TAKING THE
RACE ISSUE OVERSEAS

M y travel expenses were paid by both American and European Baptists. Now the only thing left was to find a way for my wife to travel with me.

Reverend Palmer Watson, a white American Baptist and pastor of the Mac-Arthur Community Baptist Church of San Pablo, California, managed a security firm. He gave me evening employment as a security guard to earn money for JoAnna's travel expenses. The McGee Avenue Baptist Church of Berkeley also raised travel funds for JoAnna.

EXPLORING SWEDEN

My impressions of Sweden were overwhelming. The sun shimmered and danced on the foamy waves of the Baltic Sea. Snow-capped mountains saluted the heavens in the distance. Men with long blond hair raised the forefinger and middle finger together in a peace sign. I nodded and saluted back.

The Swedish young people did not believe in war and were critical of American involvement in Vietnam. They were a reserved and reflective folk who had a deep reverence for the work of Dr. Martin Luther King Jr.

Not many days after I arrived, JoAnna's flight arrived from the States. I couldn't wait to show her this world, this Nordic paradise.

ADDRESSING STUDENTS ON THE ISSUE OF RACE

The University of Uppsala sits on a sprawling country estate. My heart pounded beneath my caramel blazer as we circled the parking lot in search of a free space. Beyond us, young people with bundles of textbooks beneath their arms took the steps two at a time.

"They are here to hear what you have to say," Dr. Rudin said. My mind flashed back to what seemed like another life now. I recalled an afternoon back in Leeds when Deacon Carter prophesied, "One day, the world is going to hear from you, James." If only he could be here.

Gothic stone angels peered down at us from their perches on the ledge of the auditorium's roof top. My eyes dilated to adjust to the dim light in the hallways. Hands reached out for my hands. Flashbulbs popped. Bright-eyed faculty members surrounded me backstage. A stout man with horn-rimmed glasses clutched me in a tight embrace. It felt like he was trying to count all of my ribs. What had I gotten myself into?

I could see Dr. Rudin as he strode from the wings of the auditorium's stage to take his place behind the lectern. "Ladies and gentlemen, I would like to present to you from America the Reverend James Alfred Smith!"

That was my cue. I glided slowly toward Dr. Rudin's side. It was only then that I got a glimpse of the magnitude of the event. I bowed slightly before a standing-room-only crowd.

That night I took them for a ride through the parchments of African American history. I recited the poetry of Countee Cullen and Langston Hughes. I cited the social reflections of W. E. B. DuBois. I took them through the oak wood doors of the African American church. Before I took my seat, I led my audience down to the boiling hot cotton fields of Louisiana where black people kept hope alive in their quest for racial justice. I led them through the southern penitentiaries where freedom riders watched their lives slip away, one minute at a time. And I introduced them to the theology and philosophy of the Reverend Dr. Martin Luther King Jr.

When I finished my last sentence, you could hear the strains of "We Shall Overcome" rise from the seats. "Black and white together, we shall overcome some day."

Here was a sea of white people hungry to see inside the naked soul of a black man. These people loved the truth and they yearned to hear it in all of its rawness. They believed that the power of love could transcend hostility and hatred.

FAREWELL DR. MARTIN LUTHER KING JR.

On April 4, 1968, I was staying at the Baptist Youth Hostel in Stockholm when someone brought me the news: Martin Luther King Jr. had been shot dead in Memphis, Tennessee. Sorrow fell down on Stockholm like a storm cloud. Sweden's leading Baptist pastor, who also served in the Swedish parliament, took me to a special memorial service convened in Stockholm. The Swedes sang "Deep River," and they sounded as authentic as the Fisk Jubilee Singers.

TOURING NORTHERN EUROPE

Over the next few weeks I embarked on a whirlwind tour through the universities of Sweden. I addressed university student groups, churches, union organizers and civic groups. They received my message with great interest and enthusiasm.

I woke up early one morning. As JoAnna lay quietly beside me, I slipped out of bed, put on my slippers, crept to the window of our flat and stared down at the narrow streets as the first rays of sun peeked through the billowy clouds. And in that mystical space squeezed between day and night, I considered the last few weeks of my life.

Through God's providence, a total stranger had twisted the door knob to the American Baptist Church headquarters at a time when only I was there. This same mysterious man invited me to embark on a speaking expedition to the other side of the ocean. As God would have it, the audience were blond people with blue eyes. In the States they might have been the people who had barred black children from walking through elementary school doors. But here, in this foreign land, they welcomed me with open arms. What was God saying to me?

A PAINFUL TWIST

Later that week a sharp pain raced through me, piercing my innards. I shot up in bed wheezing and puffing. "What is it, James?" JoAnna whispered in the darkness. I glanced at the clock. It was 5 a.m. I was scheduled to address a group of college students in two hours. The pain brought beads of sweat to my forehead. But, in ministry as in show business, the work must go on. I had preached my way through the fever and flu, through broken limbs and broken hearts, but now I was challenged with pain such as I had never experienced before.

JoAnna wrapped me up in blankets. She pressed a cold towel to my forehead and then took my temperature. She shook her head, "I told you not to eat that extra strudel last night."

"JoAnna," I cried out. "I've got to go. Help me get dressed."

"Baby, you can't do it, not this time," she retorted. "The people will understand. You are ill."

"JoAnna, help me get into my clothes. The people are going to be there waiting for a word. God called me and I've got to do what he called me to do."

She looked at me and shook her head in disbelief. In public I have always been the outgoing one; I love to be the center of attention. JoAnna is a soft-spoken person who purposely avoids public attention. I rarely walk into a room unnoticed. JoAnna, on the other hand, craves anonymity. That morning, however, she pursed her lips as though mustering courage from within. She looked at me and said, "Don't worry. I'll go and give the address. You lie down and get better.'"

I studied her, not able to believe what I was hearing.

"Can you do it, honey?" I asked, my fists clenched in pain.

"I can do all things through Christ which strengtheneth me," she replied.

While I lay on the bed, shaking, JoAnna pulled a smart, robin's-egg blue, two-piece suit from the closet. After she'd dressed, she opened my briefcase and rifled through my sermon notes. She sat down at the desk, her brow knit as she fought to decipher my hieroglyphics.

It wasn't long before a knock came to the door. JoAnna grabbed the notes and walked over to the bed. She kissed me on the forehead and left me with these words: "Be still and don't worry." When she grasped my hand, I noticed that she was trembling slightly. She smiled bravely, turned and walked out of the door. I pulled the scent of her perfume deep into my lungs as her shadow passed out of the door.

After Jesus Christ, God's greatest gift to me was the woman who bore my five children, who kept our home, and who stands by my side come hell or high water. A loving, committed marriage partner is almost indispensable in ministry. JoAnna's commitment to God, to me and to our children is the stuff of ancient love stories.

The minutes crept by like ants climbing up the great pyramid at Giza. In two hours JoAnna was back. She made a beeline for the medicine cabinet and returned with a thermometer. "Baby, how did it go?" I quizzed. "The Lord was with me," she said. "Now lay back and be still. Your temperature is still high."

JoAnna filled in for me for a few days. And then one morning, I woke up right as rain. Later I found that my wife had a transformative experience in the pulpit. The quiet woman that I treasured was morphed into a powerhouse before the eyes of those assembled.

LAST LESSON IN EUROPE

As much as I loved Europe, I was looking forward to going home. I longed to hold my children once again. I was growing homesick for collard greens and candied yams.

Our speaking tour took us to the home of a prominent Swedish pastor. His wife welcomed JoAnna and me into their home as though we were treasured family members. His eight-year-old son took to us immediately. The child would not let me rest. He wanted me to read to him from the Dr. Seuss classic *The Cat in the Hat*. Then he wanted to play catch. And when we weren't doing any of those things, he wanted to talk about the meaning of life (as far as any eight year old can carry that conversation.) At night, he pressed his blond locks and freckled face next to mine, placed a kiss on my cheek and said, "Good night, Reverend Smith." He repeated this ritual with JoAnna, and then he zipped upstairs.

Inevitably, the day for our return trip popped up on the calendar. JoAnna and I were happy to be going home, but we had found love in Europe. We were leaving with a trunk full of memories.

The blue-eyed tyke was strangely subdued over his scrambled eggs and toast. His father and I sat in the living room, a pile of suitcases at our feet. We discussed my growing interest in the abstract theologies of European Christians like Barth and Kierkegaard. It wasn't long before the doorbell rang. One of the church members had been enlisted to drive JoAnna and me to the ocean liner that would carry us to Denmark. We hugged and shook hands. When I reached for the little fellow's hand, a river of tears sprang from his blue eyes. He refused my goodbye. He ran over to his father and tugged at his jacket sleeve.

"Daddy, make him stay!" he cried.

"I can't do that, Son. Reverend Smith has a home," his father said.

"But Daddy, we love him. Can't he stay here and be one of us?" The father was speechless at his son's outpouring of emotion. Now it was my turn to cry. I couldn't formulate a sufficient goodbye that day. I squeezed the child to myself and then stumbled out of the door blinded by own tears.

I dabbed at the corner of my eyes all the way to the airport. My theology told me that love did not know the boundaries of color. Hadn't Paul, a devout multiculturalist, marched all over the known world carrying the message of Christ? He broke through tribal traditions, racial walls and nationalist arrogance to proclaim "there is neither Jew nor Greek, . . . for you are all one in Christ Jesus" (Galatians 3:28).

Why was this child so different from the white people that I had met in the United States? The answer is quite simple. The child had not been fed the rancid meat of racism or the subtle wine of racial supremacy. His father had never glanced over the dinner table and said, "What else do these Negroes want? Nobody ever gave *us* anything!"

In fact, I doubt that he knew that there was any difference between us at all. The child had not been raised in a society where race was an issue. And the tears in his eyes gave me hope, hope that perhaps we could build an America where white children like him and my children could be truly be brothers and sisters. Maybe there was yet a way to work through the years of ethnic genocide and hate to bring about a more equitable America. If God could reconcile the world to himself through Jesus Christ, why couldn't we be reconciled to one another?

JoAnna and I traveled by sea into Denmark. I'll never forget sailing past the castle described by Shakespeare. When we landed in Denmark, we found the weather 30 degrees warmer than in Sweden. Brilliant blood-colored roses burst in full glory along the bustling boulevards. Canals snaked between the tall, medieval row houses.

We found the audiences in Copenhagen just as receptive to our message as the people in Sweden. At the airport when it was time to fly to Switzerland, a little boy burst through the crowd and presented us with a bouquet of crimson roses.

The Reverend Archie LeMone and his dear wife met us at the airport in Geneva, Switzerland. Reverend Le Mone was a brilliant man, a multilingual graduate of Coozer Theological Seminary. It was he who arranged for me to address the World Council of Churches there in Geneva.

That week I walked through the dark sanctum of John Calvin's Cathedral, my eyes gazing in wonder through the fuchsia and sky-blue stained-glass windows. As I continued to walk in the footsteps of the father of Reformed

Protestantism, I thought to myself, *Grandma was right, if you trust in God and work hard, anything can happen.* Here I was, the son of one of the poorest communities in the western hemisphere, speaking for my people on the other side of the Atlantic.

I left Europe with a wider vision. Perhaps God wanted me to bring the same message to white Americans that I had brought to white Europeans. If I could do this, healing surely would come. Getting white Americans to listen without bias was going to be the hard part. But as I remembered that child's tear-stained blue eyes I thought to myself, *It's worth the fight.*

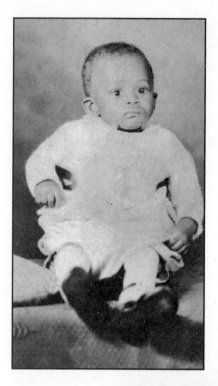

James Alfred Smith at age six months, Kansas City, Missouri, 1931.

J. Alfred Smith Sr. and his mother, Mrs. Amy Smith, after Sunday worship services, 1973.

Rev. Dr. J. Alfred Smith Sr. preaching at Allen Temple Baptist Church, Oakland, California, 1975. J. Alfred Smith Jr. is in the background.

J. Alfred Smith with U.S. President Jimmy Carter at a San Francisco campaign appearance, 1976.

U.S. Ambassador to the United Nations Andrew Young (left) speaks at Third Baptist Church with J. Alfred Smith and Dr. Ralph Abernathy, San Francisco, California, 1978.

J. Alfred Smith addresses the United Nations regarding issues about South Africa, New York, 1978.

Rev. Dr. J. Alfred Smith Sr. with Mother Beulah Richards, one of the first mothers of Allen Temple Baptist Church, 1973.

The congregation of ATBC prays for Rev. Dr. J. Alfred Smith Sr. and First Lady Mrs. JoAnna Goodwin-Smith as they prepare for travel to Sierra Leone, 1986.

J. Alfred Smith leads 12,000 people from Allen Temple Baptist Church to City Hall in a protest march against the selling of drugs, Oakland, California, 1986.

J. Alfred Smith addresses protesters at Oakland City Hall. Dr. Yusef Bey (back right) of the Black Muslims listens on.

At the 1987 Progressive National Baptist Convention conference, Kansas City, Missouri. Rev. Dr. Ralph Abernathy, Rev. Dr. Benjamin Hooks, Rev. Jesse Jackson, PNBC President Rev. Dr. J. Alfred Smith Sr., Rev. Dr. Allan Boesak.

Rev. Dr. J. Alfred Smith Sr. with Rev. Dr. Gardner C. Taylor at the 1987 PNBC conference.

J. Alfred Smith honored as a community leader by Oakland Mayor Elihu Harris (left) and U.S. Congresswoman Barbara Lee, Oakland, 1990.

Rev. Martin Luther King III with First Lady Mrs. JoAnna Goodwin-Smith after a Sunday worship service, 1993.

Professor Cornel West (left), President of American Baptist Seminary Dr. Keith Russell and Rev. Dr. J. Alfred Smith Sr. at an Allen Temple Sunday worship service, 1995.

The former East Oakland headquarters building of the Black Panthers, demolished in 1995 to make way for the Allen Temple Family Life Center.

Groundbreaking ceremony for the ATBC Family Life Center, 1995. From the left: Singer/entertainer Nancy Wilson, JoAnna Goodwin Smith, Orthell Dunn, unidentified celebrant.

Allen Temple Baptist Church receives the first faith-based initiative grant from the governor of California to provide job development services, Oakland, 2002. Governor Gray Davis (left), Rev. Dr. J. Alfred Smith Sr. and Oakland Mayor Jerry Brown (right) with First Lady Mrs. JoAnna Goodwin-Smith (seated).

J. Alfred Smith with members of the Allen Temple congregation visiting the Holy Land, 2000.

Rev. Dr. J. Alfred Smith Sr. with Dr. Charles Stith and former President of Zambia Dr. Kenneth Kaunda, 2003.

J. Alfred Smith praying with the ATBC Girl Scouts as they depart for spring camp, 2002.

J. Alfred Smith has a prayer breakfast with the ATBC Jr. Deacons, 2003.

Rev. Harry Louis Williams II (left), Rev. Jesse Jackson and Rev. Dr. J. Alfred Smith Sr., prior to a Sunday worship service where Rev. Jackson was the guest speaker at Allen Temple, Oakland, 2003.

J. Alfred Smith christening a baby during Sunday worship at ATBC, 2003.

J. Alfred Smith (left) plays saxophone during Sunday worship at ATBC, 2003.

Four generations of J. Alfred Smiths: Rev. Dr. J. Alfred Smith Jr. (left), Rev. Dr. J. Alfred Smith Sr. (center), J. Alfred Smith IV and J. Alfred Smith III (right), Oakland, 2003.

J. Alfred Smith Sr. with his wife and children after his son J. Alfred Smith Jr.'s installation services at Antioch Baptist Church, San Jose, California, 2003. Front row: Elaine Smith, Rev. Dr. J. Alfred Smith Jr., Rev. Dr. J. Alfred Smith Sr., First Lady JoAnna Smith. Back Row: Wally Sule, Amy Jones, Paul Rigmaiden, Shari Rigmaiden, Anthony Smith, Ronald Smith.

The next generations of the Smith family. Front row (from left): Joseph Smith (nephew), J. Alfred Smith III, Rev. Dr. J. Alfred Smith Sr., JoAnna Smith. Back row: Joseph Smith (grandson), Veronica Underwood, Thobecka Rigmaiden, Morgan Henderson, Mark Henderson, J. Alfred Smith IV, Asha Smith.

17

DADDY'S FUNERAL

Back in 1963 the black caucus disrupted a meeting of the American Baptist Churches over the issue of race and under-representation. Out of the uprising the Reverend Thomas Kilgore rose to the presidency of the denomination. Most likely due to Reverend Kilgore's influence, the Mission and Ministries board started hiring people of color. I was recruited to be the western area representative in 1968.

In 1969 I received a phone call from Uncle James. He said, "I hate to be the one to tell you this, but your Daddy's gone home to glory." I stood in my kitchen staring into the tiny black holes in the telephone receiver. "Uncle James," my voice seemed distant and unsteady. "I'll be flying in for the service."

Two days later I was in Shreveport, Louisiana. I rented a car and twice circled a six-block area seeking a parking space, but there was none. Cars were parked bumper to bumper, thick as bees in a hive. I drove past barber shops, barbecue pits, shoeshine parlors and storefront churches. Finally, I found a spot and left the car not knowing what to expect at the service. Daddy wasn't going to have a church funeral. He was denied that honor because he wasn't a church member. Daddy's funeral would be held at the funeral parlor itself. A string of black Cadillacs lined up in front of the tiny building pinned between the candy store and the used car lot.

I took a deep breath, cracked the door open and stepped from the humid

summer air into the cool air-conditioned darkness. The sweet tones of an organ played "Amazing Grace." The place was stuffed with men in black suits
and white shirts and women with long black dresses. Every inquiring eye
turned to the creaking of the open door. I stopped at the back pew and stared.
The faces bore a striking similarity to someone that I knew, but I couldn't place
that someone at first. I caught the resemblance in a woman's teary eyes, in the
silhouette of another man's nose and yet another woman's faint smile.

A twenty-second gaze down the row brought me to a stunning conclusion.
They all looked like the guy I saw in the mirror each morning when I shaved.
They were all my brothers and sisters, my father's children. Southern custom
had relegated them to the back of the room. Like me, they were "outside" children who were born to a number of different mothers.

Daddy's officially recognized family sat in the front row, facing the silver
casket and the bank of floral wreaths. I hugged my newfound siblings and
then made my way to the front of the church. I took a seat next to Uncle James.
A chubby woman with thick glasses clicked her dentures at my audacity.

A black man with horn-rimmed glasses approached the podium. He was a
minister hired by the funeral director for situations such as ours. He rattled off
a quick prepackaged prayer that he'd probably said a million times before, and
then he asked to see the obituary.

Uncle James, being a railroad man and not a theologian, didn't know what
the preacher was asking for. The preacher impatiently snapped his fingers.
"Man, let me see the program, *the program*." Mortified by his attitude, I stood
up. "Don't trouble yourself, Reverend. I'll give the obituary for my father."
The preacher shrugged and obliged me. You could hear the gossiping women
whisper, "That's one of Clyde's outside children, y'all. He's educated. He's a
trained man."

Since the first fellow had behaved so despicably, I decided to do more than
read the obituary, I preached with all of the eloquence within me. I saw the family sit up straight as if to say, "Now, what do you critics have to say about that?"

After the service, the long line of cars followed the hearse to the cemetery.
There I said to the preacher, "I would like to give the committal for my father."
When he offered me the book of ceremonies, I said, "I don't need the book." I
quoted the words over my father's casket from memory. After the last rose was
dropped on the southern clay, the procession found its way to Daddy's house.
The day was a scorcher, one of those hot southern days immortalized in the lit-

erature of the late William Faulkner. The people didn't know what do to cool off apart from drinking cold beer, eating fried catfish and chewing up watermelon. (Home air-conditioning units were the stuff of fantasy in 1969.)

It didn't take much spiritual discernment to see that my kinfolk were preparing to get down and party that night. "I Am a Man" by Muddy Waters was blaring from the hi-fi. My cousin Slim was lining up shot glasses at the dining room table. I was beginning to feel uncomfortable, so my next step was to get a ride to the Shreveport, Louisiana airport. That evening as I flew back to the San Francisco Bay Area, I couldn't wait to throw my arms around my own wife and children.

Uncle James and I stayed in communion after the passing of my father. He would come to visit my family once a year. He always brought us a sack of pecans from his native Louisiana. Whenever I was preaching near my uncle's house, he would come to hear me. And when Uncle James passed away, he left a request in his will that I would preach his funeral. He also left money so that my wife and I could fly first class back to Louisiana.

— 18 —

THE CALL TO OAKLAND

During the early part of the twentieth century, black refugees from the South had been settling in the San Francisco Bay Area, with San Francisco's Fillmore district and the Bayview-Hunt's Point areas becoming predominantly black. During World War II African Americans spread to West Oakland and the city of Richmond, California. The African American community was thriving. Promises of full citizenship hung in the air just beyond reach of fingertips. And then the unthinkable happened.

An explosion in an ammunition ship called the "Port Chicago" took 320 lives in San Francisco harbor. Black soldiers accounted for 202 of the lost. After the catastrophe, 328 black soldiers were ordered down into the unsafe ship's hold. The proper safety precautions were being overridden in favor of a speedy recovery of the ammo. The soldiers refused to cooperate and were arrested. Fifty of the soldiers were court-martialed and convicted of mutiny.

Thurgood Marshall of the NAACP Legal Defense Fund came to the West to fight the case, but he was unsuccessful. The black soldiers would do hard time in the penitentiary. African Americans as a whole were viewed in an unsympathetic light in the San Francisco area. Rumor had it that southern-born blacks were ungrateful and unpatriotic. People of dark hue and southern accents were labeled anti-American.

With little or no provocation, police started beating black men indiscriminately. This police brutality leaked over into Oakland, where the African American population was continuing to grow. White flight was fast changing the racial mixture of Oakland. It wasn't long before both East and West Oakland were predominately African American. The problems that haunted urban cities like Chicago and Newark began to fester here as well.

ALLEN TEMPLE BAPTIST CHURCH

In Berkeley, California, my family worshiped at the McGee Avenue Baptist Church, which I also attended when I wasn't on the road. Sitting with the congregation on Sunday mornings, I could feel the pastor inside of me stirring—I wanted to preach. On Christmas, Pentecost, Easter, Mother's Day, Father's Day—on days when the great themes of the Christian gospel would be preached—I squirmed in my seat. I wanted to prepare a text and use my gift behind the pulpit. As I listened to someone do what I was born to do, I felt like a rocket burning up in the atmosphere.

One afternoon Mr. Edward Hall, a distinguished looking man, came to the American Baptist headquarters in Oakland to pay me a visit. He came right to the point. "Reverend, we are in desperate need of an interim pastor. Would you come down on weekends and preach for us?" I replied, "Let me pray about it and get back to you, sir. Thank you for considering me."

JoAnna was already teaching an adult literacy class at Allen Temple Baptist Church. The former pastor had been a friend of mine. What harm could there be in leading the Sunday services? I love to preach and this would be an opportunity to use my gifts for the kingdom of God. JoAnna agreed.

Two weeks later I put on my new navy-blue suit. My family, dressed, powdered and perfumed, joined me in the car. We were heading for Allen Temple Baptist Church in East Oakland. As we rode the hot asphalt streets in silence, my mind began to reflect on the world that I was entering. Oakland is a major American city. Black Oakland is a world unto itself with a rich religious and social history.

African American settlers in Oakland founded Beth Eden Baptist Church in 1890 and made it the hub of the black community. Shortly thereafter, at the turn of the century, blacks began migrating West in large numbers. The sons and daughters of Arkansas, Louisiana and Texas were drawn to San Francisco by wonderful stories of railroad and seaport jobs that were opening to the "colored." But when a devastating earthquake shook San Francisco in 1906, a steady stream of African Americans fled across the bay to Oakland. By 1910 the black population of Oakland was triple that of San Francisco.

In 1919 a small group of African American Christians gathered together for church services in a hall on East 14th Street and Seminary Avenue. They later relocated to 85th Avenue, where they began to call themselves the "85th Avenue Baptist Church." By 1920 they had twenty-one members. J. I. Allen, formerly of Clarksville, Texas, served as their pastor. Years later the congregation would name itself after him, calling themselves the "Allen Temple Baptist Church."

By 1958 Allen Temple Baptist Church was drawing hundreds each Sunday. That year the church selected a twenty-four-year-old minister named C. C. Bailey to become its pastor. Several of the members had serious questions about Bailey's youth and his lack of pastoral experience. However, there was nothing to worry about. Young Bailey proved to be an insightful theologian and a gifted orator. His charismatic personality charmed young and old. He was a visionary who made daring decisions—choices that an older, more seasoned pastor might not have deemed "safe."

Pastor Bailey took a long look at Allen Temple Baptist Church's relationship with the General Baptist Association. He asked why an African American church would put itself beneath the umbrella of a segregated denomination. After he'd taken stock of the situation, he led the church to cut ties with that denomination. Bailey then led Allen Temple Baptist Church to join the American Baptist Convention.

Bailey didn't stop there. He encouraged one of his deacons to teach African American history and culture to the members of Allen Temple. This dynamic pastor also reached out to Oakland Park Boulevard Presbyterian Church, a predominately white congregation. He extended the olive branch to invite believers from the other side of Oakland to Allen Temple for a series of frank dialogues on the issues of religion and race. This may not seem revolutionary today, but he took these steps before the United States had enacted the voting rights bill!

Pastor Bailey was a man of insight, born before his time. However, after ten years of faithful service to the church, he felt it was time to move on. In 1969 C. C. Bailey left the pastorate to teach black studies at a nearby state college.

MINISTERING IN THE GHETTO

In 1969 East Oakland was an asphalt jungle sealed by razor-wire fences. Long-legged prostitutes in tight miniskirts strolled the corners, winking seductively at toothless old men. Black men of every hue stood in the shadows of the liquor stores nursing cans of cold beer. The pungent aroma of marijuana floated on the morning breeze.

I understood poverty—I knew what it meant to wear patches on my clothes—but this was more than poverty. This was the violent death of the human spirit. This was a despair that bordered on social suicide. There was a hopelessness in the air that I had never breathed before, anywhere.

My car reached East 14th Street (now International Boulevard). A blue sign with black letters screamed "BLACK PANTHER PARTY FOR SELF-DEFENSE—EAST OAKLAND HEADQUARTERS." Allen Temple Baptist Church was a large, triangular structure on the back of that block. From the outside it looked as though it might house a maximum of two hundred people if everyone held their breath.

I have never met anyone who was truly called to be a preacher who didn't love to stand behind a pulpit and preach, even if it was in a small inner-city church. I was no exception. The members afforded me great range in the pulpit. I could whoop and shout, or I could muse over theological and philosophical points that I had been contemplating since seminary. One week I could preach on the meaning of the phrase "Ye must be born again." On the following Sunday I might expound on the nature of institutional evil and the Christian's responsibility to confront it.

The people shouted at my messages. When I said "Yes," they enthusiastically responded "Yes!" When I quoted from Scripture, they finished the verses with me. When the altar call for soul salvation or church membership was announced, people responded in numbers.

The congregation seemed to like me, especially the younger members. The Black Power movement and all of its cultural trappings was sweeping America. So I grew my hair longer, and in the pulpit I wore an African garment called a dashiki. I threw quotations from Malcolm X and Martin Luther King Jr. into my sermons. Through the grace of the Holy Spirit, I crafted messages that were relevant to the times.

As I walked the desolate, unswept streets of East Oakland, I noticed a strange thing began to happen. People began to recognize me. Teenage boys with their heads wrapped in stocking hats would nod, "Hey, Rev!" Black Panthers in black berets and turtlenecks would salute me with the upraised fist. Children with sad eyes and tattered clothes would look up from a game of jacks and smile at me. And something began to tremble in my bones. Something was speaking to me. It was the voice of God.

I really didn't want to hear that voice at the time. I had a good job. My position with the American Baptists paid well. It had an enviable benefits package. There was plenty of room for advancement. I had a company credit card and a corporate account. On the other hand, Allen Temple Baptist Church was situated in a neighborhood moldering with crime and want. The members certainly wouldn't be able to compensate me with anything approaching my current salary. And few could have looked at that single building on 85th Avenue and Avenue "A" and believed that things would ever get any better. Still, I heard the Voice. I heard the Voice in my car on the way to lunch. It said, "James, what can be done about the suffering that you have seen in East Oakland?" It said, "You really should put your name in as a pastoral candidate for the Allen Temple Baptist Church."

In West Africa the European slave merchants would construct fortresses where unfortunate blacks were herded for importation to the new world. Invariably, these daunting structures came equipped with a huge wooden door that led from the castle to the slave ship. It was called "the door of no return." No one who stepped through that door was ever seen or heard from again. East Oakland was America's "door of no return." The more I prayed, the worse things seemed to get.

I had struggled my whole life to escape poverty and need. I wanted my children to know a level of comfort that I hadn't known growing up. However, I couldn't shut out the Voice. It called me at dawn. It whispered to me in the night. It walked behind me in line at the soul food cafeteria. It haunted me until the day I peeked my head into the Allen Temple deacons' room and said, "Would you gentlemen consider me for this position?" I almost could see God smiling.

MINISTRY MEETS ME AT HOME

In the evenings I would come home from my job at the American Baptist offices grateful to be finished with a hectic day. As my key turned the door lock, I visualized a nice quiet evening of reading the newspaper and eating my dinner. But invariably when I opened the door, my dreams would vanish. Six or seven teenagers in their stocking feet would be sitting around a Monopoly board, hollering as one threw the dice. My children would be clapping and shouting as though the Indy 500 were taking place in my living room. A tall boy with braces would be sitting in my leisure chair, grinning at "Gomer Pyle, USMC" on my TV.

"Good evening, Pastor Smith!" some of the teenagers would say on cue. I would wave the newspaper and walk into the kitchen. There JoAnna would be reading a book in seclusion as though protected by a wartime bunker.

JoAnna loved to see the children socializing and laughing. On the other hand, by the end of the day my mood was not quite so generous. One night I came out and asked JoAnna, "Honey, why is it that our children seem to draw other kids? Why don't some of the other families invite our children over every once in a while?

"Oh James, you're just being stuffy!" she said as she picked up a tray of lemonade on her way to the living room. I peered over JoAnna's shoulder. Could it be that God was sending me a message? Maybe they were being sent to me so that I could shepherd them.

Even though I felt that I had heard from God, there was still some nervousness. I approached the whole idea of a career move with trepidation. I was like the rich young ruler who had grown accustomed to the finer things in life. In a search for eternal wealth, the Maker of all things challenged him: "Sell all that you have and distribute to the poor, and you will have treasure in heaven; and come, follow Me" (Luke 18:22).

That story had new meaning for me in 1969. I was by no means rich, but for the first time I had two five dollar bills that could fellowship together in my wallet. I was able to buy my wife nice things to wear. We had little that could have been considered extravagant, but we were better off. And now God was asking us to take less again.

GOD SPEAKS IN NEW YORK CITY

The denomination sent me to New York on business. As providence had it, I was free on the weekend. I rented a car and drove to the Concord Baptist Church in Brooklyn. As I stepped through the threshold of that gothic sanctuary, I whispered, "Please, God, speak to me through the message." The service began, and I held my breath, but there was no direct word from God. I longed to see a finger writing on the wall, a burning pew that was not consumed—something concrete. But it didn't happen.

After the service I joined the line to shake hands with the pastor. Reverend

Dr. Gardner C. Taylor recognized me immediately. "Hello, Alfred, what brings you to this neck of the woods?" "Dr. Taylor, I need to speak with you if I may," I responded. We went into his study, and before he gave a word of counsel, he pointed at an altar. We both fell to our knees. Reverend Taylor's prayer went something like this: "Father God, you know what your servant Alfred is asking of you. Give him strength and wisdom. Let him know your will for his life. In Jesus name, amen."

"Now, Alfred, what decision are you wrestling with?"

"Dr. Taylor, I have an opportunity to pastor a church in East Oakland. But if I take it, I'll be saying goodbye to a lot of money. My family will have a difficult time."

Reverend Taylor looked me squarely in the eye and said, "Alfred, if God has called you, go yesterday. He will meet your needs."

THE CANDIDATING PROCESS

Several qualified preachers were being considered for the position of the pastor of Allen Temple Baptist Church. My name was entered in as a candidate just like the others. But there was a side of this drama to which I wasn't privy. So at this point in my story, I am going to include another voice: the recollection of Deacon Willie Wade, who first came to the church in 1945. (Unfortunately, he passed away while this book was being completed.) Deacon Wade observed: "We have a church constitution that states that certain things have to happen when we decide to hire a pastor."

"Back in 1969 we were without a pastor. At the time Reverend Smith was with American Baptist Churches of the West. He lived in Richmond, California. He came out when we lost our pastor and mediated the situation to get us from one step to the other. The process is, basically, that the church's pulpit committee calls in different ministers to preach for us. If we liked them, we would talk about bringing them here to minister on a permanent basis.

"In Pastor Smith's case, there was an impasse. The pulpit committee stated that they had problems trying to get Dr. Smith. I was kind of depressed because I'd heard Pastor Smith preach and knew that we needed him. We did not know at the time how great he was going to be. We didn't know that at the beginning, but we knew that we liked what we saw.

"Upon leaving church on a Sunday afternoon, my wife, Rosemary, and I went home and had dinner. We sat down and prayed about the Smith candidacy. We said, 'We need to talk about this because it's not getting done.'

"The pulpit committee was preparing to bring another minister here. It looked at the time like we were going to lose Dr. Smith. So my wife said, 'Maybe you should go over and talk to Dr. Smith and see if you can reconcile the difference between what the pulpit committee is saying and what he is saying.'

"So that Sunday afternoon I called Dr. Smith and I made an appointment to go over to Richmond. He was there with his wife and his children. I sat down and I talked with them. I didn't know what the impasse was because I wasn't a part of the pulpit committee. But I was a concerned deacon and a concerned member of the church.

"After that, I came back to the pulpit committee. One thing led to another and thirty years later we've got the greatest. Do you understand what I mean when I say 'the greatest'?"

OFFICIALLY INSTALLED

February 21, 1971, was one of those days that I'll never forget. It's right up there with my wedding day and the day I graduated from college. It was on this day that I was officially installed as the pastor of the Allen Temple Baptist Church. I was thirty-nine years old.

Reverend F. D. Robinson of the Pilgrim Rest Baptist Church of Kansas City had installed me in my last two pastorates, but Dr. Thomas Kilgore, a noted theologian and advocate for social justice, did the honors this afternoon.

The hymn of consecration was the Negro National Anthem, "Lift Every Voice and Sing." In the service I vowed: "Willingly do I affirm my ordination vows, believing with all my being that Jesus is the Christ, the Son of the living God, and accepting the holy Scriptures as inspired of God through the Holy Spirit; it is my sincere desire to devote my life to the ministry of the Word, administering of ordinances, and nurturing of the saints; to so live as to bring credit and not dishonor to the gospel which I preach; and to fulfill to my utmost ability the office of a good minister of Jesus Christ."

Likewise the congregation requested that "for our pastor, our church and ourselves, that God will grant us the wisdom and strength to carry out his holy will and to work together with our pastor and give him our utmost support in every way according to our abilities and opportunities, that honor and glory may thus come to the name of our Lord."

A PORTENT OF THINGS TO COME

Even though Allen Temple was a small church on a troubled block, that didn't stop many of the local dignitaries from coming to the installation ceremony. Among the political movers and shakers was a fellow that I liked: Chief Charles Gain.

Chief Gain realized that the police department needed people of color to patrol its streets. He wanted a police department that would serve and protect its citizens rather than breed fear in the community. At the conclusion of the service, the police chief approached me with an extended hand. "I look forward to working with you, Reverend. I believe that with you working with us, we'll be able to get some good things done in the community."

He and I had already worked together successfully on a drive to recruit more black applicants to the police department. He promised to be in touch, and then he was off. I went back to the business of greeting and shaking hands.

Three minutes later, Chief Gain stormed back into the church, his eyes on fire with rage. I pulled away from a parishioner and quickly stepped to his side. "Reverend," he said. "Go outside and look at my car." I raced through the door in my liturgical robes. The side window of the police car had been bashed out, and someone had ripped the radio right out of the dashboard. Broken glass littered the seats. I looked at that mess and wondered, *What have I gotten myself into?*

— 19 —

EVERYDAY LIFE AS A PASTOR

Shirley Burton moved to Oakland from Louisiana in 1969. She was searching for a church home when an elderly Methodist deacon told her, "Go around to East 85th Street. There's a short, little preacher who's really doing things for the community." She liked what she saw and joined us. Here, she shares some recollections of those early days.

"Police brutality was terrible in the early 1970s in Oakland. At that time it seemed as though if a black man just drove down the street, the police would stop him, pull him out of the car and beat him upside the head.

"It had gotten so bad that Dr. Smith would lead us down to the city council meetings. He would announce it in church beforehand. We would get a great number of members to go with us. I will never forget it.

"One particular night, we went to the city council meeting, and we were put on the agenda to speak. Well that night was the same night that some Russians were here. And the mayor gave the Russians the key to the city. Oh, he was very nice to them. And you have to remember that this was at the height of the Cold War.

"When it came to our time to speak, he was very rude. He was so rude, in fact, that he turned his chair around and turned his back to us.

"As black people, when we agree with something that a speaker is saying, we will clap our hands.

"Every time that we did this, he called for an intermission. So we had about three or four intermissions that night. We stayed at the city council until about 2 a.m., but we were not going to be undone. We stayed until we had our say-so.

"We fought to get people to register to vote, and we still do. We have a voters' registration drive on the campus. Also, when election time comes, we can't tell individuals who to vote for, but we can do a suggestion ballot telling them about issues that they can vote for. Many people do not read the papers. They don't take the time to study the issues and one little word can change everything.

"When there is a problem, people will come to Allen Temple Baptist Church first. They will ask the pastor how he feels. No matter what happens, the people know that Allen Temple is going to be there on the forefront fighting for them. The mayor and the politicians may not agree with Reverend Smith but they respect him."

A UNION SEEKS HELP

John Williams is a retired labor leader in the San Francisco Bay Area. Here he recalls how our paths first crossed:

"In the early 1970s, the Rylock Company in Union City was on strike. The unions feel that if one brother is being mistreated on the picket line, all brothers are being mistreated. So we went out there to support them.

"The company had hired this black security outfit. So we came to Pastor Smith to ask for help to get them to stop causing blacks to fight blacks. We didn't think it was fair that they were beating blacks for coming out there to try to stop the company from treating them the way that they were treating them.

"Dr. Smith was very instrumental in helping us to stop that fight out at Rylock. And he was in the center of the union struggles around the Bay Area. I've got a letter at home that he once wrote. It is a piece of history."

OPPOSITION BY THE DEACONS

I hit the ground running. I walked into the pastorate with several rooms full of new ideas. I was a man of prayer and felt as though the Spirit of God was leading me. The problem was that I could not get the leadership of the church to go along with my suggestions. I had faced this before, but I had always been able to overcome it. Here, in East Oakland, I had met my match.

When I came to Allen Temple Baptist Church in the early 1970s, I told the church that I wanted us to build housing for the poor and the elderly. There was some hesitation and plenty of fear. The shocking thing was that in 1972, the leadership went ahead and organized the community development corporation, but they left me off the board.

The Reverend Dr. Arthur Scott was the vice president of a bank and a trustee here during that time. He told the people: "You won't get anything going and no one will pay attention to you unless your pastor is on board and involved." An invitation to join was forthcoming.

DEACON MONDY REMINISCES

Today Deacon Joseph Mondy is the senior member of our deacon board. He and I have weathered many a storm together. Here he reflects on some of those early battles.

"In the military service, I had seen a lot of leaders, guys come from West Point, Annapolis and variety of other places. Reverend Smith had a unique style of leadership. He loved people. He wanted to do things. He was aggressive. I said to myself, 'This man is a dynamic leader.'

"When he came in we had about three or four deacons. They had been there for many years. And every time that Pastor Smith came up with a new idea, these men would question it. They gave him a hard time. They made him sweat underneath the armpits.

"Finally I began to think to myself, *I wish I could be the chairman of the deacon board because I think that I could help this man out. I think I could protect him from these guys.* And they made me the chairman of the deacon board.

"So about the second meeting that we went to, I made an announcement: 'There will be no more roasting of this pastor. This pastor is going to do what God called him to do. I'm just letting you guys know. I'm just putting you on notice. We will have discussions in these meetings, but there will be no more bashing the preacher. We are going to work with him, and with him we can do great things.'

"They weren't particularly interested in doing a lot of new things. They wanted to stick with the old."

It wasn't that the leadership of the church was deliberately trying to be mean. I was a young preacher with an unorthodox style of doing things. They thought that I was going too fast. They were trying to protect the church.

NEW WINESKINS

It seems that the people who give you the most trouble never go anywhere. Despite their intransigence, God has a way of working around them. He sends new people, new leaders. That's just what happened at Allen Temple. As the church grew, so did the number of deacons. Many of the new deacons were more progressive in their outlook. We shared a broader view of what the urban church could be. I brought on seven new deacons, six of whom eventually left us to become pastors or missionaries.

God sent Mary Morris to us. She was a brilliant Sunday school teacher who had standing-room-only crowds. She had a great deal of respect for the office of pastor. She loved the pastor and taught others to do the same.

Mother Ruth Young distinguished herself as a fine Christian and a missionary. She would whisper in my ear at the conclusion of the services: "Pastor, you preach the gospel, and I will fight the hard-headed naysayers for you."

I usually took a good look at the visitors on Sunday mornings. One time I noticed a tall, well-built fellow who sat in the back nodding at each phrase that I uttered. He never blinked. Sunday after Sunday, he took that same pew. Who was he? I walked over to him at the conclusion of a service one Sunday morning and said, "Brother, why don't you give your heart to the Lord today?" Usually people do not refuse such a request, but he had an answer.

"Preacher, you don't want me in your church. I am a gambler." He couldn't have been more wrong. He was just who I wanted in my church. Immediately Christ's words flashed before my eyes. "For the Son of man has come to seek and to save that which was lost" (Luke 19:10). Without thinking, I reached out and threw my arms around him. Shock pushed me back. When I'd embraced him, I felt a steel bulge beneath his jacket pocket. This worshiper had smuggled a .38 snub nose revolver into the house of the Lord. No wonder he'd been so reluctant to join the church!

For this man, following Christ was going to mean more than reciting a pretty prayer and putting his name on a church roll. Repentance was going to mean some distinct changes in his lifestyle. Rumors began to circulate around the church. The grapevine had it that this brother was a loan shark and that he owned a pool hall. Yet something kept drawing him to the Sunday morning church services each week. I believe that it was the power of the Holy Spirit. It wasn't long before he made up his mind about the life that he wanted to lead. He sold the pool hall, gave up any other extracurricular activities and got an honest job working for Amtrak. A year later Bill White became part of a new team that I was training to become deacons. He and I became close friends. It is a friendship that has endured for thirty years.

CHOOSING ANOTHER DEACON

A phone call came through one afternoon from a Berkeley police officer. This fellow attended services at Allen Temple, but I hadn't had the chance to really get to know him. He'd never called before. His voice sounded strained, nervous. "Pastor Smith, I was called upon to respond to a suicide on Sacramento Street last night. The man had killed himself by cutting his wrists and throat, and he bled all over his apartment. When we walked in, the stench was almost beyond your imagination."

"Before he died, he had ripped pages out of the Bible and with his own blood stuck them against the wall. He left a suicide note that said he had done what could never be forgiven. He had blasphemed the Holy Spirit. For that reason he killed himself.

"That was the most grotesque scene, with his body, his blood and the Bible all over the place. There were flies everywhere. It was unbelievable. Pastor, I called my mother and said, 'Mama, would you think about this?' She told me to call you. What does it mean to blaspheme, and why couldn't he be forgiven for that?"

That afternoon I sidestepped the theology. There would be plenty of time for that. I told Reggie that God is the God of the second, third, fourth chance and so on to infinity. I said, "Reggie, I want to meet you. I want to get to know you."

The next Sunday morning during service, I called him up and had him sit next to me near the pulpit. For the next six or seven years that was his seat. In the following years, Reggie Lyles became a trusted deacon (and a police captain) who traveled all over the globe with me. Today he serves as the chair of the Allen Temple deacon's ministry.

A FUNERAL SERVICE IN WEST OAKLAND

By now, you've probably guessed that I am pretty unconventional as preachers go. I have never fit into the stodgy mold that society expects of ministers of the gospel. This became evident on many occasions. Take the night I received an urgent plea from the pastor of the Zion Missionary Baptist Church in West Oakland. "Brother Pastor," he drawled, "I'm on my way out of town for a denominational conference. One of my members just passed away. Would you come and do the services?"

"No" has always been the hardest word in the English language for me to utter. True to form this time, I didn't even try. I simply said, "Yes, Brother Pastor. Just give me the name and address of the church."

I circled the streets of West Oakland hunting for the church. Finally I found a hearse parked in front of a church with Roman columns. Mourners in black struggled up the marble steps of the grand structure. Their own tears blinded them. I tucked my Bible beneath my arms and followed them inside.

An elderly woman leaning on a black cane shuffled past me. Her floppy black straw hat hung down over her eyes. "I'm so sorry about your loss," I whispered. Her voice was choppy and broken: "God bless you, Reverend."

I had arrived at the church early on purpose. How these home-going services are performed varies from church to church and from place to place. I needed to find the funeral director and quiz him concerning the protocol in this church. I needed to ask which family members might want to say a few words. Who might sing a song? What did the funeral director know about the deceased?

Unfortunately, he knew nothing about the deceased and even less about how funerals were conducted at this church. Frustrated, I hunted for a deacon but found none. I would have to wing it. The only thing left was to follow the old axiom "Act as though you know what you're doing, and people will never guess otherwise."

I requested a printed program from an usher and started up the red-carpeted stairs to the pulpit. The lights shined down from the ceiling like seraphim angels lighting up a black hole in space. I cleared my throat and looked down over the dais. People in black suits and dresses were packed tight from the front almost to the rear.

Then I saw something that caused my heart to skip a beat. The casket was open. At Allen Temple we never host open-casket funerals. We glorify the risen Christ. We celebrate the resurrection of the dead on that great day of the Lord. We don't celebrate the earthly body.

Well, I wasn't at home, so when in West Oakland, I thought, do as West Oaklanders do. I opened in prayer. The service was going smoothly until a chubby man in an ill-fitting, mud-brown suit rose from midway down the sanctuary. He clumped down the aisle until he reached the body. He then put his hands on the side of the casket and peered inside. I was shocked. I had done many funerals, but never had I seen anyone interrupt the sanctity of a service in that manner. I held my breath. After a few seconds, he sat down.

I cleared my throat and continued preaching. After two minutes the man was on his feet again. He marched back down the aisle and peered inside the casket again. This time he moaned the deceased person's name. I stiffened, ready to spring into action. A minister must maintain order and decorum in a service. A funeral can deteriorate into bedlam and chaos in seconds if the presiding minister doesn't control the situation with a firm hand.

I have attended funerals where it appeared that one of the bereaved was going to climb into the box with the deceased and holler, "June Bug, take me with you!" With this in mind, I moved to keep order. "Uh, sir, if you cannot keep your seat, I am going to ask the deacons to remove you."

I was firm but not cross with him. Still, my reprimand didn't go over well. People hissed and booed. "Let him alone," a man cried out. An older woman hollered, "Leave him be!"

I tried to apologize: "I am sorry. I am from East Oakland. I don't know the way that you do things over here in West Oakland. It was certainly not my intent to offend anyone." But some of the faces peering back at me were stern and unforgiving. I tried my best to ignore them as I continued my sermonette.

Two minutes later the mourner in the brown suit was on his feet again. He jumped up from his pew, sauntered up to the body and leaned over the casket. This time a long, shiny object dropped out of his jacket pocket. The green object thudded to the carpet and then rolled for an eternity before it crashed against a wooden pew with a pop. It was a Mad Dog 20/20 wine bottle. The mourner had been sipping happy sauce!

A persistent smile twitched at the corners of my mouth. I licked my lips, struggling to hold it back, but it wouldn't stop. The smile broke into a silly grin. A tingling that began in the bottom of my stomach soon erupted into laughter. Tears gushed from the corners of my eyes as I held my sides.

The mourners looked up at me open-mouthed. Some of the relatives laughed right along with me. My grinning outburst proved to be the end of the funeral service. I straightened myself up and then closed in prayer. After the amen, I turned the proceedings over to the undertaker and walked out—quickly.

MY DAUGHTER'S REQUEST

My wife and I were blessed with five very intelligent children. My daughter

Shari Lynn enrolled in a school exchange program that allowed her to go to Chile. I encouraged Shari Lynn in this endeavor. I wanted her to be exposed to as many broadening experiences as possible.

One afternoon I got a phone call from Chile.

"Hi, Baby! How are you?" I chirped into the telephone.

"Daddy! We have had an emergency here," she screamed.

My stomach tightened like nuts and bolts. I began to wonder what airline I would call for tickets and how long it would take for me to get to Chile.

"What kind of emergency, Honey?" I queried.

"It's not me, Daddy. It's Esmeralda's mom. You gotta help her, Daddy. If you don't help her she's gonna die!"

As it turned out the woman had been diagnosed with a heart ailment. The Chilean doctors, for whatever reason, were unable to treat her.

"What do you want Daddy to do, Sweetheart?"

A week later my daughter and Esmeralda's mom disembarked from a plane in San Francisco. JoAnna and Amy set up sleeping quarters for the ailing woman. My friend, Congressman Pete Starks, pulled some strings and helped me find some emergency healthcare for her.

As it turned out, the woman's heart was fine. She was suffering from a relatively minor discomfort called hyperventilation, a condition that can be controlled without the aid of medicine. Esmeralda's mom was grateful, so grateful in fact that she did not want to go home. JoAnna had taught her how to speak and write English. She developed a penchant for McDonald's cheeseburgers and American television.

She had a husband and a handful of children back home. Still, I had my hands full trying to persuade her to go back to Chile. Until I could accomplish this feat, she became part of the eclectic crowd that could be found at my dinner table on any given day of the week. We broke bread with hippies with waist-length hair, anti-war activists, labor organizers, politicians, famous preachers (who were passing through the Bay Area) and the occasional homeless neighbor. It was a crazy time, but we had a lot of fun.

THE PREACHER IN OVERALLS

In my youth I tried to push something down the throats of traditional church folk who just weren't ready for it. I should have learned a lesson, but I didn't.

One Sunday I looked down from the pulpit and saw a commotion. Two women were whispering loudly enough to be heard over the soft organ interlude. Then a poor neighborhood woman who had wandered in wearing blue jeans ducked her head between her shoulder blades and scooted out of the door.

I thought that I had a firm sense of what I'd seen. However, after the service I approached a nearby usher. "Brother, what happened when that sister left the service abruptly like that?" I asked. "Oh, Pastor," he said, "the ladies were talking badly about her because she didn't have on the right church clothes."

"I see," I said, looking down at my shoes. I really didn't see at all. What difference does it make what somewhere wears to church as long as they're there? We were hosting a worship service, not a fashion bazaar. The more I thought about it, the more my blood boiled. I came from a poor family. Did that mean that we were less than others who had nice clothes?

The next Sunday I decided to address the issue head on. Heads turned and mouths opened as I walked down the aisle and into the pulpit decked out in a pair of worn-out overalls. If people wanted to be outraged over the way someone dressed in church, I came ready to give them a reason.

The younger people loved it. Many of our poor neighborhood members laughed. Others found overalls in the pulpit an abomination unto the Lord. Their eyes burned laser beams through me as I opened the Word of God that Sunday. Subtlety had never been my strong suit. However, I was finally going to learn my lesson.

—20—

THE HONEYMOON IS OVER

Not long after the overalls incident, we received word that a Billy Graham crusade was coming to Oakland. Members of my church shouted, "Hallelujah!" You see, Allen Temple is located within walking distance of the Oakland Coliseum.

It promised to be a tremendous event. Churches were coming by the bus loads from northern California, the San Joaquin Valley, the coast and mountainous regions of our state. It seemed as though everyone was going to be there—except me. That's right, I refused to go.

Many members thought it disgraceful that I would not walk with them to the crusade. To add insult to injury, the Reverend Billy Graham had asked for his African American brethren of the cloth to sit on the stage with him. A number of my colleagues in ministry counted this an honor and a privilege not to be missed. Still I refused to have any part in it. The members couldn't understand my rationale for not attending, and they were livid.

Here's my thinking in a nutshell. I knew that when the revival was over, my neighborhood, East Oakland, was going to remain unchanged. Business people attending the crusade were not going to contact me about hiring young people in our congregation who needed employment. Many of the social ailments in our community would continue to fester and bleed long after Billy Graham had packed his bags and left for the next city.

I wanted something more, something that would radically transform the lives of our people. I felt that if some man recently released from prison went to that crusade and made a verbal commitment to Christ, the crippling environment that once drove him to a life of crime would still be waiting to tempt him when he returned home. I also thought of the man who beat his wife out of frustration because his inability to provide for his family made him feel like less than a man. And I wanted Mr. Graham, George Beverly Shea and the rest of my white brothers and sisters to do something more than sing "I Surrender All."

The Black Muslims and other black power groups were calling preachers "ecclesiastical pimps." They were saying that the black preacher and the black church were a part of the dilemma that plagued black people rather than part of the solution. One well-known Bay Area revolutionary had threatened to shoot the black Christian preachers and simply be done with it.

I wanted the Christians who lived in more affluent communities to become yoked with their struggling brothers. Here we were trying to build bricks without straw, and they were saying, "Pull yourself up by your own bootstraps." And when our white Christian friends would accept an invitation to come to out to Allen Temple, they were nervous wrecks, on pins and needles the entire time.

I refused to go to that crusade because I believed that the gospel has to transform the way that the poor and the powerful relate to each other. I'd seen white churches send missionaries to distant lands and yet turn their backs on the poor living in squalor and deprivation just blocks from their own lavish digs. I refused to celebrate such hypocrisy. I stayed home that night and watched preseason football.

A PHONE CALL AND STRANGE DRIVE

After the crusade my wife and I took our yearly vacation, and that's when the attempt was made to oust me from my position at Allen Temple. I was still oblivious to my peril for some time after I returned from vacation—until I received a phone call from a retired minister in the congregation. Reverend Douglas, my trusted mentor, was calling with a strange request. He said, "Come, son, come and get me. Take me for a ride."

Well, a pastor's schedule is often filled from morning till evening. The work accumulated during my vacation left me seeking a way to squeeze sixty-one minutes out of an hour. I simply couldn't spare the time. But then Reverend

Douglas said, "You'd better do it. What I'm about to tell you is serious. It's going to determine whether you are going to be able to stay at that church or not." I picked up my hat and walked out of the door, my troubled mind racing a mile a minute. It was 1971. I felt overwhelmed.

I took a deep breath as Reverend Douglas slipped into the passenger seat. Without even so much as a "Hello," he said, "Show me how you drive this car on this street." It was a narrow street so I drove slowly. A few moments later we were cruising down International Boulevard, which is a much busier thoroughfare. Once again Reverend Douglas said, "Show me how you drive this car on this street." The traffic was flowing quickly so I had to pick up speed. Reverend Douglas wasn't finished. He said, "Take me out to the freeway. Show me how fast you drive on the freeway." Without question or comment, I complied. Then Reverend Douglas said, "Now come back to East Oakland and let's drive through the alley near the church."

Well, I had to drive very slowly through the alley. Finally, he said, "Take me home." The wheels began to turn in my mind as we approached Reverend Douglas's front door. Throughout our impromptu tour of East Oakland, he had remained silent except to mutter his cryptic driving instructions. And now he was unlocking the passenger door. So I quickly blurted out, "You were going to tell me how not to get fired."

Reverend Douglas paused momentarily. His face was devoid of emotion, and he said in a most deadpan monotone, "You [have to] pastor a church just like you drive an automobile. When it's necessary for you to travel slowly, you drive slowly. When it's necessary for you to speed up, you pick the speed up. When it's necessary for you to travel at a freeway pace, you travel at a freeway pace. Now, goodbye." And with that he slammed the door, turned his back and walked into his house.

LESSONS LEARNED

Did I lead my church to that Billy Graham crusade? No. I have never been to a Billy Graham crusade to this day. But I did learn that the shepherd has to honor the minds and the will of his flock. The pastor must explain his rationale on issues. The pastor must teach before he or she leads. Change comes gradually within the four walls of a church building. I had to slow down. I was pushing the people too hard. I got so far out in front of the people I was trying to lead that they thought I was the enemy. No general can fight without an army.

— 21 —

LOVING OUR
BLACK PANTHER NEIGHBORS

In a church good ideas come from everywhere because God can speak through any member. That's what I thought when Arthur Burnett, a cashew-complexioned deacon with ivory-colored hair, came with a strange suggestion. Deacon Burnett said: "Pastor Smith, the Black Panther Party for Self-Defense has their headquarters right around the corner. I mean, we're on the same block with these youngsters. Why don't we invite them over and see what they have to say?" I agreed with him.

THE RISE OF THE BLACK PANTHERS

In 1966 police brutality was an epidemic in Oakland. Black men were being beat up, denied due process and systematically harassed like war criminals. Huey P. Newton and Bobby Seale decided that enough was enough. They formed a political party called the Black Panther Party for Self-Defense.

There is a famous portrait of the two in those early days. Newton is holding a shot gun. Belts of shells crisscross his torso. Minister of Defense, Bobby Seale, has a sidearm on his waist. Both men are dressed in black leather jackets and black berets. The concept caught on like wildfire. The black world had never seen anything like them.

The Black Panther Party rejected the nonviolence of the civil rights movement. Newton and his compatriots faced down the Oakland Police Department with pistols and shotguns. To quote from a now-famous Black Panther manifesto: "Black people have begged, prayed, petitioned, demonstrated and everything else to get the racist power structure to right the wrongs which have been historically perpetrated against black people. . . . The Black Panther Party For Self-Defense believes that the time has come for black people to arm themselves against this terror before it is too late." Black Panther chapters sprang up in major cities all over the United States. International cells opened around the globe.

The American press tried to play the Panthers down as a ragtag gang with illusions of grandeur. Nothing could have been further from the truth. These young sons and daughters of the ghetto were full-blown revolutionaries. They were heavily armed and quoted liberally from Sartre, Mao and Fanon. Their leader, Huey P. Newton, had met with the leadership of the North Vietnamese government during a time when our nation was at war with them. Newton and Palestinian leader Yasir Arafat were friends. Newton was also a guest of Fidel Castro. FBI director J. Edgar Hoover referred to the Black Panther Party as the "greatest threat to the internal security of the country." At Allen Temple we were contemplating these facts as we looked forward to our first face to face, tête-à-tête.

BLACK PANTHERS IN THE HOUSE OF GOD

The deacons drifted through the doors one by one on the evening of the proposed meeting. By 8:30 p.m. everyone was present except for one man who was struck with a most unusual and sudden attack of strep throat. (However, through the tremendous power of prayer, he was healed and present the next day for worship.) The usual banter about the game or the weather was strangely absent. Solemn stares and brief handshakes marked the occasion. We sat in silence.

The sounds of East Oakland on a Saturday rattled the windows. Harley Davidsons burned rubber up and down the avenue. Car horns and coarse banter trickled in through an open window.

I took a look around me at my deacons. They were bus drivers, school teachers, restaurant workers, carpenters, retired military personnel and people in the banking industry. Tonight they were dressed down in blue jeans and Le Tigre sports shirts. They rested on metal folding chairs, peering anxiously at the door in rapt anticipation of our famous guests.

"Pastor, what are you preaching on tomorrow morning?" someone asked. "I might be preaching a funeral tomorrow morning," I joked, trying to lighten the mood. Only one deacon snickered.

Then I heard deep, husky laughter and the sound of jackboots stomping on the concrete sidewalk outside. The door flung back with a bang. The deacons stiffened. Black leather shadows drifted in from the darkness. A deep bass voice was singing the lyrics to the soul hit "(For God's Sake) Give More Power to the People." There were ten of them, just a representation of the army that was now famous world over. The leader was a tall, slim man about thirty years old. His most distinctive features were the eyes that blazed like onyx when he lowered his head to glare at me from over the top of his sunglasses.

Being a pastor is a lot like being the underdog in a pick-up game of basketball. People always spot you a few points. The title "Reverend" is universally respected within the African American community. It's usually good for ten points at the beginning of any interaction. However, the narrow, penetrating stares that I was getting told me that I was going to have work for everything I was going to get tonight.

Deacon Burnett leaped to his feet. He walked over to the cadre with a forced smile. I followed, pressing my hand into one young hand and then another. The Panthers, however, were brimming over with anger, and as quickly as I could introduce myself, it came out.

The brother with the blazing eyes said through clenched teeth, "You bunch of bootlicking Uncle Toms. Y'all ain't nuthin' but popcorn pimps, ripping off fools and old people."

I gasped for breath. I had been called a lot of things in my life, but this was a new combination of epithets. Somehow I kept my composure, though I could feel the temperature rising all around me. I put my hand behind my back, signaling to my deacons to stay cool. And then I asked, "Son, why do you see me as a traitor to our people?"

A younger fellow with freckles tattooed across the bridge of his nose cut him off. "Marx was right," he said. "Religion is the opiate of the masses. The police are trying to crush us beneath their boot heels and the church is silent. We're struggling to get housing built that is fit for human beings to live in but y'all ain't saying nuthin'. The Oakland schools ain't preparing brothers and sisters to do nuthin' but clean white folks' houses and flip burgers. And what's the church sayin' 'bout it?"

He drew nose to nose with me, tilting his head and pointing into my face. "Ya see, you're the worst kind of traitor. Tellin' our people to accept oppression on earth because in heaven they get milk and honey. You oreo, sellout mutha . . ."

That was the final straw. Vulgar language is a desecration of sacred ground in the African American church. He had committed sacrilege. The deacons jumped to their feet behind me. People were shouting on both sides now. Tonsils were ringing, fingers stabbed the air, hands slammed down on table tops. Outside, it must have sounded like a riot.

"Let me tell y'all a little sumthin'," one younger deacon said with a distinct southern twang, his veins bulging on his neck. "Ain't no Uncle Toms in heah. I got to Oakland one step ahead of the torch and the rope. And I been here in this church worshipin' my God and scrappin' for justice in his name ever since. And we ain't about to be but so many traitors up in heah!"

Other deacons testified. Some had been whipped with the same police billy clubs that the Black Panthers had faced. Others had faced job and housing discrimination and a myriad of subtle atrocities that black life in California had to offer. If there is any positive application to the term "Christian soldier," these men exemplified it. None of us had abdicated our responsibility to fight for human rights in East Oakland in favor of a pie-in-the-sky-when-I-die religion.

It was time for me to put in my two cents' worth. I said, "Brothers, my religion offers people the choice to resist evil or be a party to it. If we don't raise our voices against the oppression of people of color in America, we might as well get white cone hats and join the other side. If we don't raise Cain because the health system in East Oakland is costing black people their very lives, then shame on us. We believe that God holds people accountable for their silence in the face of atrocity. I believe it. I live by it. Ask anybody who knows me or anything about me."

The air was peppered with "Amen" and "Say it, Pastor." I started reaching for reconciliation.

When the world looked at the Black Panthers, it saw AK-47 assault rifles and black leather jackets. I saw the sons and daughters of our community. Some of these folks had grown up in our Sunday school. Black Panther chairman Bobby Seale's mother and sister were (and are) core members of the church. We didn't want enmity. We wanted understanding. We wanted—no,

we needed—our young people to understand our faith and what we represented.

RAPPROCHEMENT WITH THE PANTHERS

The Panthers asked for our help that night. I said, "Name it. We'll do anything
to help you that we can. Just don't ask us to carry any guns."

That broke the ice. Everybody laughed. In the end we decided to let the
Black Panther Party for Self-Defense use our social hall as a place where the
wives and children of imprisoned Panthers could meet while waiting for bus
transportation to the San Quentin and Santa Rita correctional facilities. We also
allowed them use of our kitchen facilities.

In the coming years we mounted a massive voter registration drive with the
Panthers. Father Earl Neil, an Episcopalian priest, served as the Panthers' Minister of Religion. When he was transferred to another parish, the Panthers began to call on me to open public forums in prayer, to pray for their sick and
incarcerated, to bless their buildings and to preside over their funerals. They
began to call me "friend." Our newly forged friendship with the Panthers had
an unexpected benefit. People thought twice before accosting one of our members on the way home from prayer meeting. Graffiti artists left our building
alone. The word on the street was "Hands off the preacher and the church."

— 22 —

VICTORY AND TRAGEDY

On any given day, any number of opportunities or challenges might come through the front door of the Allen Temple. In those early days an offer was presented to me that I snapped up quickly.

Ted Keating, the president of the American Baptist Seminary of the West, wanted a professor of preaching and church life who could train budding pastors. He offered me the opportunity to mentor these preaching virtuosos.

This part-time position gave me the opportunity to have one foot in the pulpit and the other in the academy. As a seminary professor I've had the opportunity to influence so many lives. I've taught preaching to students who proclaim the Word of God to the four corners of the world. There have been Iraqis and Scandinavians, Harlemites and East Indians in my classes. And I have learned at least as much from journeying with them as they have learned from me.

MANY HANDS MAKE POWERFUL WORK

The Lord had given me a philosophy of ministry that I could sum up in a simple phrase: "Get out of the rocking chair of lazy religion." So I told the church members, "You didn't come to this church to watch me work. Get involved! Join a church ministry. Find somewhere to serve in the House of the Lord." Soon the work was growing so fast at Allen Temple that the task of guiding the church grew beyond the capability of one person.

Well-to-do blacks began to come back from the comfort of their hilly suburbia to serve their God in the flatlands of East Oakland. Their tithes and offerings were the beams and timber that supported miracles. A church full of active people took a lot of weight off my shoulders.

As time went on I trained others to do the work that is typically seen as the work of the pastor. We gathered evangelistic teams to go into the streets to preach the gospel of Jesus Christ. A public ministry group was assembled. No longer did I have to lead the battle at city hall. I could send a team to wage war with the forces of political power while I committed myself to prayer and the study of God's Word.

ANOTHER BIG CHANGE

In those days there were no women on the ministerial staff at the church. Women were allowed to read announcements or occasionally gave an address from a small lectern at the base of the pulpit. I took it upon myself to change this—*slowly*. I began to preach about women of the Bible like Huldah. I taught about the women who were the first at Christ's empty tomb. Through this teaching I introduced the concept of women in ministry to the church.

The first ladies I ever ordained were Dr. Elvina Stephans, the head of our prison ministry, Reverend Dr. Ella Mitchell, and Reverend Dr. Josie Lee Kuhlmann, a missionary who returned from the Philippines. Today we have more women in ministry at Allen Temple than men. On Good Friday the women preach the seven last words of Christ—the men sing.

HOWARD THURMAN COMES TO ALLEN TEMPLE

In 1973 I began graduate studies at the Graduate Theological Seminary in Berkeley. Reverend Dr. W. Hazaiah Williams brought the great mystic Dr. Howard Thurman to the institution to teach courses on spirituality. He was a towering intellectual figure and had a great spirit. Dr. Thurman would begin the class by quoting the 139th Psalm. When he spoke in a hush, we felt as if we were being ushered into the very presence of God: there was a feeling of awe, of reverence, of being in the presence of a Power greater than ourselves. Dr. Thurman had no assigned reading list for the class. He was the textbook. No one could be in his presence for long without developing a hunger for prayer. At the conclusion of a class, I would walk out to the pay phone and call JoAnna.

My greeting was always the same: "Honey, he has me on a high!"

Even though Dr. Thurman was not well known to Allen Temple Baptist Church, I invited him to address us on Martin Luther King's birthday. He graciously accepted. I left for the church late that day, and I wasn't sure whether anyone would be there. When I got to the church I was shocked. Motorcycle police were directing traffic. Many people had traveled great distances to be with us. And there were as many white people there as there were black!

We had invited a band comprised of Black Panther members to provide music for us. I wondered how they would take to the soft-spoken prophet. There was no real need to worry. Dr. Thurman held people in rapt attention with his tales of racism in Florida. For example, when his daughter asked why she couldn't play in the public park in Jacksonville, Dr. Thurman told her, "You are so special that it takes a whole state to legislate laws to keep you out." That response struck a chord with the Black Panther band. They beat on the drums. They sounded the horns. People clapped. It was a wonderful experience.

FACING OAKLAND'S EDUCATIONAL CRISIS

Our church is located right across the street from the Highland Elementary School, and on crisp autumn days the sound of children singing and playing filtered through my windows. So I decided to walk across the street in order to introduce myself. I shook hands with the administrators. One of the office assistants took me on a tour of the school building. We slipped into a classroom and took seats in the rear. I listened to the children read from a workbook. I was disheartened as student after student read. Some of the children read so poorly, I knew that something had to be done.

The principal and I developed two significant educational projects. The first was called the High Rise Tutorial program. I enlisted volunteers from Allen Temple to tutor young Highland students after class. These volunteers worked closely with both teachers and parents. Second, we created Project Interface. Together we drew a group of educational professionals together and created a program that would help inner-city children develop science and math skills.

Through this experience I became a part of Oakland's educational circles. I attended the board of education meetings and was eventually elected to a seat on that board. I advocated for better schools and higher salaries for the teachers.

MARCUS FOSTER MAKES A DIFFERENCE

Oakland brought in a man who was well-suited to make a difference. His name was Marcus Foster. Coming from Philadelphia, Foster hit the ground running. He instituted sweeping reforms in Oakland's schools. He fought for parental input in the educational system. He decentralized the bureaucracy that had monopolized control of the schools.

I really liked Marcus Foster. He was a spiritual man, so I invited him to preach one Sunday at Allen Temple. After the presermon hymn had been lifted up, he pulled a pocket New Testament from his vest pocket and began to read about Paul's shipwreck from the book of Acts. He preached a brilliant sermon without the use of notes. I was deeply impressed and was glad he was in Oakland.

On November 6, 1973, Marcus Foster was walking to his car when a multiracial band of men and women walked up to him and shot him dead. They called themselves the "Symbionese Liberation Army." (They would go on to achieve even greater infamy for the kidnapping of heiress Patty Hearst.)

The community was in a collective state of shock. A blanket of fear stretched over Oakland. Word had it that these virtually unknown radicals had targeted other prominent leaders in the African American community. Police cars circled my house day and night, maintaining a vigil.

I miss Marcus Foster. I think about him from time to time. I wonder what would have happened had his dreams for our children had time to grow.

—23—

MAN OF THE YEAR?

In November 1975 I was selected as the twenty-first recipient of the Sun Reporter/Metro Reporter 1975 Man of the Year. I was the first clergyperson ever to receive such an honor. The Oakland *Tribune* said: "The yearly award is given to those individuals who have made a most significant contribution in the service of their fellow man."

The publisher, a physician named Dr. Goodlett, said the following words, which greatly encouraged me when the award was presented: "During the perilous times in which 25 million blacks find it difficult to secure a mooring or a shelter, in an age of an incipient revolution, the importance of the black church as a refuge and a beacon light of hope to men everywhere becomes more deeply manifested.

"We honor you, however, based upon your concern for developing new dimensions of the Christian gospel, in that you have taken the meanings of a revolutionary Christianity into the byways and highways of not only the community in which you live but also in the Northern California-San Francisco Bay Area.

"We are particularly impressed by the fact that in a short space of time of approximately five years, you have taken a small parish church and made it into a tower of strength in your community."

STRATEGIC PARTNERSHIP

Why do some of the children of the inner city frequent its street corners? Why do some teenagers enter into crime and vice at such a young age? The answer is simple. So often there is no place for them to go and little for them to do that might be considered constructive. What better way to save our children from the ravages of the streets than to build a youth center, smack dab in the middle of our community? But where would we find the tens of thousands of dollars needed to build it?

The Allen Temple family and other community members developed a grassroots campaign to create a youth center in the Elmhurst District. My friend Robert Shetterly of the Clorox Corporation caught our dream. He presented it to Clorox. To our great delight, that corporation offered to put up the construction costs for the East Oakland Youth Development Center. They also raised an endowment which would keep the center funded for years to come. This victory taught me that if the church builds partnerships with the private sector as well as the public arena, great things can happen.

ANOTHER DEGREE

In 1975 I received a master's degree in American church history from the American Baptist Seminary of the West. I still felt a need to strengthen my biblical studies background. So I applied and was accepted to the doctor of ministry program at Golden Gate Theological Seminary. Fred Fisher, the New Testament Greek scholar at Golden Gate, agreed to do an independent study program with me.

The theological seminaries I had studied at were fairly liberal. However, at Golden Gate Theological Seminary I became immersed in biblical studies and I found theology and ethics that helped to give me a balanced perspective.

Dr. Francis DuBose taught urban ministry and a course titled "The Church in Community." While I was a doctoral student, he enlisted my services as a teaching assistant. For eight years he and I conducted urban church seminars together.

WEIGHING A TEMPTING OFFER

In 1975 the Reverend Dr. Thomas Kilgore Jr., the mentor who had installed me in the Allen Temple Baptist Church, contacted me about an incredible opportunity. Reverend Kilgore, who had become the president of the board of trustees, invited me to come out to Atlanta to serve as the dean of the Morehouse School of Religion. What a prestigious opportunity, one that many preachers dream of over the length of their ministries.

Allen Temple members George Elliot, Clem Daniels and Don Barnett got wind of the offer from Morehouse. In a demonstration of their love and commitment to my ministry to the Allen Temple family, they led a community-wide testimonial celebration for me. Tickets were sold for the event and the proceeds used to send my wife and me on a Caribbean cruise.

In the coming years other incredible offers came across my desk. I was offered the office of the Executive Secretary for the National Ministries of the American Baptist Churches, USA. Princeton University offered me the position of dean of the chapel. One of America's most renowned seminaries invited me to candidate for its presidency.

I always lifted these opportunities up to God in prayer, but each time I felt his assurance that I was to remain at Allen Temple Baptist Church. My place is in the pulpit.

A STRANGE CHRISTMAS

If I could go back and change one thing about my life, it would be the priority that I sometimes gave to ministry over my family.

My busyness came to a head one Christmas morning. The Christmas season is a sacred time when my family comes together and rehearses important family rituals. I love to hang sprigs of holly from the silver vines of garland. I love the dance that the multicolor lights do on the Christmas tree. That Christmas Eve, my family and I had sat around drinking eggnog and telling jokes.

I went to bed late that night with my whole Christmas day planned out. I would sleep in, catching up on some long needed rest. Then I would arise to watch my children peel bright red and green paper from the boxes of their gifts. It was a great plan. But in the middle of a good early-Christmas-morning dream, my wife's voice rudely brought me back to reality. As I fought to regain consciousness, I could hear tension in JoAnna's voice. "James, there's a problem. You had better throw on a robe and come into the living room."

My eyeballs felt like they had been rubbed with sandpaper. My muscles ached. I threw my legs over the bed and grabbed my robe. I opened the bedroom door and went to meet the problem.

A woman in a raincoat stood with her arms folded. Her eyes were pinned on the bows, ribbons and boxes beneath our tree. My children, dressed in their pajamas, eyed me silently. I could read their faces, "Is Daddy going to leave us on Christmas?"

Without a "Hello," a "How are you?" or a "Merry Christmas!" the woman tossed her request at my feet. "Reverend Smith, you know that my husband didn't buy the kids any presents. What are you gonna do about it?"

My children stared at me with bewilderment in their eyes. This was a nightmare. "Sister, have a seat. Let me make some phone calls." JoAnna offered the woman some tea. She has always been loving and sympathetic to those who interrupted our family privacy.

I called a deacon who said that he would go out and find the woman some presents. She was full of thanks, but the damage was done. *James Smith* was the one who answered the call of God on that bandstand in Vanita, Oklahoma, so many years earlier. I thank God for a patient and understanding family that has traveled the Jericho Road with me.

THE CROSSROADS

Souls were being won to Christ in well-attended revivals. Wednesday night Bible studies were attracting larger crowds. We were doing sickle-cell anemia testing, neighborhood cleanup projects, after-school tutorials, job placement and credit repair workshops. We were putting our pennies together to provide scholarships for neighborhood young people who wanted to go to college but lacked the tuition. We worked hard to get these kids a fighting chance. We were seeing lives resurrected and families restored. You'd think that everyone would be excited about the good news, wouldn't you? Many times it had just the opposite effect. Politicians labeled me a dissident and a troublemaker. They wondered out loud why I wasn't baptizing more souls at the church instead of looking over their shoulders and meddling in civic affairs.

Local preachers turned me into the prince of darkness himself, a liberal usurper who turned the church into a clearing house for black empowerment and social uplift—two things that they believed had no business in the house of God. These people of the cloth rarely missed a public opportunity to bash me. Yet when someone from the neighborhood came to them with a need that involved housing, clothing or food, they gave them the address of Allen Temple Baptist Church.

Despite the success that the Lord had sent, many of the long-term members didn't know what to make of what we were doing. They had grown up in churches where the pastor led the annual Easter egg hunt and confined his ministry to sermons, baptism and Communion. Back in the Louisiana bayou, the pastor had not gone down to the city hall to make public the mayor's neglect of the black community.

Some of the members were afraid of the numerical growth that we were experiencing. They had grown accustomed to seeing the same faces for years; now people from every walk of life were joining on a weekly basis. Old social networks were being tested and transformed. Some new person who didn't know any better might sit in a family's favored pew. That caused hard feelings.

These things left me spent and discouraged. I was so tired. Allies seemed so few, and the battle raged so hot. Wasn't I the man of the year? What had gone wrong?

In the midst of my melancholy, the phone rang.

—24—

A FRIENDLY CALL—
A TRAGIC END

O
ne of the most prominent preachers in the state of California was calling
me. His voice was bright and vibrant. I was surprised to hear from him.
Though his church was located in nearby San Francisco, we didn't run in the
same circles.

"How are you doing, Pastor Smith?" he inquired.

"So-so, I guess," was my not-so-enthusiastic response.

He heard me clearly and said, "You sound a little down."

I explained the overwhelming opposition that had arrayed itself against
me. He countered by saying, "James, I know just how you feel. If you weren't
seeing any opposition to the work, you'd have to question whether you are
headed in the right direction. Doesn't the Scripture say, 'Many are the afflic-
tions of the righteous: but the LORD delivereth him out of them all'? Doesn't
the Scripture say, 'Weeping may endure for a night, but joy cometh in the
morning'? My Bible says, 'Let us not be weary in well doing: for in due season
we shall reap if we faint not.' " I was instantly glad that this preacher had
called me. I felt faith stir in the innermost quarters of my being as he quoted
Scripture after Scripture from memory.

"James, is there anything I can do for you? I want to invest in your calling,"
he said.

In fact there was something he could do. I told him that I had penned a collection of prayers that I yearned to see in print. Christian publishers had answered my queries with a string of rejection slips. I wanted to go the self-publishing route, but that was costly.

"How much money?" he inquired. When I told him, he said, "Consider it done. Tell me where to send the check."

Joy flooded my soul. I rose from my desk and stared out of the window. The sun had risen like a ball of fire in the sky. A smile crept across my face. It had turned out to be a lovely day after all.

A few weeks later, a knock came to my office door. An amiable man in green khakis had come from San Francisco. He had three cartons of books with him. The title of the work was *In the Name of the Elder Brother*. I was referring to Jesus as our elder brother. (However, in the light of what would happen later, I see a touch of irony in the title.) I was so grateful for the publication of my prayers that I put in a call to the famous preacher who helped me. I said, "Brother, I want to come over to San Francisco to see you."

"Come on over, James! Do you know how to find us?" he asked. I knew exactly where his church was located. He was in the Fillmore district, a traditionally African American community that was falling somewhere between poverty and gentrification. The congregation had refurbished a building that once served as a Jewish synagogue. We set a date and a time. I looked forward to hanging out with him. My spirit was revived through the kindness of this near stranger.

Many of the local black preachers in San Francisco didn't like him. The explosive growth of his multiracial congregation had drained their own churches of thousands of members and tens of thousands of dollars.

Because of his huge following he had a lot of power over the local branch of the NAACP, a fantastic feat for a white man. Frankly, I didn't give much thought to his skin color. It was his deeds that I was looking at. He was a good man whose church was doing tremendous ministry. He had broken down the walls that separate Christians like no preacher I had ever seen. Rich and poor, black and white, Asian and Latino prayed and served as equals there. I believed in his leadership.

On the afternoon that I went to his church, he greeted me like a brother. He grasped my hand in both of his hands. He invited me into his sparsely decorated office, where we sipped strong coffee and discussed the ins and outs of ministry. The pastor was well schooled in the academic side of theology. I was impressed.

As we walked around the church, I came to the conclusion that people were living communally inside of the church complex. Men and women slept dormitory style on bunk beds. This proved unnerving. A feeling of foreboding fell over me. I couldn't shake it. Everybody was smiling and grinning. Come to think of it, they seemed a little too happy. They called the preacher "Dad." Questions floated in my mind, but I quickly suppressed them. If this man wasn't a Christian, who was?

"DAD" DOES A TERRIBLE DEED

Months later a news flash interrupted a college basketball game. There, plastered on the screen was my friend, the San Francisco preacher, Jim Jones. As it turned out, he had led almost a thousand people from his church in San Francisco to the jungles of Guyana. His brainwashed henchmen forced these men, women and children to drink from vats of poisoned Kool-Aid. Those who refused were shot to death. The flesh of babies and children turned blue and cold in their mothers' motionless arms.

That next day a representative of some of the bereaved families called our church. The bodies of the suicide/murder victims were being shipped back to the United States. They wanted to know if I would perform a mass funeral for hundreds of lost people at East Oakland's Evergreen Cemetery. I felt that this was the least that I could do.

SAYING GOODBYE TO THE INNOCENTS

I could look at a crooked politician from across the table and pick out what lie he was going to spit out before he even opened his mouth. In the ghetto people who need help always show up with a story. I was good at sifting through what was actually true and what was not. However, this preacher had fooled me and a boatload of powerful preachers and politicians who probably should have known better.

Tears streamed down faces. Shrieks of agony echoed through the graveyard as we stumbled past granite angels and stone crosses. A tall, bald-headed white fellow in an expensive periwinkle suit dropped to the fresh dirt, screaming his daughter's name again and again. Television cameramen angled around for a better shot of these tormented souls. Rows and rows of metallic boxes were lined up on the grass carpet. Clouds blocked the California sun. Satan cast his ominous shadow over the sea of tombstones. It was bizarre.

"When Religion Becomes Sin" was my sermon title. I preached about the eternal comfort in the tireless arms of the Lord that awaits the children of God. I bid the wounded to look beyond the clouds because even through the senselessness of lost life and misery, I believe that Almighty God exists, that he is passionately concerned and engaged in the lives of his children on this wandering planet called Earth.

In my mind I heard Bessie Smith sing the blues, and I saw my preacher-friend from San Francisco peering at me through his ever-present black sunglasses. I have done more funeral services than I can count, but I will never forget the anguish that fell in the wake of those who died in the Jonestown tragedy.

— 25 —

BIG TROUBLE STRIKES

On a national level the tide was turning in our favor. Affirmative action legislation had created court-mandated space for minorities in government offices, public universities and construction bidding wars. Members of our church, our friends and our family saw the doors of the plush suburbs open to the sons and daughters of Louisiana, Mississippi and Arkansas. Black people were headed for sectors of the society where we had been barred since the creation of the Republic.

One day a politician from the South came to Oakland promising us even more opportunities. He began talking about "justice" and "social equity." This definitely tickled my ears. His name was Jimmy Carter. I promised him my support. I burned up the streets telling everybody who would listen to help this man get the Democratic Party nomination. I met with lots of cynicism. I heard things like, "He's just another pol-*lie*-tician. He'll tell us anything and then we won't be able to find him after he gets into office."

"No," I retorted, "This man is different. I just have a feeling about him. I think that he'll come true to his word."

Andrew Young, who would later serve as ambassador to the United Nations, came to the Bay Area. He had been a trusted lieutenant to Dr. Martin Luther King Jr. During a barnstorming tour for Carter, he stopped by to encourage me to continue my efforts on Carter's behalf. I liked Andrew Young. We had some things in common. He was an ordained clergyman and a member of the United Church of Christ. His commitment to justice came without question.

When Jimmy Carter won the Democratic nomination, I knew that we could get him into the White House. I worked with members of Allen Temple in building a massive voter registration drive. If he didn't win, it wouldn't be because we didn't do our part in the San Francisco Bay Area.

The election was a landslide. After the balloons fell from the ceiling on election night and the last victory songs had been sung, our eyes were looking toward Washington, D.C.

DINNER WITH THE LEADER OF THE FREE WORLD

One day an invitation arrived in my office from Washington. The new President was inviting me to come visit him at the White House. A tear dripped down my cheek as I held the card in my hand. Life in parish ministry was like a roller coaster ride. One afternoon I was petitioning business leaders to invest in a recreation center for our children; the next I was seated across from the leader of the free world asking, "Would you please pass the pepper?"

My instincts about Jimmy Carter were correct. He was a good man, a fair man. That evening at the White House I was impressed by his down-home charm. His political powers had not dulled his manners. After dinner we were escorted into a small theater in the White House. An actor walked on stage and recited the entire Gospel of Mark from memory as the President, his wife Rosalyn and I looked on. I went back to my hotel room refreshed. It was as though God was sending me a message. He was saying, "Hang tough, James Alfred Smith Sr. I am with you even until the end of the world."

MAMA JOINS US

Back in Kansas City, Mama's health was growing more delicate. With my brother and I both living in California, there was no one to cut the grass or chop the firewood. In 1978 my wife and I decided that it would be best for Mama to live with us.

The kids loved their grandmother. Her relationship with JoAnna was more mother-daughter than mother-in-law to daughter-in-law. If JoAnna and I ever disagreed about anything, Mama invariably took JoAnna's side.

A NEW CHURCH BUILDING

If the fire chief had ever made a surprise inspection at the Allen Temple Baptist

Church on a Sunday morning, he would have shut us down. Worshipers were coming to Allen Temple from all over the San Francisco Bay Area. Despite all efforts to accommodate them, people were being turned away at the door because the building was too full. Insistent worshipers stood outside of the windows, peering in at the worship. We were so crowded that one Easter Sunday when the choir marched out of the church as part of the morning service, the choir members couldn't return to their seats because a sea of worshipers occupied them.

After this debacle I called the deacon board together. Some of the older, hard-line members seemed to know what I was going to say. They tightened their lips and folded their arms over their chests. I said, "Gentlemen, we've got to build another church."

"Out of the question," one of the leaders remarked. "We told God when we asked him to help us pay off this building that we wouldn't ask him for nothing else." I had plenty that I could have said in response, but I bit my tongue. My patience was wearing thin, but years of ministry had taught me to keep my mouth shut. I just prayed that they would catch the vision. After listening to them I said, "Well, if you don't want another building, let's build a balcony in this one. The board saw that as a fair compromise. "Well, Brother Pastor, if you find some architect to put a balcony in this building, we'll support that."

We hired an architect to see what could be done. He walked into the sanctuary, took a quick look around, shook his head and said, "It won't work. This building structurally won't support a balcony." I smiled broadly and said, "Well, gentlemen, I guess that settles it."

I had learned that the pastor can't do it all, so I turned to Deacon Mondy and gave him the responsibility of leading the fundraising drive and getting the new sanctuary built. I trusted this man. During the ensuing building committee meetings, I sat quietly in the back of the sanctuary as Deacon Mondy chaired the meetings from the front. I knew that he wouldn't let me down. And he didn't.

RAISING THE MONEY

Money is always a sticky subject in church. People are naturally distrustful of church fundraisers. Everybody in the African American community has seen a crooked preacher. There is always somebody who has an aunt who gave Pastor So-and-So a large sum of money in exchange for a "miraculous" healing. In every church there are a bunch of people who were pastored by some Scripture-spouting con artist who ran off with the building fund. So when a pastor asks for money to build something, members' hearts are rarely receptive.

One Sunday morning my mother was sitting in church when a woman behind her said, "Oh no, here he goes again talking about money. Doesn't he have any other sermons?" Mama was crushed by the woman's insensitivity.

At Allen Temple the people could see where their money was going. We used their tithes to buy food for the hungry, to provide medical care, to support missions and to carry out other ministries. The financial demands of this ministry continued to mount. We needed to raise $11,000 for emergency food relief for our neighbors who had been displaced by the closure of factories that had employed people for generations. Across the ocean in Somalia, civil war was destroying the lives of little children. We pledged $6,000 as a token of our love and solidarity.

What were we going to do? A new worship house was going to cost $1.8 million. Undeterred and believing in God's faithfulness, we solicited pledges from our members. We asked them to give generously—sacrificially—beyond their normal tithes. If they were giving 10 percent, we needed 15 percent. Vision costs money. It takes sacrifice. Certificates of Deposit had to be cashed in. Vacations had to be postponed. And I never asked anybody to give without going into my pocket first.

God is good! One day the sanctuary was finished, all 16,000 square feet of it. We marched into the church singing, shouting and praising our God. Local priests, preachers and politicians were packed into the new sanctuary. We were walking on air. Allie Whitehurst, a faithful Allen Temple member, agreed to lead the continuing campaign to get the church building paid off in five years. (God blessed her efforts, and we came in under the wire.)

Ten years earlier, I had walked into a struggling church in the Elmhurst community. But that night there were thousands of us standing in a brand-new building, holding hands and vowing to stay the course in our struggle to make God's will a reality on the earth. It felt good.

— 26 —

BUILDING ON THE BLOCK

T here were forces beyond the invisible walls of the ghetto that transpired to keep the people inside poor and uneducated. One of the methods that they used was called "redlining." This is when banks refuse to loan money for people who desire to build in poorer sections of a city. Redlining is actually illegal, but it's hard to prove. It has been one of the largest problems we've faced in East Oakland.

By 1981 East Oakland operated so far outside the country's economic mainstream that there wasn't a single bank in the entire community. However, nature abhors a vacuum. A man with evil intentions decided to profit on the empty pockets and broken hearts of our people. He made loans available to poor people at 50 percent interest.

Even now I have to ask God for forgiveness for the thoughts that raced through my mind when I found out about him. This man was a soulless bottom-feeder, taking bread from babies and stealing their Pampers. After the waves of rage passed, I thought and prayed about what could be done. The church can only give out so much money before the coffers are depleted. How could we teach people who had never seen much money how to save it, invest it, store it up for their children? How could we help people get enough money to buy their own homes?

An idea came to me. What if we could build our own financial institution?

After much prayer I started exploring the idea with key church leaders. They were excited about it. So I went to an advisory board who in turn laid out the idea before the whole church. We took recommendations as to who should sit on a new board to pursue the dream. From there I took the idea downtown to local politicians who were sympathetic to our cause. One councilman was particularly enthusiastic. His name was Frank Ogawa. Ogawa was a nursery man, and he blessed us by sending over beautiful plants and flowers.

We purchased a building across the street from the church. The only thing left was to raise the huge sum of money that it would take to build up the credit union assets. We threw everything into a large-scale fundraising drive. Dreams of this magnitude are incredibly expensive. Members divested from their own banks and put their savings in the Allen Temple Baptist Church Credit Union. Local black churches caught the vision and banked with us. They encouraged their members to do the same thing.

People who had never held a bank book in their hands now had a financial institution set up with them in mind. We put people in their own homes for the first time in generations. Allen Temple gave start-up money to minority-owned businesses. At one time the credit union controlled $10,000,000 in assets.

How were we able to convince so many people to invest so much in a shaking fledgling project, you might ask. The people had seen the hand of God raise Allen Temple. They had seen the good that we were doing in the community. I personally had developed some hard-won street credibility. People knew of the struggles that I had faced and the obstacles that I had to climb to do ministry on these mean streets. To put it bluntly, they knew that I was for real. You can find a million people to make a speech but few who will struggle when the lights go off and the camera bulbs stop flashing.

BUILDING HOUSING FOR THE COMMUNITY

When I had worked for the Ministers and Missionaries Benefit Board of the American Baptist Churches, I worked closely with the American Baptist Churches of West Retirement Homes. The denomination had constructed homes for retired missionaries and clergy. But because few people of color could afford to reside in such places, it would have been easy for me to think: *Well, this isn't for African Americans and it's not what I'm called to do. So why apply myself? Why learn anything about this? Why learn about how these things work?* If I had not applied myself 100 percent, I would have missed out on God's plan for my future. Instead I learned how to raise money and how to plan for large-scale buildings projects. I couldn't see it at the time, but as I began to craft a plan to do these multimillion dollar projects, I realized that God had me work at the American Baptist headquarters to learn to do what he was calling me to do.

So often God does his greatest work in our lives in the dark, in secret. And in these painful times it may seem as though our ministry is heading toward the grave. However, this may be when something fantastic is being birthed in our lives. The secret is to be diligent—even in things that seem insignificant and that have no relationship to what you believe God has called you to do. With God, nothing is wasted. The time that I spent shuffling papers for the American Baptist Churches of the West taught me how to put a roof over the heads of hundreds of elderly people.

BIG BARRIERS TO BUILDING

Having the know-how was only a small part of the equation. (If God had put all the pieces together too easily, I would never have reason to trust him.) This project was going to take an extravagant sum of money. Tithes and offerings would cover only a part of the building and staffing costs. We were going to need some help from both the local and federal governments. This was easier said than done.

Years of activism on my part had created a wall between the political leadership of the city and myself. John Reading was a hard-line Republican conservative who looked at me as a radical Democrat who was always jumping down his throat about something. And now I was asking for his help. He didn't exactly welcome me with open arms. As I was mulling this problem over, an idea came to me. C. J. Patterson, a member of our church, was active in local Republican politics and was the head of the Golden State Business League, a local chapter of the National Black Chamber of Commerce (founded by Booker T. Washington). I called C. J. and shared the vision with him. Then I told him we needed his help. He responded with, "Yes, I see, I see." After our call was finished, he made a personal visit to the mayor's office.

Through the grace of God, Mr. Patterson was able to convince the mayor that this was something that had to be done in East Oakland. What the mayor thought of Reverend Smith had nothing to do with building affordable housing for the citizens of East Oakland. The mayor agreed. He gave us the green light to work with Mr. John Williams, the head of the Oakland redevelopment agency. A prominent businessman named Leo Sorenson came alongside us, as did Oakland City Councilman Frank Ogawa.

After Mr. Patterson had opened the door, I was on my way to Washington—with good company. John Williams, Frank Ogawa and Leo Sorenson went with me to meet with the Secretary of the Department of Housing and Urban Development. The Secretary told the mayor that in order for us to build low-income housing in East Oakland, we had to designate the East 14th St. corridor as a federally enforced code area. The mayor complied, setting aside the territory from 82nd Avenue to the San Leandro border for this purpose. The city sold us that land at a cheap price and held it until we could come up with the funding.

A STALLED PROJECT

Even though we had secured the city's help, we still needed a friend with some political clout. I went to see my old friend Congressman Peter Starks. He believed in what we wanted to do and said that we could count on his help. Allen Temple Baptist Church was able to hire a top-notch housing consultant who taught us the ins-and-outs of proposals for funding. We created our proposal and submitted it to the authorities in Washington, D.C. We were knocking at the door to victory. We were gazing into the Promised Land. The first check should have come in during the span of two or three months. But it didn't; our dream went comatose.

Despite our incredible proposals, HUD hesitated to loan us the millions we needed to begin. We were deeply perplexed over this monumental setback until Congressman Starks came back from Washington with a report from behind closed doors. The people considering our proposals were quietly saying, "He's in a ghetto! Does he think that we're going to give him that kind of money to put in a rat hole like that?"

Sometimes I would drive my car down International Avenue to the proposed sight of the proposed building: the Allen Temple Arms. I would grab my Bible and walk around the site, praying out loud, beseeching God to extend his intervening hand to make a way out of no way, as he had done for our ancestors. I know that he heard me, but God's timing is not our timing. Almost seven years went by and not a single brick was laid down on the site.

After the Sunday services, elderly mothers of the church would whisper into my ear, "Pastor, if we get that Allen Temple Arms built, I sure would like to move in. I can hardly make the rent anymore. Things are just so expensive here in the Bay Area." And I would smile and say things like, "Hang in there, sister, God will see us through." But as more elders inched their way through the crowd to shake my hand, I would be choking back tears. My heart was broken.

My faith had almost turned to dust. I would make periodic visits to Congressman Starks's office. We would talk about the proposal and wonder what had happened. Occasionally, we would stare at each other in bewilderment. We had done everything that possibly could be done.

A FULFILLED PROMISE

We had seven proposals turned down. I was on the verge of giving up when one of Starks's staff members, a practicing Roman Catholic named Mrs. Teresa Límon, whispered, "You can't give up, Pastor. The Lord told me to work with you. We're going to get it this year." At that point Congressman Starks assigned her to our project full time.

What Límon was promising was impossible by human standards. However, she had attached these important words: "The Lord told me." Sure enough, within one year of her bold proclamation, a check came from the California Finance Housing Authority, who was working in conjunction with HUD. At that time, California had a governor, Jerry Brown, who was very sensitive to social justice issues. Governor Brown's enlightened leadership made this grant possible. For that I will always be grateful.

At dawn one morning I walked out to the lot designated for the building. As I lifted my hands to consecrate this land to God, I cried out to him. I brought the names of our senior citizens before him, and he heard me. On that morning there was a huge crane dangling a thirty-foot steel girder high above the very spot where I sought God's face. In 1981 the doors to Allen Temple Arms opened.

One Sunday-morning the congregation marched from the sanctuary to the Allen Temple Arms. The police escorted us, sirens blaring. Oh what a jubilant moment it was. The elderly folks who came to Oakland from the Deep South brought a saying with them: "The Lord may not come when you want him to, but he's always right on time." This is indeed true.

God gave us the Allen Temple Arms, and we treated the building accordingly. We surrounded our facility with daisies, lilies and begonias. The sidewalks were swept frequently. A staff was hired to keep the place sparkling and fresh. We treated our tenants with love and tenderness.

BUILDING ON THE BLOCK

Allen Temple Arms was a success. The building quickly filled to capacity. Still, the elderly called on us to help them find affordable housing in their golden years. After much prayer, we assembled a team to create a proposal for Allen Temple Arms II.

Hours of painstaking groundwork went into the planning stages, but history repeated itself. Despite the fact that we'd been successful, Washington officials again seemed hesitant to invest in East Oakland.

We needed an advocate; someone with both political savvy and high-level connections. Our old friend C. J. Patterson came to mind immediately. Even though he was confined to a wheelchair, his determination to fight for housing on behalf of East Oakland's elderly had not waned.

Mr. Patterson and his private nurse flew to Washington, D.C., where he met with Samuel Pearce, the secretary of the Department of Housing and Urban Development (HUD) who happened to be a black man.

As soon as Mr. Patterson began to give his argument for housing in East Oakland, Secretary Pearce shook his head. He opened his desk and retrieved a large manila envelope. He reached his hand inside and extracted several newspaper clippings. The articles (which he had gone through some trouble to assemble) contained quotations of me lambasting the Republican administration.

Mr. Patterson, who had picked up the tab for a banquet thrown in Pearce's honor during a recent visit to California, spoke to Pearce as one Republican to another. "Look," he said. "You're not doing this for Pastor Smith. You're doing it for the people of East Oakland." Finally, Mr. Pearce saw it our way. He awarded Allen Temple Baptist Church the building capital from his own discretionary fund. Allen Temple Arms III followed in 1988 and Allen Temple Arms IV in 1989.

— 27 —

HUNTING THE HUNTER

I have always been a firm believer that the gospel must go beyond the four walls of the church. The church is a daunting and potentially frightening place to those unfamiliar with life behind the stained-glass windows. This is why we must take the message of Christ to the lost who wander up and down the busy streets, searching for someone, anyone, to tell them they are loved, to remind them that God really and truly cares.

In the early 1980s I led our evangelism team to the streets that surrounded our church. I would put on my overalls and sneakers and take the gospel to the streets. Some of our members would walk beside me, toting copies of the Gospel of John and boxes of tracts. The routine rarely varied. Someone would lead a few songs, and then I would grab a bullhorn and preach like Jesus was coming back in a half hour.

Some of the most impassioned messages that I have ever preached were delivered to the crowds that surrounded us on the corner of 85th and East 14th Street.

One overcast day in the late summer of 1981, I noticed a trim fellow with a thick mustache. He eyed us from across the street with a distinct frown marring his visage. He stood flatfooted, hands clasped behind his back and a toothpick dangling from his lips. He rocked back and forth on his heels, eyeing me coolly. Clearly he was up to something. Young African American men huddled around him, whispering and pointing across the bustling boulevard at us. He bared his teeth and twisted his head back and forth. He seemed to be sneering at me.

One of my members whispered into my ear. "You know they sellin' dope over there 'cross the street." "Whose the man?" I asked. "That's Frank Rucker. He just got sprung from Quentin on a 187 bid." [Translation: Frank Rucker had been recently released from San Quentin State Prison after serving hard time for murder.] "Rucker runs East 14th Street. We standin' in his bidness right now. We driving away his customers. They too ashamed to do bidness with the church out here."

I had seen Frank Rucker's "customers." They stood on the corners in sleep-eyed stupor, their legs bending beneath them as heroin coursed through their systems. Rucker's clientele drifted up East 14th like unwashed cadavers, searching for lost pennies in the cracks of the sidewalks. I felt that anybody who sold something to people that turned them into what I was looking at was committing genocide. So as I stood there with the bullhorn in my hands, I thought to myself, *Frank Rucker won't be making any money here this afternoon.*

I raised the microphone to my lips and shouted: "This corner does not belong to the dope dealers. It belongs to Jesus Christ. Drug dealers are sell-outs and Uncle Toms. They are selling death to their own kind. They are selling their own people into slavery. Jesus Christ offers you hope. He offers you freedom. You can have forgiveness for your sins. Come forward and let us pray with you. God has had mercy on us. He has visited us in the person of Jesus Christ. Come let him wash your sins away. He offers abundant life—eternal life. I'm not talking about pie in the sky; I'm talking about eternal life that starts right now."

A teenage girl in a blonde wig and red high heels pressed her way through the crowd, tears falling freely from her eyes. A pipe fitter in construction boots who'd stopped on his way home from work removed his hard hat and came forward. Young and old followed. I told my makeshift choir to keep singing. "Come on forward," I shouted. "Today is your day to be liberated from sin."

Somewhere during the last sentence, my eyes inadvertently landed on Frank Rucker. His eyes were encased in pure hatred. His boys were flashing their middle fingers at me. They yelled, "Shut up! Shut up!" If they thought that I would be intimidated, they had miscalculated. Some of the members surrounding me countered by hollering, "Preach on, Pastor!" I put the bull-horn down and said to a fellow behind me, "How can I turn this thing up?"

BACK AGAIN

That evangelistic meeting met with such success that we came back the next week and the week after that. Each time that I opened my Bible, Rucker's venomous stare locked eyes with mine. His purveyors of death were forced to take an unwelcome break from their stock and trade when the church came out to the block. But then I went too far. I made a statement in the local press about the unchecked drug trade around Allen Temple, and I demanded that the police do something about it.

It didn't take long for Rucker to answer back. A few days later I called the office to retrieve my phone messages. Marie Johnson, my office manager, answered the phone. She screamed my name, her voice trembling with terror. "Pastor Smith, don't come in today. Frank Rucker was here with two men." My heart began to beat began like a jack hammer. "What did Rucker want?" I asked. "He said, 'You tell that preacher to stay off East 14th Street. Tell him to leave East 14th Street to us. His place is down here at the church.' Pastor Smith, he said that he and those hoodlums are going to run up in here next Sunday, drag you out of the pulpit and beat you down in front of the entire congregation. What are you going to do, Pastor?"

I didn't know what I was going to do, but I did know what I wasn't going to do and that was run. I had learned the basics of the pastoral ministry from Reverend F. D. Robinson back in Kansas City. And item number one in the unwritten preacher's manual stated that the shepherd (the pastor) must do whatever is necessary to protect the sheep. If the shepherd is chased off, the sheep will scatter and become prey for the wolves. If I were to let Rucker run me out of town, the church would become demoralized. Some members would go back to the world.

On the other hand, I had no doubt that Mr. Rucker was serious about his intentions for me. For people in his profession, the homicide of a man of God would be a simple business decision. Drug dealers are capitalists, and evangelists affect the bottom line.

Look at it like this: Mary has a $500-a-day drug habit. Mary becomes a believer. She gets help for her problem and becomes a productive, tax-paying citizen. What happens to the man who was supplying her with the drugs? Answer:

he is out $2,500 a week. What happens if he loses three or four such customers?

Ultimately the drug lord doesn't care if the addict prays, fasts or stands on his head as long as the drug lord can pay for his gold car rims. However, the preacher or anyone else who tampers with his ill-gotten gains will quickly find him- or herself in trouble.

Rucker believed in peaceful coexistence: the pastor should hide out in the church building and the drug dealers should own the streets. I disagreed with his analysis. It is a sad day when the preachers lock themselves inside a build-ing, believing God is only for those few individuals brave enough or fortunate enough to walk through church-building doors.

Christ's ministry took place beyond the walls of the established place of worship. He shared the intimacy of the table meal with a cross section of hu-manity that was ostracized as "sinners" or "unclean." If Jesus were here today, he would certainly be rubbing shoulders with the thugs and thugettes who are slapping down playing cards at gin and juice parties. And as far as I was con-cerned, the Spirit of the Lord was leading me to preach the gospel to the poor wherever I might find them. I was now on a mission.

DETERMINED TO STAND

I drove down to the establishment where Frank Rucker was known to fre-quent. The place was as dark inside as the fifth level of hell. A wad of chewing gum stuck to the sole of my shoe. B. B. King whined from the jukebox, "The thrill is gone."

I squinted, trying to adjust to the dim light. The place stank of cheap beer and urine. A toothless man chomped on a hot dog and ogled a prostitute in a platinum wig. I leaned over the bar and motioned for the bar-keep to come close. He looked startled.

"What you want here, Preacher?" he mumbled.

"Where is Frank Rucker?"

"How am I s'posed to know? I don't know."

"Well, why don't you know?" I hollered. His jaw popped open in shock. "You tell Frank Rucker that J. Alfred Smith Sr., pastor of Allen Temple Baptist Church, was down here looking for him!" The place got as quiet as a Quaker prayer meeting. I turned on my heel, leaving the patrons staring at my back. Next, I headed for the church.

Ms. Johnson had been busy since we had last spoken. She'd been on the phone to all of the church's leaders. The congregation was in an uproar. We had plenty of Allen Temple members who had climbed out of the same world that had spawned Frank Rucker, and they were more than willing to climb back down into it to save me, should I just say the word.

I certainly didn't want that to happen, and I said so in no uncertain terms. Sure, I wrestled with my personal adherence to the principles of nonviolence. However, I knew that he who lived by the sword (or the .44 magnum in this case) would die by it. To call out the dogs of war would have meant the betrayal of my ministerial calling. I told my more street-oriented members not to touch a hair follicle on Rucker's head.

The deacons made an emergency call to the Oakland police department. It was Rucker's turn to be hunted. There was an all-points bulletin out to bring him back alive. Cops combed East Oakland with black and white mug shots of him.

In the meantime the district attorney offered me twenty-four-hour police protection. I wore a bulletproof vest. Deacons watched my house at night. By day bodyguards traveled with me from one destination to another.

I still looked over my shoulder. Every car that backfired sent me ducking for cover. I had faith in the Lord. I knew that he was watching over me, but every once in a while a tinge of fear would pinch me, then I would scout the rooftops for sniper fire.

SHOWDOWN

One evening, Deacon Joseph Mondy's phone rang. It was a woman who introduced herself as Frank Rucker's wife. "Frank wants to meet with the pastor. He wants to make peace."

I was immediately skeptical. This could easily be a trap. Did Rucker think that preachers were fools? His wife did her best to convince us that her intentions were honorable. She was a church-going woman. She gave us her word that no harm would come to me. However, she completed her plea with three words that caused me to shiver with doubt. She said. "Come alone, Pastor."

Against everyone's better judgment, I left my security detail that Saturday night. I was to meet Rucker inside a church building in North Oakland. I sang all of my favorite hymns in the car that night. Streetlights glared through the foggy mist. My car pulled up a few blocks away from the church.

A voice from deep down inside said, "J. Alfred, you better get back in this car and go home. Frank Rucker might blow your head off when you walk in that church." If I were to tell you that I wasn't afraid, I would be lying. The church door creaked open. There were no lights on inside. It was quiet as a crypt. There, in the darkness, I saw two figures. I recognized the outline of Frank Rucker's frame. The inner voice said, "Run. Save yourself!" but my feet kept walking forward.

It's difficult to explain the sensations that flooded my soul when I got close enough to look into Frank Rucker's face. I felt a warmth, a compassion for him. I felt the mercy of our Savior, Jesus Christ, wash over me. At that moment I wanted nothing more than to embrace Frank Rucker as a brother. And I did.

FORGIVING RUCKER

Rucker turned himself in to the police, and then I called one of my deacons, attorney John Harrison, telling him that I wanted him to defend Rucker against the charges of terrorist threats. He respectfully declined, saying, "Pastor, if something happens to you, I won't be able to live with myself."

When he found that I would not be dissuaded, he approached his law partner, Leo Brazille, to work on Rucker's behalf. The judge released Rucker, and the deacons and trustees hired him to work at Allen Temple Baptist Church as a custodian.

Not all of the members totally agreed with these decisions. Some were convinced that I had lost my natural mind. I ignored the criticism. These were the same members who had begged me for years to sound retreat and move the congregation to a safer part of town. I thanked the Lord that he had chosen me to show mercy to Frank Rucker. Paul said, "All have sinned and fall short of the glory of God" (Romans 3:23). In God's eyes Rucker's sin might not have been any worse that our own. Besides, he was a model employee.

OAKLAND'S NEW MAYOR

We had shed blood and money, but sacrifice was producing results. The government was finally beginning to listen to us. Back in 1973 Bobby Seale of the Black Panther's put his beret up and donned a neatly tailored suit. The chairman of the revolution ran for the office of mayor of Oakland. My son J. Alfred Jr. worked diligently on Seale's campaign. In the end he fell just short of victory, though he made an impressive showing, gathering 44 percent of the popular vote.

Much was gained by Bobby Seale's candidacy. The youth of Oakland were energized by the idea that they had a voice and vote that could be heard. Seale's campaign set the stage for the African American judge Lionel Wilson to consider a run for that seat in 1978.

When Judge Wilson ran, we hit the streets. Allen Temple volunteers registered an army of people all over East Oakland. Election night found us sitting around the radio with folded hands and whispered prayers. It was a tight race. However, when the final precincts were counted, a shout went up in the streets. For the first time in its history, Oakland had an African American mayor.

I saw a difference immediately. No longer was I public enemy number one at city hall. The new mayor welcomed me with open arms. He was interested in everything that I had to say.

—28—

TO SERVE, NOT TO BE SERVED

In 1983 the American Baptist women's auxiliary held one of the their annual meetings at our church building. Though it was a meeting strictly for sisters, I was present, shaking hands and directing guests to the appropriate area. Most of the women present were white folks from Northern California. There were a few that I remembered from my early stint with the denomination. I was so glad that they'd made the trek down to East Oakland.

In midst of shaking hands, I noticed someone who seemed out of place. A tall man with a scraggly beard and blue jeans tried to blend inconspicuously into the crowd of white-haired women from the other side of Oakland. His eyes hunted and scoped, dancing from one dangling pocketbook to another. He licked his lips and rubbed his fingertips together.

I approached him with a greeting: "Hello, friend, can I help you?" When I drew closer to him, he smelled like a grape vineyard. Alcohol seeped through the pores of his flesh.

"Get away from me, man. Mind your business," he drawled.

"I beg your pardon. This is my business. I'm the pastor," I countered.

He turned his back toward me and walked steadily to the sanctuary where singing and clapping could be heard. I grabbed his arm before he could enter the sanctuary door. The fellow whirled around, shocked that I touched him. When he turned, the overhead lights reflected on a glass object in his left hand, a wine bottle. Before I could blink he had smashed the bottle against a wall. The stranger crouched down into a wrestler's stance, dancing on the balls of his feet. I moved to his right, slowly with a shuffle of my feet. I circled determined to keep him at bay. We danced a surreal ballet.

He lunged, slashing out with his homemade bayonet. I ducked. I was determined to grab him, but he was too fast. He feigned a movement, and when I shifted away, he dove forward, gouging the flesh of my forehead with the jagged edge of the tinted bottle.

Some latecomers stumbled upon us. They shrieked as the blood gushed like a flood from my forehead. My white shirt and blue blazer were drenched crimson. Blood-curdling screams startled my assailant. He lowered his head and sprinted for the first open door—with me in a dead run right behind him. I wanted him to pay for his crimes.

We cut through the parking lot. He wove through parked cars and past the sidewalk. I glanced behind me to see two figures giving chase. The man closest to me was a deacon of the church. He was followed by the church custodian—Frank Rucker ran like a deer.

The assailant took off down a brick canyon sandwiched between two tenements. It was as dark as midnight in that alley. I heard his footfalls but I could no longer see him. I started in after him but the deacon who had caught up to me snatched my arm.

"It's a police matter now, Pastor," he said.

Frank Rucker glanced at my blood-drenched suit.

"It's a police matter now, Frank. The police have been called. Let them handle it," the deacon repeated matter-of-factly.

Rucker looked at the deacon as though he'd just walked out of a Martian spaceship. "Oh, yeah, right."

And then he marched into that dark alley as boldly as if it had been broad daylight outside. I heard shoving and the smack of a hand against flesh. Then there came a sound like combat boots stomping down on something soft and mushy. A scream that sounded like it belonged to a woman pierced the night. Who could it be? I knew that there were only two people in that alley. The crash of garbage cans startled us. There was a noise like a dry twig breaking in a forest. Someone was calling on the name of the Lord. It didn't sound like Rucker. And then everything got hazy.

I had lost a lot of blood by the time the police finally arrived. Somebody opened up a car door, and I was on the way to the hospital. The doctors stitched me up. A thick gauze patch was strapped to my forehead by two white adhesive strips.

Ironically, as I was being escorted to the door, who should be brought in but my assailant. He was handcuffed to a gurney and attended to by two policemen. He looked like he had just crawled out from beneath a plane wreck.

A REASON TO BE THANKFUL

St. Paul said, "For by grace you have been saved through faith, and that not of yourselves; *it is* the gift of God, not of works, lest anyone should boast" (Ephesians 2:8-9). I know that Paul is talking about salvation of the immortal soul in that passage, but when I looked in the mirror the morning after the attack, I couldn't help but apply that verse to my life. You see, it's only five inches from the forehead to the jugular vein. A scar across the forehead might have damaged my vanity, but if the jagged edge of the bottle had ripped my throat, this might have been the end of my story.

For a few days, I was the talk of East Oakland. And then things settled back to normal, or as normal as they get in a place where someone walks into the house of God and cuts up the pastor.

RUCKER MAKES A DECISION

Frank Rucker became a part of the Allen Temple Baptist Church. I have to admit, life was a lot easier having him inside of the church instead of across the street from it. He was a dedicated worker who made the church building shine. He was also intensely loyal.

One Sunday morning the choir sang like cherubim on Easter Sunday. The praises of God rang out through the sanctuary windows and saturated the air over East Oakland. People in the church were on their feet clapping and shouting. In the midst of this, I saw a figure march down the aisle. He made his way from the rear of the dim sanctuary and then fell to his knees at the foot of the altar. I came down from the pulpit to embrace him. "What must I do to be saved?" he asked. It was Frank Rucker.

JAMES JR. MAKES A DECISION

Frank Rucker wasn't the only person that God was dealing with. I was surprised to receive a call from my son J. Alfred Jr. He didn't call so often now. I missed the sound of his voice. I think that he must have sensed that in the tone of my voice.

"Daddy," he said. "Last night I walked the beach at Santa Cruz all night. I was wrestling with the great philosophers and theologians who walked this planet down through the ages. And I am convinced of one thing, Daddy. Jesus Christ is truly Lord. I want to serve him, Daddy. I'm coming home."

I thought of the threats, the stabbing, the backbiting and the wars that I had fought to do ministry in the inner city. And when I heard those words, I thought to myself, it's all been worth it. JoAnna wept when I told her what our son had said.

One day I stared across the kitchen table as J. Alfred Jr. rambled on about some philosopher or another and a tear rolled down my cheek. In that moment, I realized just how alike my son and I were. He became deeply involved in the life of Allen Temple. He worked diligently with the church's teenagers, teaching and staging dramatic productions. My son developed into a man of prayer and Bible study.

"I believe that God is calling me to the ministry, Daddy," he remarked over lunch one day. J. Alfred Jr. had expressed that calling as early as 1972. I had sensed such a call on his life but just to hear the words flow from his lips caused the tears to start cascading once again. You see, my son understood the triumphs and tragedies of ministry from observing my life. I wasn't some prosperity preacher who flew into the ghetto in a helicopter and flew out after the second offering had been taken. My life was poured out daily for the urban poor who called East Oakland home.

J. Alfred Jr. knew that the Son of Man had not come to be served but to serve. I had taught him by life example that the minister must follow the example of the Master. The future was safe for my son with Jesus walking by his side. I gave thanks and praise to God.

— 29 —

A Surprise Awaits
in Cincinnati

—⟡—

By the spring of 1984 I was spiritually exhausted from the rigors of ministry. I was burned out, and I needed rest and retreat if I was going to continue the journey. I knew just the place. The Progressive National Baptist Convention was having its annual convocation. This year it was scheduled to be held in Cincinnati, Ohio.

In 1961 the Progressive National Baptist Convention was formed by dissatisfied black clergy who left the National Baptist Convention fold. Allen Temple Baptist Church was dually aligned with both the American Baptist Churches in the USA (ABC) and the Progressive National Baptist Convention (PNBC).

The PNBC combined the teachings of eternal life with concern for the "least of these." There was a focus on not only the spiritual but the social and political dynamics that affected black people in America. It became the first African American Baptist denomination to adopt a pension plan for pastors, church missionaries and other employees. It was also the first to employ a general secretary and staff. Nearly half of the preachers selected by *Ebony* magazine as the fifteen best preachers in America have been members of the Progressive National Baptist Convention.

I drew nourishment from these yearly gatherings. Here I found new avenues for effective urban ministry. The times of corporate prayer revived my soul. Each year the greatest African American preachers in America are chosen to say their "Thus saith the Lord" at the PNBC annual convention. But on top of all that, there is nothing like getting together with a room full of black preachers. We laugh and joke until our sides split. These are healing times, nourishing times, strengthening times, times when new friendships are forged and old friendships are rekindled.

CHOSEN TO RUN

The normal process for being selected to the presidency of the organization started when the nominating committee produced a slate of officers who desired the position of second vice president. Back then the second vice president served a term of two years (now four years). He would subsequently be promoted from that post to vice president. When that term was finished that vice president would almost certainly be elected president.

I landed in Cincinnati on a shoestring budget. I got there by counting out loose quarters for spending money. The thought of renting a car was out of the question. Upon arrival, someone pointed me toward the city buses. I fought with the rush-hour commuters, inadvertently banging knees and ankles with my suitcase.

Finally I arrived at a low-budget hotel on the outskirts of the city. Bored young men with hollow eyes and stocking caps wrapped around their heads lounged on the hood of a gold Oldsmobile 88 set up on cinder blocks. They welcomed me with a round of nods. I nodded back. I checked in and then dragged my suitcase up three flights of stairs to my room. I opened the door and gasped. Room 313 smelled like onion soup. I tested the mattress; it had all the flexibility of a grave marker. Someone had replaced the television antenna with a coat hanger. A strange rumbling came from the closet. It sounded like a tennis ball trapped in a tumbling clothes dryer. I threw my shoe in the direction of the noise. It stopped immediately. Well, the room would do. I hadn't come to Cincinnati to hang out in a motel. I washed up, changed my suit and went downstairs. I wanted to get to the convention center for the evening services.

The brothers in front of the Olds hadn't budged an inch. "Say, Bloods," I asked. "How can I get to the convention center?"

"What, you lost?" one young man inquired, rising up in sudden interest. Before I could answer, one of his homeboys jerked his thumb toward the bus

stop across the street. I nodded my thanks and then made my way as night began to descend on the ghetto.

A half an hour later I was downtown, walking through the doors of the con-
vention center. I was truly in my world. I wandered through the crush of humanity searching for a familiar face. Finally, among the throng of thousands I
saw a preacher that said, "You're Reverend Dr. J. Alfred Smith Sr.! Reverend
T. L. Willis is looking for you!" That was no surprise. T. L. Willis, the pastor of
Pilgrim Hope Baptist Church of Los Angeles, California, was my close friend.
When I went to my first Progressive Baptist meeting at Ebenezer Baptist
Church in San Francisco, Pastor Willis spotted me sitting in the back row. He
came to my pew and extended his hand. We were instant friends. Each year he
would call on me to preach a revival at his church.

Today he wasn't smiling when I walked through the door, which was unusual. He said loudly, "James, why are you just now getting here! What is
wrong with you? We are gonna run you for the second vice president!"

I was so shocked that I forgot to breathe. I was trying to make sense of that
last sentence. I knew that eventually the second vice president would become
the president of the PNBC. It was practically a given. I tried picturing myself
as the CEO of an organization that had 1.2 million people in it. It took a few
seconds for those words to sink in. I said, "Man, I can't run for the second vice
president. I'm not even the nominating committee's choice."

Reverend T. L. Willis was a big man. He walked over and placed his heavy
hands on my shoulders. "James, we are going to run you from the floor. After
the nominating committee finishes in their report, we're going to stand up and
put you in nomination." I said, "No, I'm not going to do that." Reverend Tillis
bellowed, "Yes, we are!" The California preachers stood behind him and
voiced their agreement. Those attending the women's convention cried out in
unison, "Yes, you are!"

Well, it was my turn to ask the logical question. I asked, "What are we going
to do about the Eastern Region? The Eastern Region has its own candidate,
and it is the most powerful region in this convention." But the California con-
tingent would not be moved. Someone said, "Wyatt Tee Walker (a former lieutenant to Dr. Martin Luther King Jr.) of the Canaan Baptist Church in Harlem,
New York, is going with us. Reverend Charles Adams is going with us. Dr.
Marshall Shepherd Jr. from Philadelphia is with us."

It was clear that they had already done the political footwork in gathering prominent East Coast pastors to endorse me. However, I was still not sure that this was going to be enough. The pastors from the South had already given their commitment to the Eastern Region's candidate.

The Eastern Region's candidate had money, and he was spending it by hosting delicious barbecue dinners for potential voters. T. L. Willis had a solution for that. He walked right into their camp and told those preachers, "I know that you were at the dinner that he hosted. And I know that he has your allegiance, but let's look at what's good for the PNBC."

Wyatt Tee Walker and Charles Adams were true to their word. They went back to their respective delegations and said, "We know who you have chosen, but we are going with Reverend Dr. James Alfred Smith Sr. out of Oakland, California. We think that he should represent our denomination."

NOMINATION NIGHT

On the big night, some of America's most powerful black preachers engaged in a battle of oratorical skills. They sang the East Coast candidate's praises. The smart money said that it was a done deal. The vote was a mere formality. Few figured that he would be opposed at all. True to his word, before the proceedings came to an end, Reverend T. L. Willis stood up in that great arena and said, "I would like to enter the name of the Reverend J. Alfred Smith Sr. of Oakland, California, for second vice president."

A collective gasp went up in the house. Who would dare to stand in the way of what was inevitable? People were whispering, "Who is J. Alfred Smith Sr.?" Adrenaline raced through my veins. Since the idea had been posed to me, so many thoughts had raced through my mind. If I were elected president, I thought I would push for greater spending for foreign missions. I would increase our denomination's commitment to historically black colleges. I would bring the PNBC into the thick of the antiapartheid struggle. If only I had the chance.

GOD SENDS HELP

I walked through the convention hall introducing myself to preachers from all over America. I would say, "Hello, my name is J. Alfred Smith Sr. You may have heard last night that I am running for second vice president." I seemed to be making a little headway, but it was like moving Mount Everest with a plastic teaspoon. And then a miracle happened.

Reverend Robert Gordon, one of my "sons" in the ministry from Allen Temple, showed up in Cincinnati out of nowhere. He said, "Pastor, I was visiting my family in Detroit when the Lord spoke to me. He said, 'Go to Cincinnati and help your pastor.' So here I am, sir. Where do we start?"

The first thing that Reverend Gordon did was to rent a car. We drove all over Cincinnati, wherever convention goers could be found, shaking hands and trying to garner votes. We put placards with my name and picture into the hands of potential voters.

The day before the election, we struck out at dawn, coaxing, arguing and persuading preachers to vote for an unknown candidate from the San Francisco Bay Area. By 6:00 p.m. I was bone weary and wet with perspiration. My suit stuck to me like a damp bed sheet. "Take me back, Reverend Gordon. I'm ready to call it a day." I said. The only things I desired from life at that point were a shower and a chance to stretch out again on that concrete slab of a bed. Whatever was going to happen on election day was just going to happen.

My aide-de-camp wouldn't hear of it. He responded, "Pastor, I know you are tired, but the people are eating meals in these hotels. They are not going to bed after the sessions. I am going to take you from hotel to hotel, and you are going to tell people who you are." I was too exhausted to argue.

It took the whole afternoon to count the ballots by hand. Some of the people in my camp, like the late Reverend M. J. Williams of Oakland's Bethany Baptist Church, insisted on being present to make sure that no ballots were miscounted or thrown out. I went back to the hotel and fell into a fitful sleep.

ELECTION NIGHT

Reverend Robert Gordon picked me up and drove me to the evening session, where the election results would be announced. On the way into the hall we bumped into two of the greatest African American preachers of our time, both of whom had served as president of the Progressive National Baptist Convention. Reverend Gardner C. Taylor and Reverend Nelson Smith of Birmingham were like twins.

Reverend Taylor asked, "Alfred, did you win?" "I don't know," I said. But I was trembling in anticipation. Electricity was in the air. The hands of strangers reached out for mine. More than one older preacher called out, "God bless you, son."

I walked all the way to the top row of the auditorium. In my heart, I knew

that I didn't have the votes to win. To tell you the truth, I was slightly embarrassed at letting myself be drawn into this contest. I just wanted the results
read and the thing to be over with at that point. I folded my hands and bowed
my head, praying for the grace to bear the inevitable.

Ten minutes into the ceremony Dr. Charles Butler, a Morehouse College
scholar, stood up and announced the election results. Sheer pandemonium
broke out. People stomped, screamed and whistled. It sounded like a contro-
versial decision at a heavyweight title fight. I bowed my head. I can still hear
his words ringing in my ears: "The winner is the Reverend Dr. J. Alfred Smith
Sr., senior pastor of the Allen Temple Baptist Church in Oakland, California."

To the shock of many, I had beaten that powerful East Coast preacher. I was
the convention's choice for second vice president. That night I was called
down from the most obscure place in the building to sit on the dais. God had
brought me a long way from Leeds.

COMING TO JESSE JACKSON'S DEFENSE

In that same year, the Reverend Jesse Jackson made an announcement that
electrified the African American community. The famed civil rights leader decided to run for the presidency of the United States of America. From the barber shops to the barbecue pits, from the choir lofts to the country clubs, black
America was buzzing with the news. There was jubilation in our world, but
not everyone was smiling.

Some of the Democratic Party's most respected leaders came out against the
Jackson presidential bid. When the murmuring reached my ears, I went into action, penning an opinion piece for the *Los Angeles Times*. Ted Koppel of *Nightline*
got a hold of the article, and as a result I was invited down to Los Angeles to be
on his show along with Benjamin Hooks (then president of the NAACP) and
an African American newspaper reporter from Chicago, Vernon Jarrett.

Well, they were all over Reverend Jackson. They had nothing but negatives
to shower on his character. I responded, "Jesus had his Judas and Caesar had
his Brutus. Now Jackson will have his Jarretts and his critics." That line appeared in *Jet* magazine the next week as a "Quote of the Week."

—30—

SOUTH AFRICA

—⁂—

Awhite South African named Alan Paton wrote *Cry, the Beloved Country*, which had a profound impact on my understanding of the apartheid regime in South Africa. It was the fictional account of an Episcopalian priest whose parish was located in the slums of a segregated township. In this place blacks had to produce passbooks when moving from one police checkpoint to another. Their lands were taken from them, and like beasts they were herded into barren wastelands. Intemperate white police often pulled blacks out of bed in the middle of the night without provocation or just cause. Black people were routinely tortured in police custody and sentenced to prison without legal due process.

The story reveals the suspicion, hatred, verbal abuse, alcoholism, prostitution and family disintegration that segregation produces when practiced in an affluent society. I saw in Paton's book the faces of my people, black people struggling far away in a land that I had never seen. I related their struggle for dignity and empowerment with the struggle of African American people in East Oakland. From the time that I turned the last page of *Cry, the Beloved Country*, I coveted any reading material concerning the history of South Africa and the struggle that was being waged for freedom.

FIGHTING FOR SOUTH AFRICAN FREEDOM

At Allen Temple we waged our own war to free South Africa. We raised money for the African National Congress. I personally began fasting for two days each week, praying that God would grant our people freedom on that distant shore. I was even arrested in San Francisco (along with other clergy) for blocking the entrance of an oil company that refused to divest its holdings in South Africa.

From time to time I would sit down to tea with expatriates who had fled from the oppressive regime, and as I listened to their tales of struggle, two names would often surface: Bishop Desmond Tutu and the Reverend Dr. Alan Boesak. These courageous men were the spiritual leaders of the black people of South Africa.

In South African townships, black roughnecks had a brutal way of dealing with police informers. It was called the "hot necklace." An old tire filled with gasoline was placed around the neck of the suspected traitor and set ablaze. On occasion Boesak and Tutu would wade into angry crowds, placing their own lives at risk to liberate those who had been marked for death.

Bishop Desmond Tutu rose to become the first black bishop of the Anglican Church. In 1984 he was awarded the Nobel Peace Prize. When F. W. de Klerk, the president of South Africa, realized that concessions would have to be made or the country would be lost, he called out for Dr. Boesak and Bishop Tutu.

I had to meet these men, to embrace them, to hear their stories firsthand. I wanted my people at Allen Temple to hear them.

BISHOP TUTU COMES TO EAST OAKLAND

In May of 1985 an unmarked charter bus rolled through the heart of the Oakland slums and pulled up in front of Allen Temple's door. The sounds of laughter and sporadic shouts of "hallelujah" rose up in the coolness of approaching twilight. I was among those who left the sanctuary that evening to watch the visitors descend from the bus. Our Congressman, Ron Dellums, was there with us. (Rep. Dellums was perhaps the most outspoken member of Congress on the subject of apartheid.)

Several luminaries from San Francisco descended from the bus. They walked toward us that night, their faces beaming. And then I saw him, a crown of white hair glistening on top of his head. He was not much taller than I. His smile is what I remember most. It was peaceful and serene. His teeth were pearl white. But the thing that impressed me about him most was his humility.

I walked toward my guest with tears in my eyes, "Good evening, Bishop Tutu." I could barely get the words out. Then I welcomed him and our other guests into my study. Dr. Janet Marshburn had prepared peppermint tea and shortbread cookies. My children and grandchildren sat on folding chairs in my little office. I gave the bishop my own seat.

In him I found a kindred spirit. I looked upon lips that had uttered ten thousand prayers; eyes that had shed ten thousand tears and feet that had walked ten thousand miles. And as I beheld this slight man who peered at me through rimless glasses, so many pieces of my own life seemed to fit into place. Here was a fiercely determined man of God who had faced death threats and beatings. He had led a denomination and raised the voice of a prophet in the wilderness against the sin of racial hatred. Bishop Tutu found it his Christian duty to stand up against oppression, to empower those who had been marginalized and left out by the powers that ruled the land. And this rebellion against injustice was more than a reflex. It was his calling.

I stood before him, a preacher in a segregated ghetto almost beyond the reach of America, bowed but unbroken. The attitude of the American church toward matters of social justice had left me somewhat disillusioned. I had grown sick inside from the criticism of ministerial peers and obstinate church members.

But as I stared into Tutu's timeless and patient brown eyes that night, I understood that freedom is not free. Only when people are willing to work, to suffer, to cry out to God in the darkest night will change ride in on the wings of the dawn. But first, there must be suffering.

At the end of the evening, I followed the little man with the lilting accent back onto the bus. The multitudes eyed me cautiously as I bent down before him and kissed the tops of his shoes. It was a symbolic gesture meant to exemplify the Scripture that reads: "How beautiful are the feet of those who preach the gospel of peace" (Romans 10:15). Before Bishop Tutu's bus left, we gave him an offering that was raised to aid those fighting for democracy in his homeland. The brown paper bag we handed him was filled with $15,000 in cash.

REVEREND DOCTOR ALAN BOESAK COMES TO AMERICA

I did not get to know Bishop Tutu well, but the day was coming when another South African freedom fighter would step out of the pages of the history books and into my life. I had read so much about Dr. Alan Boesak that I knew his story by heart.

In 1982 the World Alliance of Reformed Churches held a historic summit in Ottawa, Canada. In an unforgettable move, that denomination declared the doctrine of apartheid, or the separation of the races as divinely ordained by God, a heresy. It then proceeded to suspend the Dutch Reformed Church, which was the largest of the white Afrikaner churches. But the Alliance wasn't finished. The members of the Alliance elected Alan Boesak, a black South African freedom-fighter-clergyman to the presidency of that huge body of believers.

In August 1983 when South Africa's United Democratic Front (UDF) hosted its first gathering, it called Boesak to be the keynote speaker. The UDF was composed of a cross section of South Africans, black, white and mixed people. It included trade unionists, educators and people from every walk of life who loved freedom. The gathering, held in Cape Town, was illegal. In its wake Dr. Boesak was arrested, but not before he could say: "The time has come for white people in this country to realize that their destiny is inextricably bound with ours. . . . They will never be free as long as they have to lie awake at night worrying whether a black government will one day do to them as they are doing to us."

Dr. Boesak realized that racial reconciliation was more than blacks and whites sharing a hymnbook at a church service. It involves sharing political power and economic resources. People can't say, "I am your brother," in church and then be unconcerned about the injustice that sends me to the slums when they return to the suburbs or the hills after the benediction is pronounced. According to Boesak, the most impassioned voices for equality in any country should rise from the pews of the local Christian church. His message resonated with me. When I heard that Dr. Boesak was going to be speaking in Berkeley, California, my heart leapt wildly within me.

MEETING THE PROPHET FROM SOUTH AFRICA

Reverend John Turpin, a Presbyterian pastor in Berkeley, was a good friend of mine. He was a white fellow who loved the black church. He savored the different preaching styles within the black church tradition the way a French chef treasures pastry recipes. His church had put together the travel expenses to bring Dr. Boesak to America for a series of lectures. Some of my church members accompanied me into Reverend Turpin's pastoral study to meet Dr. Boesak before the service began.

How can I explain what it was like to meet Dr. Boesak that first time? I was like a rabbinical student presented with the opportunity to meet Moses. Dr. Boesak was a ginger-colored man with round cheeks and sparkling eyes full of the joy of life. He and I became instant friends. We began to discuss passages that inspired us from Tillich, Niebuhr, Rauschenbusch, Cone and King. We shared a love of jazz music and travel.

Before we walked out to the pulpit, Dr. Boesak said, "James, Caucasian churches bring me to America, and I find myself speaking to almost all-Caucasian audiences. However, I really would like to speak to some of my African American brothers and sisters." The wheels were turning in the back of my mind as he spoke. Here was a man who had fought against one of the greatest evils to confront modern humanity—and he won. Here was a man who rose to the top of an organization that had once held people of color under lock and key in the name of the Christ to whom we prayed. God had raised this man up and given him a voice that African Americans needed to hear. And I told him so.

That night he lectured to a quiet audience. When it was over, I shook his hand at the door and said, "Friend, if I ever get a chance to bring you back to America to speak to black people, I will." And it wasn't long before I was able to be true to my word. That was the beginning of a brotherhood that has spanned two continents and three decades.

31

THE PRESIDENCY,
DRUGS AND GANGSTERS

—⁂◯

The second vice president of the PNBC attended regional meetings and did some fundraising for the organization. The pastors must have liked what I was doing because they elected me to the vice presidency in 1984. And in 1986 I was nominated and elected as the president of the Progressive National Baptist Church. I was seated in a place that many of the great African American preachers of the twentieth century had occupied. I trembled at the swearing in, feeling the weight of the awesome task ahead of me.

The first thing that I did was to call for the books. Before I laid out my vision before the people, I wanted to see what we had in the coffers. In America even dreams cost money. That is why I held my head in my hands after a ten-minute glance at the financial statement. The PNBC was broke. Thus my immediate future was laid out for me. I would have to fly all over America to raise money to keep us from sinking into bankruptcy. I embarked on a grueling schedule: St. Louis one night, Phoenix the next, and perhaps New York City after that. I began to suffer from a puzzle that plagues many pastors—I couldn't figure out how to be in more than one place at the same time.

The leadership of Allen Temple Baptist Church made a decision that helped the church function effectively in my absence. They elevated my son J. Alfred Smith Jr. from the position of assistant pastor to that of copastor.

This allowed him to make crucial decisions in my absence.

We needed a prophetic presence in God's house because a cloud of death and violence had come to hover over the housing projects of East Oakland; its name was "crack."

CRACK TAKES OVER

If a Surgeon General's warning could be found on a vial of crack cocaine, it might say, "One hit is never enough, and one thousand are never too many." The ravages of crack addiction transformed clear-faced high school girls into the two-dollar whores who walk International Boulevard night and day. It morphed once proud men into panhandlers.

Crack is a combination of cocaine and several other cheap chemicals. It produces an intense rush that usually lasts for five minutes or less. Crack was an equal opportunity destroyer. Businessman who dabbled on the weekends, thinking that they could handle crack, became handled by crack. They joined the barely visible multitudes stretching soiled hands to total strangers and begging for "spare change." These users develop such a lust for that initial blast that they will do virtually anything to recapture that high.

The addict's insatiable thirst for this new narcotic created a new kind of street entrepreneur. He was younger and quicker to settle any dispute with violence. Cheap handguns flooded East Oakland. And while once we performed funeral services for those who had lived full lives and then went home to be with the risen Christ, now we were burying teenagers who had lived fast and burned out before their time. East Oakland morticians had to become creative about covering up gunshot wounds.

HEROIN KINGPIN WREAKS HAVOC

Many people wonder why violence has taken root in black America. We are living in a postindustrial society. When I first came to East Oakland, there were factories where an unskilled laborer could make a livable wage. Those days are gone (along with the factories). By the advent of rock cocaine, there were few jobs in the inner city and masses of unemployed people. Many of those people have been out of work for a year, two years, even three years. Some have given up hope of ever again finding gainful employment.

The school system was failing. Families fractured and broken by adversity created lost, rootless children. They looked at the material world that television flashed before their eyes and lusted for sneakers, luxury cars and expensive jewelry. Prison for them became gladiator school, a rite of passage, a badge of honor. Many of the young people in our community had never had an elder to show them the way. The church has failed them miserably in most cases because it is unable or unwilling to adapt to the rapidly changing seasons.

THE ORIGINAL GANGSTAS

Into the abyss stepped Felix Mitchell, one of the most infamous gangsters that the West Coast has ever manufactured. Even today, if you were to walk down International Boulevard and whisper his first name, nine out of ten people would immediately know who you were talking about. He grew up in the 69th Street housing projects, a gaggle of drab green two-story buildings where the grass grew high and the law of the magnum handgun prevailed. Like many of his peers, Felix dropped out of high school. He became just another unemployed black male roaming the streets of East Oakland—until he stumbled across an idea.

Felix revolutionized the way that heroin was sold. He knew the law. It clearly states that in order for the police to arrest someone for drug sales or possession, a hand-to-hand sale must be observed by an informant or a policeman. Felix found a way around all of this. His efforts bought him two homes, three legitimate businesses and a fortune estimated in the millions.

This is how heroin was sold in the 69th Street housing projects. Six or seven young black males would stand around on a corner laughing, joking and staring. Gold chains and diamond earrings gave them the appearance of Nubian Pharaohs. Their pockets bulged with folded wads of paper money, blood money. A string of emaciated men, near cadavers in oily blue jeans and with disheveled hair would approach them. Three or four of these well-dressed heavy hitters would be holding pistols, to thwart any attempts at a hold up. Two young men collected money from the addicts. The last man was a shot caller, a lieutenant who never touched drugs or money. He controlled the actions of the others with a nod, a whisper, a flick of the head.

When the money was received, he looked toward an apartment building about a block away, pulled out a walkie-talkie and whispered a number, the number of heroin packages that the buyer had just purchased. Coworkers in the apartment building, who would have rented this space for about $500 a day from a welfare mother, then lowered the drugs down through a garden hose to the addict below. The money and the drugs were never in the same place.

Preteen boys on the corner were paid lookouts. They hollered, "Rollers! Rollers!" when an unmarked car turned the corner. This caused the six or seven thugs to run, each in a different direction. The shot caller remained behind. He had no drugs and no gun. He wanted to see which officers arrived on the scene, taking a mental photograph of their faces and names.

Somewhere behind it all was a charismatic drug lord. He would rarely come near that corner. He didn't have to; he was a multimillionaire. He owned Rolls Royce limousines and other high priced, four-wheeled toys.

The 69 Mob purchased Air Jordan sneakers for neighborhood athletes and sponsored Easter-egg hunts for toddlers. Still, there was a dark side. For example, a fourteen-year-old had his life snuffed out. A carload of hit men flashed by and started spraying bullets. They allegedly murdered him in a case of mistaken identity. His bereaved mother said, "My son was a born-again Christian, and I believe with all of my heart that he died so that others might live."

The FBI was eventually able to put a racketeering case together with Felix's name on it. He took flight but was finally caught and brought to justice. In the Leavenworth Federal Penitentiary, the king of the Oakland underworld was stabbed to death over a $10 debt. He was 32 years old.

FELIX'S EXTRAVAGANT FUNERAL

The story doesn't end there. Felix's funeral will long be remembered as part of the Oakland folklore. His grieving loved ones purchased a gold-plated casket and, taking a page from the funeral of the late Martin Luther King Jr., a team of horses pulled a wooden cart containing Felix Mitchell's body through the streets of East Oakland. Gangsters, hustlers, the famous and the infamous followed in tuxedoes. Most of them drove luxury cars.

Young children stared at the spectacle, drinking in the message their culture was sending them. If you sell drugs you'll get rich, and one day others may celebrate your death by parading your body through the streets of East Oakland on a horse-drawn cart.

OUTRAGE IN OAKLAND

East Oakland had finally made the headlines of the *New York Times*. The funeral procession was broadcast on network television and seen all over the country. The next day, which was Sunday morning, Deacon Reggie Lyles

walked into my office distraught and furious. He had seen the funeral procession firsthand. He and many other good police officers were dismayed.

I too was as hot as the blazes of hell. And that morning, being Sunday, I let
everybody know about it. Before I began the sermon I said: "Just what have
we come to in Oakland? Instead of honoring people who are giving their lives
to educate our children or to protect us from the criminals, we lift up this infamous druglord who destroyed lives through the distribution of drugs. He destroyed children who stayed out of school to sell his drugs. He destroyed families. Scores of people are in their graves before their time because of this man.
And people are marching to celebrate him?" I continued, "How many innocent children playing tag outdoors have stepped on a hypodermic syringe
filled with blood and 69 Mob heroin? I say we ought to have a march for righteousness. And Deacon Reggie Lyles is going to lead it!"

Reggie's eyes stretched open in shock. I hadn't pondered the logistical
problems of such a march before the words came out of my mouth. To this day
I believe that the Holy Spirit breathed his inspiration upon me at that moment.

TAKING A STAND AGAINST THE CRACK GAME

Taken from my outburst in the pulpit, the name "March for Righteousness"
stuck. Reggie Lyles was just the man to get the ball rolling. Before long there
was a coalition standing behind that simple phrase. Many of the African
American churches stood with us. Hispanic, Asian and Caucasian residents
of our city called Allen Temple asking how they could help. The Bay Area
Black United Fund, The Richard Allen Institute, Oakland Parents in Action
and the San Francisco/Oakland Boys and Girls Scout Council were just a
handful of our partners.

On Saturday morning, November 23, 1986, more than twelve thousand
people gathered in the streets surrounding Allen Temple Baptist Church. That
was a much larger number than had been on hand to view Felix Mitchell's final procession. The eleven-mile march started in front of our church and continued to the front steps of city hall. Marchers held up signs that said "No
Hope in Dope," "Guess What? Hell Is Real," "Try a Dose of the Holy Ghost,"
"Crack Kills—Christ Heals," and "Oakland Not Cokeland." People joined us
at each juncture of the route, others hung halfway out of their apartment windows cheering us on.

A woman named Denise Stovall was found by a reporter pushing a baby carriage. She had already marched seven miles. Ms. Stoval said, "If I get blisters, its worth it. We're showing our kids that the real hero isn't Felix. It's Jesus. And Jesus never snorted cocaine." Another East Oakland resident said, "I really feel good about the church doing something about the drugs in the neighborhoods. I've felt so long like a prisoner in my own home. There has been so much drug activity right outside my door that I was afraid to go outside."

Allen Temple did not stop its anticrack efforts when the march was over. The next week community activists descended on Allen Temple Baptist Church to do some long-range logistical planning. We created an antidrug network. On December 20, Allen Temple sponsored another antidrug rally down on the corner of our street. We gave out free hot dogs, ice cream, soft drinks and helium-filled balloons. We also had food baskets, free clothing and toys on hand for those whose refrigerators were empty and their children's closets bare. I said in the December 21, 1986, edition of the *Oakland Tribune*, "We are reaching out to the people who are living in this troubled neighborhood. We are telling them that they can find strength in the Lord. We're reaching out to tell them God loves them." Some of the members of our church who were also part of the law-enforcement community started going to known crack houses and pull lost souls out into the streets to hear the gospel. They would tell the shot callers, "You're out of business today. Jesus is taking over."

THE CRACK GAME AFFECTS US ALL

Our efforts have barely slowed down the leviathan that stalks the streets of the ghetto or the violence that accompanies it. One evening after a staff meeting here in the church building, my son James Jr. decided to stay behind to play his saxophone. After he had finished practicing, my son flicked on the lights in his office. Out of nowhere a metal chair came crashing down on him. An unseen person slammed it against his back and his head. They began to wrestle. My son's wallet dropped out in the fray. The intruder picked it up and scurried for the door with James in pursuit. Some of the neighbors saw the man running with my son behind him. They too gave chase but the thief escaped.

Deacon Reggie Lyles came to the scene moments later and took my son to police headquarters to make a statement. James Jr. suffered a concussion and back injuries from the attack. His saxophone was ruined.

What was our church's response? *Love.* That next Saturday we gathered together two hundred members and we marched through the neighborhood proclaiming the gospel. We told the people that God loves them and that we love them.

The man who attacked my son might well have been a crack addict in search of a quick blast. If my guess is right, he was trying to find money to put in some crack dealer's hands. And for so many, robbery is a legitimate way to fast money. The young people in the ghetto hear many voices telling them that "grinding" and "hustling" is a legitimate way to make it under certain circumstances. We must act to let them know that those who sell drugs become agents of destruction to their own kind. They must understand that genocide and self-destruction *are never* good alternatives.

32

FIGHTING THE
SUPREME COURT NOMINEE

As a pastor and the leader of a denomination, I have been careful to discern which issues would affect people of color in the inner cities. Politics is more than a pastime for the rich and famous, and I understood that lawmakers and politicians who sat in key policy-making seats determined to a large extent the quality of life for people in places like East Oakland, Watts and the south side of Chicago. This caused me to pay close attention to who was running for office, what issues were at stake and where the candidates stood on issues.

Judge Robert Bork was Ronald Reagan's nominee to fill a vacant U.S. Supreme Court seat. Bork's voting record on civil rights troubled me. God had used the Supreme Court to grant minorities and people of color so many rights. We couldn't afford to let someone that we perceived to be hostile to that progress be nominated. So I led the Progressive National Baptist Convention on a campaign to block the confirmation of Judge Robert Bork to the Supreme Court. We urged the members of Congress to vote against Judge Bork. A letter from Congressman Walter E. Fauntroy in response to my efforts follows:

Dear Dr. Smith:

Thank you for your letter urging my opposition to the nomination of appeals court Judge Robert H. Bork to the U.S. Supreme Court.

Please be assured that as a Member of Congress and as President of the National Black Leadership Roundtable, I will be working with a broad coalition of civil rights, labor, progressive religious, and women's rights organizations to defeat this nomination.

Again, I thank you for your letter and I look forward to working with you in the effort to oppose the confirmation of Judge Robert H. Bork.

Sincerely yours,
Walter E. Fauntroy
Member of Congress

Who says that our voices won't make a difference? Look at the aftermath of our struggle. Judge Bork may have written his odes to conservatism and collected his lecture fees, but he never sat on the Supreme Court. We won.

PNBC GROWTH AND PERSONAL ACCOLADES

There were more victories to savor. The Progressive National Baptist Convention was rising from the financial ashes. During my first year in office, we collected a record sum of money to be donated to historically black colleges and seminaries. We raised $30,000 for a well-digging project in Malawi, Southeast Africa. We made great headway toward paying off the mortgage for Progressive National Baptist Convention headquarters.

In 1987 *Ebony* magazine named me one of the "100 Most Influential Black People." My picture appeared on the same page as General Colin Powell and Stevie Wonder. Another issue of *Ebony* listed me as one of "America's 15 Greatest Black Preachers." These are among the highest accolades that one can hope for within the African American community.

AMBUSHED BY "FRIENDLY FIRE"

Again, not everyone celebrated my success. My fellow clergy should have said, "Praise God from whom all blessings flow. If God can use James Alfred Smith Sr., God can use me." That is exactly what some preachers were saying; yet there were others who snarled in private, "Who does that California Negro think he is?" In their jealousy, they plotted to embarrass me. I was pretty oblivious to all of this until an older preacher approached me in the hallway one night at a PNBC meeting. I hardly knew the gentleman, but I listened to him courteously as he spoke in a voice that was slightly above a whisper.

"Now, President Smith," he said, "because of jealousy, some of your competitors are going to try to embarrass you at the next board meeting. Your adversaries have the secretary in their pocket, and they have convinced her to sabotage you. When you call for the minutes to be read, she's going to say, 'Well, I'm so sorry. I inadvertently left home without them.' " Then this wily sage counseled me with the advice: "In order to save yourself and your mission, bring your own secretary to the meetings and have her there by your side and make sure that she's taking the minutes."

If God had not intervened on my behalf through the elderly preacher, I would have fallen into disaster. Without the approved minutes we would have flown all the way to Washington, D.C., for nothing. The efficacy of my leadership would have been brought into question.

How he obtained this inside information remains a mystery to this day. But sure enough, it came down just like the preacher had warned me it would. At the beginning of the meeting, the secretary said, "Oh my, I seem to have left the minutes at home." You could hear people gasping and moaning. Someone said, "What are we going to do?"

I stared at the faces around the table. I was as calm as a pearl in an oyster's mouth. Then I said in words just above a whisper, "Well, my brethren. Let's not be too hard on our secretary. All of us make mistakes. Haven't you ever left home and realized that you didn't have something that you really needed? Well, my own personal secretary, Mrs. Margie Lawson, was taking minutes so we have a backup. I have always learned in my ministry that it is good to have a backup plan."

One of my friends jumped up and said, "I move that we accept the minutes of the president's secretary." Another friend cried out, "I second the motion. All in favor say aye." It was unanimous. They had set a trap for me, but it failed. Most members clapped and said "Thank the Lord," but not everybody was smiling. In my heart I gave thanks for the insight of my elderly pastor-friend.

This little episode told me to approach denominational work with my eyes wide open. Even the people at the highest level of church structure sometimes have varying commitments to Christ. Ambition and backbiting can worm their way into the scheme of things. I learned that I must rely on prayer and discernment. If I became too heavenly minded I could have my head chopped off while others shouted "hallelujah." The Scripture admonishes us to be "wise as serpents and harmless as doves" (Matthew 10:16).

COMING HOME FULL CIRCLE

In August 1988 the PNBC annual convention was held in Kansas City, Missouri. My heart fluttered as I descended from the 747, my wife, mother and children in tow. I could only think of the incredible distance that the Lord had brought me. I was born here in the shadows of a garbage dump, the child of a single mother. Now I was returning as the president of one of the largest Christian organizations on the face of the earth.

The conference booked a hotel suite for me that held special significance. When I was a boy, my mother had served in that same establishment as a chamber maid, making other people's beds and scrubbing the floors. Walking through the lobby as a patron was something akin to waking up while still inside a sweet dream.

That night I scooped JoAnna up in my arms and held her as the summer breeze washed over us. "Jo, see that?" I pointed my index finger at a clump of buildings at the edge of town, the lights sparkling beneath the rays of the Big Dipper. "That's Leeds. That's where I grew up." In the silent moments that followed, I reminisced about my old neighbors back in the Paul Lawrence Dunbar District who had fled to the Midwest in search of a better life. I wondered what had happened to my old baseball team. I pulled JoAnna close and pointed down at the rooftop of a large department store. "See that place, Jo? I used to be a stock boy there."

JoAnna held my neck in the crook of her arm. I had traveled so far, propelled forward by a calling that first got my attention on a bandstand in Venita, Oklahoma. I had been around the world—from South Korea to England to Africa and Mexico and all points in between. By this time I had lectured at Harvard, Yale, Duke, Morehouse, Virginia Union and Howard. God had blessed me to lead thousands to himself.

That afternoon, people from all over the United States and the Caribbean embraced me and shook my hand as I wandered through the halls with my blood kin and church family. Rarely did I pass a dignitary or a delegate without saying, "May I introduce you to my mother, Ms. Amy Smith?" My mother didn't say much. Yet I could see pride blazing through the pupils of her eyes. The next morning at breakfast, Mama touched my hand and smiled broadly. "We've come home, son, in a big way."

— 33 —

GOING HOME TO AFRICA

If I forget you, O Jerusalem, let my right hand forget its skill" (Psalm 137:5). These are the words of David, a son of Zion.

But I too felt a connection to the soil where my ancestors lie, Africa. Like the prophet Nehemiah, who up to his adult years had never seen Jerusalem yet loved it so, I loved the people of the African continent.

In the mid-'80s Reverend Dr. Henry Gregory III invited me to preach at the historic Shiloh Baptist Church in Washington, D.C. Before I arrived he arranged for me to meet with one of his members, Mrs. Marie Hamilton. That afternoon I was blessed to sample delicacies from the African nation of Sierra Leone.

This meal was about more than fellowship. Mrs. Hamilton requested that I lead PNBC leaders on a fact-finding mission to Sierra Leone.

Sierra Leone was a hot spot on the globe. Television news reports brought the carnage of black-on-black civil war into our living rooms. There was live footage of child soldiers toting rifles through the backwoods on their way to fight insurgent forces.

Sierra Leone is a tropical paradise where white crosses cast their shadows down on the beaches, and black-skinned children with toothy smiles run up to visitors to shake hands. The people there promised to fill the church where I would be speaking.

PREACHING TO AFRICANS

The church was as warm as the inside of an oven when I set my Bible down on the pulpit and began to preach. Rows of men, women and children sat in their best clothes. They listened intently, absorbed by the sermon. No one spoke. No one stirred. No one clapped. There wasn't an amen in the house. But after I closed in prayer, they clapped like manna had just fallen from heaven.

Before we left Sierra Leone, we sat down with President Momoh, a man trying to make peace in this war-torn nation. Blood was being shed over black-market gems. Diamonds were being smuggled out of Sierra Leone daily, wrecking its economy. The president had his hands full. He was happy for any help he could get from his brothers and sisters across the big water. Mrs. Hamilton also introduced us to the nation's religious and civic leaders.

We sent thousands of dollars in aid back to Sierra Leone. Today we support the Sierra Leone Bible College, which educates indigenous people. The JoAnna Goodwin Smith Scholarship aids needy students each year in their quest to attend the college. One of the present religious leaders of Sierra Leone received help from that fund. We have also encouraged churches to sponsor missionary endeavors in Sierra Leone.

A POOLSIDE BAPTISM

Later that week as we sat poolside trying to stay cool, a thin man drenched with sweat ran up to us. We could see his heart pounding through his shirt. "I have come to be baptized," he announced. It turned out that this young man had been corresponding with members of our party from Detroit. He had missed our visit to his home village by minutes. Determination pushed him through the backwoods and finally to the city where he knew he would find us three days later.

I went up to my hotel room and came back in my baptismal garments. Then I pointed toward the swimming pool. Wealthy tourists wrinkled their noses. I didn't care, and I'm sure the exuberant brother next to me didn't either. Water is water, right?

"I have come to be baptized." His determination to follow Christ's command inspired us all, even after our African journey was over.

PROPHESYING AT THE UNITED NATIONS
HEADQUARTERS

On April 4, 1989, I was summoned to testify before a United Nations committee in New York City concerning the efforts of people in the Bay Area to end apartheid in South Africa. I said, "As a third-world pastor of a third-world people in a first-world country that practices deception and duplicity in a program of destructive engagements with South Africans and a justice-oriented preacher of the gospel of liberation for both the oppressed and the oppressor, I come to articulate not only my beliefs but also to express the intensity of the convictions of thousands in Allen Temple Baptist Church and in Oakland, California, who are broken in spirit and bruised in emotions because justice sleeps while black South Africans are painfully and destructively trapped in the degrading, dehumanizing, oppressive structures of apartheid. Like Zechariah of our ancient past, we scream:

> Come, O Zion! Escape you who live in the Daughter of Babylon. For this is what the Lord Almighty says: "After he has honored me and sent me against the nations that you have plundered—for whoever touches you touches the apple of his eye. I will surely raise my hand against them so that their slaves will plunder them. Then you will know that the Lord Almighty has sent me." (Zechariah 2:7-9)

The press photographers showed Reverend Frank Pinkard of Oakland's Evergreen Baptist Church and me holding up in jubilance the hands of a South African exile named Patrick Mtoto. Allen Temple had been instrumental in assisting the young man in his attempts to obtain asylum in the United States.

—34—

A REVOLUTIONARY'S LIFE

I had enjoyed my time as president of the Progressive National Baptist Convention. It had given me a chance to work for the Lord on a national level. I also received opportunities to share the gospel all over the world, including speaking before the World Baptist Alliance in Seoul, Korea. We dedicated our national headquarters during my watch as president. I left the organization with its books balanced. But it was time to get back to the business of full-time pastoring in Oakland.

One Sunday morning at Allen Temple, I slipped on my black, waist-high rubber boots and waded into the baptismal pool. The deacons led a man down into the waters from an adjacent stairwell. The brother bowed his head as he drifted down the blue tile stairs until he was waist deep in water. He faced the painted backdrop of John the Baptist and Black Jesus, and then he turned toward the audience.

The years had not been kind to him. His hairline had receded. His youth was gone. But his eyes still sparkled like the distant stars on a rainy night. He was searching for the path to healing and holiness. I cradled Huey P. Newton in my arms, the flesh-and-blood embodiment of black struggle clothed in a white, floor-length baptismal robe.

"Huey P. Newton, I baptize you in the name of the Father, the Son and the Holy Spirit. Amen." He squeezed his eyes tight. The muscles in his back tightened. The organ and the piano blended into the sweet melody of "Take Me to the Water." Hundreds of voices lifted the chorus through the roof, as a deacon plunged Huey through the chilly waters of repentance and regeneration. The clapping of hands was deafening. Voices cried out, "Hallelujah! Thank you, Jesus! Great is God!"

Baptismal water dripped from Huey P. Newton's hair and the bottom of his beard. He shook his head, spraying me with beads of cold water. He embraced me; then the deacon pointed him through the waters to the stairs.

Hours earlier, he and his wife had sat in my office clutching hands. We talked about the Christian faith. He knew what he wanted to do. *If only he had continued to walk with us.* Not many days later, my secretary put an emergency call through. Huey P. Newton had been shot in West Oakland. I felt as though a grapefruit had lodged itself in the pit of my stomach.

"Dead?" I repeated. "Dead," the voice confirmed. I dropped into my desk chair, my head resting in my hands. Rumor had it that Huey had been sucking on the glass pipe. It takes only one pull to draw a human being into the steel jaws of its brutal addiction. Huey P. Newton had lost the tug of war for his soul long before the grim reaper met him on a desolate corner of our dangerous world. All of that intellect, that promise and hope swallowed up in a moment of senseless gunfire. Huey's last words were: "You can kill my body but you can't kill my soul. My soul will live forever."

As I sat there that afternoon, I remembered Huey's eyes, those laughing eyes and that gentle smile. I recalled his Southern manners. The phone rang again. The Newton family wanted Allen Temple to host Huey's home-going services. Would Allen Temple host his home-going service? Yes, of course we would. They asked me to preside over the event.

FUNERAL FOR A PANTHER

We held his funeral on Monday, August 28, 1989. One of my deacons, Randall White, remembered that day in a recent conversation: "There were people here concerned that there might be trouble at the funeral. Because of all the sensationalism, people felt insecure. This car pulls up and Newton's right-hand man steps out. He says, 'Are you gonna search my bag? Do you know who I am?' I look up at him and say, 'Whoa, I know you're Bobby Seale. I know who you are. Everything is cool.'

"Everybody in the community was here. We had like five different black

Muslim factions. One of the deacons who had a background as a police officer was kind of on edge because some of these people like to come with their own security and take over the show. Rather than getting upset with them, I tried to find a place to include them in the goings on.

"You know how at funerals everybody who hasn't been part of what's been going on wants to be included. They don't necessarily care for the person who was being honored. There's this weird dynamic where people have to elbow their way in and get their piece. That was going on here, but on a huge scale.

"Some of these brothers tried to sneak in machetes rolled up in rugs. Plenty of the old Panthers were there. We had a lot of folks in the city government who were now respectable but at one time were part of the movement. Every revolutionary movement you can imagine was there. Members of Allen Temple were also there.

"The police were nowhere in sight. They were gathered in mass with their attack squad out at the Oakland Coliseum a few blocks away, ready for this thing to jump off so that they could come in and make a mess. You couldn't find a police officer within a two-mile radius of Allen Temple.

"To make matters worse, the water was mysteriously cut off during the service. The place was packed with people and we couldn't flush the toilets. The church building itself was surrounded with folks thirty deep. You couldn't get in or out of the gates. Right in the middle, agent provocateurs were trying to cause a scene so that they could come in and make a mess of Huey P. Newton's funeral."

There were so many people in the church that it looked as though the walls were breathing. Hundreds crowded around the fence that surrounds the building. They were angry and heartbroken at the news that the church had no room to squeeze them in. They wanted to say goodbye to their departed warrior. Bobby Seale went outside to defuse a potentially explosive situation. He shook hands with the mourners at the gate and offered words of peace.

When Bobby Seale stood up to speak in the sanctuary, the electricity on the entire block shut down. That has never happened before or since. I opened Huey P. Newton's eulogy with the words "In the fifty-fifth Psalm, David wrote, 'Oh, that I had the wings of a dove! I would fly away and be at rest—I would flee far away and stay in the desert. Selah. I would hurry to my place of shelter, far from the tempest and storm. Confuse the wicked, O Lord, confound their speech, for I see violence and strife in the city. Day and night they prowl about on its walls, malice and abuse are within it. Destructive forces are at work in the city, threats and lies never leave its streets.' "

I had recently held Huey P. Newton in my arms and baptized him. Now I was saying the last words over his mortal remains. And so ended the 1980s.

— 35 —

CHANGE IS IN THE WIND

—◈◈◯

B‍y the 1990s black people all over the country began to open their eyes to a truth that rose on the horizon like the dawning sun. The opportunity to be served at a lunch counter did not equate to full citizenship. Huge numbers of African Americans had been left behind in crumbling inner cities like East Oakland. For these people it was as though Dr. Martin Luther King Jr. had never existed.

So many people in the urban areas lacked access—access to computers in the age of the microchip, access to public transportation that would get them to jobs in the suburbs, access to schools that would provide them with a quality education, access to adequate healthcare. They lacked access to just about every inalienable right that the framers of the Declaration of Independence might have had in mind when they penned the phrase "Life, liberty and the pursuit of happiness." And what compounds their pain is the fact that few Christian preachers who have the power to exercise incredible influence on American society on behalf of inner-city people will use their vocal cords to do so.

Relatively few pastors have ever read an African American history book or studied urban sociology. When racist policies displace inner-city Christians, prominent ministers skirt the issue completely, or even worse, they throw out some utterly asinine remark like "There'll be room for everybody in heaven." By the early 1990s I realized that the church had to do more than provide social services for the community. We had to fight for social justice. We had to do more than desegregate lunch counters. We had to seat people on the other end of the table at city hall.

PIPELINE TO POWER

Do I believe that spiritual principalities dominate a world wracked by sin and evil and ruled by the prince of darkness, Satan? Absolutely. Do I believe that some strongholds are only destroyed by prayer and fasting? Without a doubt. However, the years have taught me that not every evil is a demon that has to be cast out. There are times when evil can be exorcised with a pull of a lever in a polling booth at election time.

In a free society the government works for you. Government officials are your representatives. You are paying their salaries. They are voted in by citizens to serve citizens and their interests. Some of them even live in public housing. Christian, you can hold them accountable.

Through the years I have mentored many people who went on to attain public office. I taught them to "do justice, love mercy and to walk humbly" with their God (Micah 6:8), to govern with love and to speak truth based on God's Word, no matter who likes it or who doesn't like it. At one time some of the most powerful figures in Oakland city politics were members of Allen Temple. Some of our members even held key positions in the state capitol and the nation's capitol. One newspaper referred to this disparagingly as the "Allen Temple Pipeline."

ALLEN TEMPLE MEMBER BECOMES CHIEF OF POLICE

For years Oakland had struggled with the plague of police brutality. We had fought against this scourge without denigrating all police officers. I am a large supporter of the Oakland Police Department. I am proud of the men and women of any police force who put their lives on the line to protect citizens. Through the years, several of Allen Temple's members have been law enforcement personnel. Joe Samuels is one of them.

Brother Samuels is a tall, stately man with square shoulders. When he first joined Allen Temple, he was a foot patrolman. However, his conscientious service soon propelled him through the chain of command. In the church he became one of my prized deacons. In the secular world Joe Samuels became Oakland's first African American police chief.

Chief Samuels hired a large number of women and minorities to round out his staff. He instituted a no-tolerance policy on police brutality, causing the rate of incidents to decrease dramatically. The crime rate in Oakland fell. Unfortunately, not everyone was as thrilled with the chief's performance as was the community.

A NEW MAYOR HITS TOWN

Jerry Brown had once been California's progressive governor. I liked him. But his mayoral campaign platform troubled me. His team called itself "We the People." They promised to bring ten thousand new people to Oakland. That bothered me. You see, East Oakland sits in the middle of the most expensive real estate in North America. Few families in the inner city can afford to purchase their own homes. By the 1990s rents had begun to escalate beyond the reach of the working poor, forcing some to share an apartment with two or even three other families. Some of our former neighbors are now spending their nights beneath a freeway underpass. They've been damned to this hell on earth by greedy landlords and politicians.

Jerry Brown won the election. Under Mayor Brown's rule, building began in the downtown areas. His idea of affordable housing seemed to be housing for those who could afford it. Modest studio apartments in some of the Oakland condominiums began to climb toward the $350,000 mark. And in November 1997 Mayor Brown was awarded powers that no other mayor in this city had ever had the good fortune to wield. He used his extended authority to hire city manager Robert Bobb. Bobb sent out a sea of pink slips.

One day I received one of those terrible late-night phone calls that deprives one of sleep. The caller said, "Joe Samuels's head is on the chopping block, and it's going to roll tomorrow." Sure enough, in March 1999 Chief Samuels was fired.

I was disheartened because I love Joe and his family. I had officiated at their wedding. I had dedicated their baby son to the Lord. I saw his leadership in the police department as the answer to our prayers. And now the mayor was snatching him away from us. I burned up the phone lines calling the other preachers in town. We staged demonstrations and press conferences. Finally, we were granted an audience with the mayor and members of the city council. The mood in the room could only be described as tense. The politicians had adopted a patriarchal "we know what's best for you" style of leadership. They began to pat me on the back and say things like, "Now, now, calm down, Reverend. Remember, you're a man of the cloth."

I hate to be patronized. If you want to pet something, get a dog! It wasn't long before my temper got the best of me. Jaws dropped as I jumped out of my seat and made my way toward a startled city council member. I got as close to that prominent elected official as I could before they grabbed me and then I threatened to apply the heel of my shoe to the seat of his trousers. (Well, perhaps not quite that politely.) Later I regretted my actions. My angry outburst was reported in the newspapers to my own personal embarrassment.

During the entire Samuels matter, the city fathers and mothers played the role of nonbenevolent subdeities. They didn't want to hear from East Oakland or its community representatives. They didn't want to reason with us. They just wanted us to go away. These are the same leaders who want to be front and center at our churches on Sunday morning. They want to be introduced and to have the opportunity to say a word. They want our endorsements for their campaigns. How much pure gall can people possess? When we went down to the halls of power where the elected officials are supposed to be working in our best interests; they didn't want to hear from us. I felt deeply insulted. Sure, I felt like kicking some seats!

They took away Chief Samuels and brought in Chief Richard Word. Chief Word is a good man, but Oakland's murder rate has gone through the roof. Right now a group of ex-police officers nicknamed the "Riders" are on trial and facing heavy prison time for police brutality. They are accused of having stopped black men in West Oakland at random, beating some and planting dope on others. The leader of the Riders jumped bond and is rumored to have left the country. The city ended up paying out $10 million in out-of-court settlement fees before the trial had even reached its conclusion.

The Oakland Police Department is still struggling, but Chief Samuels landed on his feet. He became the chief of police in the city of Richmond, California. He is also the head of an international body of police. I couldn't be more proud of him.

THE CREDIT UNION CHANGES HANDS

The Allen Temple Credit Union went through a period of phenomenal success. We grew from 365 members in 1989 to 1,650 in 1995. In 1993 the local NAACP merged its credit union with ours. When Citibank made the decision to serve underserved inner city people, it knocked on the door of the Allen Temple Credit Union. Pacific Bell and its parent company, Pacific Telesis, each invested $90,000 with us. The credit union expanded its range of operations, eventually becoming classified as a community development credit union.

In June 1998 International Longshore and Warehouse Union (ILWU)-Teamster coalition invested $150,000 in the Allen Temple Credit Union. Somebody noted that Allen Temple was yielding one full percentage point less than the going interest rate. A Union official answered the complaint by stating, "The ILWU is willing to do that so individuals in the community who otherwise wouldn't qualify can get loans."

The financial expertise that we were able to bring to East Oakland was like rain in a desert. People who had never been able to share in the American dream came to our annual Conference on Economic Empowerment with pen and paper in hand. Financial experts taught community residents the ins and outs of credit, investing, business planning and employment. Pastors and members of other local churches put pettiness and jealousy aside. They worked shoulder to shoulder with us to build this institution, which lifted so many people out of poverty. The Allen Temple Credit Union merged with Kaiser Credit, which allows our members to have checking and credit card services.

CHINA VISIT

One day my secretary, Carlotta Herbert, came into my office with a message from Irvin Jones. A smile came to my face when I heard his name. She said, "Mr. Irvin Jones called and said that you once helped him early in his career. He would like to return the favor by sending you and five other guests to the nation of China."

I was thrilled at the prospect of a visit to the Far East. I sat back and contemplated who I would take with me. First, I thought of people in the church whom I might get far away from home so that I could pitch some new ideas that I had for the ministry. But the more that I prayed about it, the deeper the impression on my heart became that God was telling me to take my wife and five children with me. They had all grown up and moved away, and this would be an opportunity for us to spend some quality time together. So we went as a family. Mr. Jones arranged for us to stay at a plush five-star hotel. We visited Hong Kong and Shanghai, both beautiful and modern cities with skyscrapers that rivaled New York's expansive skyline.

We had a chance to talk and rebond as a family on this trip. We were about to face another bend in the road. My beloved wife, JoAnna, recently had been diagnosed with the early stages of Alzheimer's disease. The trip to China was a chance for all of us to share strength and love for the journey that lay ahead.

JAMES JR. LEAVES ALLEN TEMPLE

No pastor has ever had a better copastor than I had in Reverend Dr. J. Alfred Smith Jr. He was a wonderful preacher and a gifted theologian. He grew to be a friend as well as a son. But one day he came to the realization that God was calling him beyond the walls of Allen Temple Baptist Church. I was sad to see him go but excited as well, because I knew that God had great things in store for him.

36

TIME TO BUILD AGAIN

—⧜⧝○—

Our community had problems that had to be addressed. So did our church. One of those problems was a lack of space. When we built the new church building, we didn't include any classroom space. I felt the need to lead Allen Temple in the creation of a space that could help us meet the people's needs from the womb to the tomb. So I began to ask the church leadership how we were going to do outreach ministry to a needy community without the proper accommodations. I argued that in order for a church to be more than a one-day-a-week institution, it has to have the appropriate facilities. We had to have a building to help us meet the needs of both the here and the hereafter.

FAMILY LIFE CENTER

In disadvantaged urban communities, there are centers of death scattered throughout the neighborhood. There are too many liquor stores on each block. You'll find crack houses in residential communities. You'll find thugs crowding the corners and young toughs kneeling in a circle, cracking dice against the curb.

Allen Temple, contrary to the death centers, was providing life-giving activities. We are an oasis in an urban wilderness. The question was, where would we house our new dreams?

Ironically, the answer came from Huey P. Newton before he was murdered. As the Black Panther Party faded into oblivion, chased to its end by the federal authorities, it was forced to divest itself of all of its holdings. The leadership of the party went to Huey Newton and asked him, "What shall we do with the building that once housed the East Oakland headquarters." Huey said, "Sell it to the church [meaning Allen Temple], they'll know what to do with it."

The Black Panther Party for Self-Defense sold us the building at far below the market price. Huey was right; we did know what to do with it. And on the place where the Panthers may have once stored caches of Uzis, magnums and street sweepers, we built the Allen Temple Family Life Center, a thirty-classroom structure that also houses a full gymnasium, church offices, a library and a computer learning lab.

HOW CAN WE STOP THE KILLING?

How can we stop the killing? That's the question on everybody's lips in Oakland these days. Last year Mayor Jerry Brown took a trip behind the walls of San Quentin State Penitentiary to seek advice from the inmates on how to quell the killings in the streets. At the church we have been praying, researching and crafting our own solutions.

Reverend Eunice Shaw came to us from my hometown of Kansas City, Missouri, by way of Houston, Texas. She is a single mother of three who clawed her way through college and seminary. (Presently she is completing her doctoral dissertation.) Reverend Shaw came with a heart for the lost on the Jericho Road. My son and I decided without question that she should head up our health and social services ministries.

God gave our sister in faith a vision. When Reverend Shaw shared it with me, I waved the checkered flag and offered any support that I could. She felt compelled to organize anger management classes for men and women down here in the killing fields. And today you'll see our men—dreadlocks, sagging jeans, sneakers and all—as they walk through the doors of the Allen Temple Outreach Center seeking healing and release from the demons that plague them. Sometimes there are tears. Often there is repentance. The success of our anger management program has not escaped the notice of our criminal justice system. Parole agents and judges are sending court-mandated parolees to us. Our numbers are swelling.

God's goodness is shining on us. And only he knows how many marked-for-murder Oaklanders will live to hug their toddlers next Christmas day because some potential life-taker had his (or her) life rerouted through this program.

REUNITING THE FAMILY

One of urban America's untold stories is the tale of the unwed father who seeks contact with his child but is denied that access. The problem is more widespread than most people would imagine.

The writer of Ecclesiastes got to the root of the situation when he said, "Money answereth all things" (Ecclesiastes 10:19). And without a pricey lawyer's counsel, an economically challenged dad may never touch the hands of his babies. The cries of these men who want to do the right thing but don't know how to navigate the system shook us.

In 2002 we received a grant in conjunction with Cosmopolitan Baptist Church, one of our East Oakland neighbors. Together we created the "Malachi Project" to provide advocacy for noncustodial parents. This grant allowed us to offer parenting classes as well. We are teaching the noncustodial parent how he or she might effectively contribute to the spiritual, financial and emotional well-being of their children. Child-support payments have been made more manageable. We also work with the courts to arrange visitation for the noncustodial parent.

NEED JOB SKILLS?

In May 2002 Governor Gray Davis showed up at our door with a check for a half-million dollars. The money from his discretionary fund was earmarked for a training academy that would benefit ex-felons. This is important to note because a huge number of homicides are committed by people sent back to the streets from California's penitentiaries. The governor told us that there were some things the state could not do, and in those times they turned to the church and other faith-based institutions.

Research taught us that the construction trades rarely barred ex-offenders from their ranks. Therefore, we created a preapprenticeship construction trade class. Through a second module focusing on office automation skills, people with lengthy prison backgrounds are taught computer skills.

Vision dictated that we find a building that could house this new venture, a proposed social service clearinghouse where community residents could get

G.E.D. training, case management and special job education.

For years we had petitioned the owner of a building adjacent to the Allen Temple campus to sell us his property. He was never interested; his business was too profitable.

It was our building council chairman, Othell Dunn, who was finally able to convince the gentleman to sell us the property. Dr. Robert Scott, the Allen Temple AIDS ministry co-chairman, arranged financing for the property through a local bank. As the project began to come to life, the building council recommended that it be named after me. The loving members of Allen Temple accepted the recommendation. The training program and the building are known as the Dr. J. Alfred Smith Training Academy. A student sent me the following letter about his experiences with Allen Temple:

Dear Dr. Smith:

I am so amazed at the amount of help I receive through the ministry of Allen Temple. I have never met you personally, but in you I see a black man who had a dream and with the grace of God made his dream a reality. If I had a choice of a role model for my 10-year old son, it would be you.

The impact on my life through the outreach program for ex-offenders that serves the East Oakland community through the Allen Temple Housing and Economic Development organization has been incredible.

As a prior drug dealer as well as a white collar criminal, I have spent a lot of my adult life in and out of prison. Each person here has shown me that I don't ever have to go back to a life of crime or return to the penitentiary. Everyone here treats me with more respect than I have ever experienced in my life. I will *not* return to prison because of the genuine love and actual help that I receive here. Someone here addresses every problem in my life. I am not a member of this church but this church has opened its arms to me.

The organization helped me with concrete financial needs that often become the frustrating hurdles that turn an ex-con back to crime.

God bless you, Pastor Smith. He created a great work in you.

Sincerely,

Terry Lovett

37

ALLEN TEMPLE TODAY

When I first came to East Oakland, I was the only clergyperson on the church staff. Today Allen Temple's ministerial staff consists of about forty ministers. We have full-blown children's and youth ministries. Deacon Billy Mayfield heads our Boy Scout troop. We have been blessed with a phenomenal number of young men who achieved the rank of Eagle Scout under his tutelage. Reverend Ruben Hurtado heads our work in the Latino community. God has blessed our prison ministry as well as our community evangelism team. Allen Temple has members who do mission work overseas. Indeed, Allen Temple's ministry is worldwide in scope.

Years ago I became aware that there were several institutions in Oakland that train people for ministry, but none were headed by people of color. However, the issue of higher education and the church is a thorny one. Many Christians believe that the anointing of God to preach precludes any need for theological inquiry. The person who has given his or her life to matters of faith need not pursue education. I vehemently disagree. The preacher who does not study the Word of truth in an academic setting eventually will be shamed. So I felt the need to create an institution of higher learning that would offer theological training from an Afrocentric base.

Reverend Dr. L. P. Lewis, Allen Temple's minister of community affairs, and Dr. Jess Perry, a University of California, Berkeley, graduate came alongside me. Together we formed the Allen Temple Leadership Institute. Classes are held on Saturdays, which allows students to pursue a degree without disrupting their work lives. The institute has drawn students not only from our church but from churches all over the Bay Area. Credits earned at the institute are transferable to several colleges. A number of our graduates have gone on to seminary and the ministry.

Allen Temple Baptist Church became the first black church in the nation to address the AIDS crisis by building a housing complex for those members of our community who are HIV positive. Recently, former Lakers basketball star Magic Johnson came to the church to discuss HIV and AIDS with the community.

Through the years, notables from Maya Angelou and Jesse Jackson to James Cone and Cornel West have stood in the pulpit of our church. We have certainly been blessed.

WHAT NEXT?

Perhaps you remember the movie *New Jack City*. Wesley Snipes plays a Harlem drug lord called "Uptown Nino Brown" who has taken over "the Carter," a housing project. The police had arrested scores of would-be drug barons over the years. However, they had never seen one with technological and legal expertise that Nino Brown possessed. One detective, played by Mario Van Peebles, suggests that the police bring in two young cops. His rationale: "We need a couple of New Jack cops to bring down a New Jack gangster."

A seasoned pastor realizes that God raises up prophets for each generation. And in the East Oaklands of the world, the church is going to have to raise up some New Jack preachers to bring down some New Jack demons. In light of this, I have developed a theology of mentorship modeled by the pastors and teachers who mentored me through the years. As a professor of preaching and church ministries at the American Baptist Seminary of the West and the Graduate Theological Union, I pour myself into young people who are called to serve Christ. As a pastor I'm constantly seeking to mentor preachers that God has placed in my care. The results are more than gratifying.

I believe that Allen Temple Baptist Church has sent more students to the American Baptist Seminary of the West than any other church in the country. We've sent clergy to Fuller Theological Seminary, Golden Gate Baptist Theological Seminary and the Pacific School of Religion. Some of our preachers have gone on to the Samuel DeWitt Proctor Theological Seminary of Virginia Union University, Morehouse School of Religion and Howard University School of Divinity. Many of those whom I've been blessed to mentor went on to serve in the military as chaplains; others serve as hospital and college chaplains. One of my sons in faith serves as the general secretary of the ecumenical churches in Iceland.

Allen Temple ministers-in-training complete both college and seminary degrees. They come from all ethnic groups. Reverend Ray Johnson is in charge of missions work in Southeast Asia and is stationed in Malaysia. Dr. Dwight Hopkins is a professor of theology at the University of Chicago. Dr. Anthony Lloyd of Gardenia, California, is a college professor and a pastor. Dr. Johnny Wilson had the mark of God's call on his life when I met him. After he finished college, I encouraged him to attend the American Baptist Seminary of the West. Afterward he became a Navy chaplain and then went on to become the first African American chaplain at Keuka College. From there he pastored in the state of New York. The Reverend Cheryl Ward preaches all around the country. As a fifteen-year-old she expressed God's call on her life. I helped her to identify her gifts and then to sharpen them. Dr. Charles Hudson was an airplane mechanic who was called to the ministry as a young adult. He wanted my blessing. I encouraged him to complete his studies. He finished seminary and graduate school and then went on to become a U.S. Navy chaplain. Today he is serving as a pastor. I licensed Dr. Majorie Rice to preach. I also ordained her and installed her in her first church. She graduated from the American Baptist Seminary of the West with an M.Div. degree. She had already earned her Ph.D. from Temple University in Philadelphia. Today she ministers in Denver.

God has blessed me with the opportunity to mentor twelve different ministers who have gone on to earn a doctorate degree. Three persons on our pastoral staff are in the process of completing a dissertation. Three of us on the staff have earned doctorates. Of the seven persons on the pastoral staff, five are women. They call on me for counsel, ideas or simply a shoulder to weep on. I am honored by their sacrifice and devotion to excellence in ministry. They are my pride and joy.

MY CURRENT GOALS

God has blessed me to see so many of my dreams come true. As I walk through our expansive Allen Temple Family Life Center, I remember the days when every church activity had to take place in the small building that we now use for the church fellowship hall. I count my blessings when I pick up the phone to pray with a political figure, when I lay hands on a young child and speak a word of hope into his or her ear, when I stand in front of a full congregation on Sunday morning and bow for corporate prayer. Yes, I have seen my dreams come true. But I have seven more goals for my ministry on the Jericho Road.

1. As long as God allows, I will strive to use my gifts to prepare younger leadership for prophetic ministry that will enable the church to be an instrument of God's will in the twenty-first century.

2. I will diligently work toward an Abrahamic unity among Jews, Muslims and Christians that will diminish global conflict and wars.

3. I will continually intercede for the sins of the nation just as Abraham did for Lot and his family and for Sodom and Gomorrah.

4. I will be an advocate for women in Christian ministry and stand in solidarity with all persons who are the objects of racism, sexism, ageism, classism and homophobia.

5. I will teach responsible stewardship and economic justice, particularly seeking the release of the Two-Thirds World from its economic captivity to the West.

6. I will participate in the long process of eradicating modern towers of Babel in order to experience a new multilingual, multiethnic Pentecost.

7. I will attempt to deepen American spirituality with the rich prayer tradition of the African American church and to share with the whole world the African American spiritual tradition of discovering joy in sorrow, strength in weakness, hope in despair and triumph in tragedy.

MY DISAPPOINTMENT WITH A DENOMINATION

Dr. Martin Luther King Sr. said that "there can be no disappointment where there is no great love." That saying definitely serves me well when I think about my relationship with the American Baptist Churches of the West. Our American Baptist brothers and sisters have gone further to the right than they were when I served the denomination in 1968. Then they at least had someone on staff to deal with social justice issues. Today the major buzzword is "church planting." But I ask, planted to do what? No one is even discussing this because it's not an issue; neither is race, politics or the church in society. The attitude seems to be: Let's see if we can create a megachurch like Willow Creek or Saddleback. They seem to have put social justice issues on the back burner (or even removed them from the stove). Will things change? I am not terribly optimistic. That is why our church is dually aligned with the American Baptist Churches USA *and* the Progressive National Baptist Convention.

THE PROGRESSIVE NATIONAL BAPTIST CONVENTION'S FUTURE CHALLENGES

Many of our younger African American preachers have been sucked in by the allure of TV preachers who fill stadiums to stage neo-Pentecostal entertainment productions devoid of any social justice agenda. Our challenge as a denomination is to hold on to our roots in social justice-oriented ministries. We have to find our way back to the foot of the cross where, following the example of Jesus, we will be renewed in our commitment to the least, the lost and the left out.

I have a picture in my home office of two black men. One brother is at the bottom of a wall reaching up. The second man has already hoisted himself to the top of the wall and now he is reaching back for the hand of his brother. We must teach our more affluent brethren to reach back in similar fashion.

We've done enough catering to the white-collar crowd. We must lead people into the streets and down to the Jericho Road if we are to see our institutions continue to thrive.

I DO SEE THE DAWN

Because of the exciting young people who are in my classes at the American Baptist Seminary of the West and Fuller Theological Seminary (as well as the many other seminaries), and because of the many dedicated young adults who are publishing Christian prose, poetry and psalms, and because of the young minds who are not content to be prisoners of either a dead past or a static present but who are stitching new wineskins for new wine, I see a beautiful and bright future for the American church.

These young people will stand on our shoulders, and they will see farther than we see and accomplish greater things than we have. They will speak to the brutal dehumanization and the crass materialism of our time. They will find solutions to the absurdities of our culture that create such pain and unfulfillment. They will recapture the quest of Howard Thurman's "search for common ground" and passionately seek Dr. Martin Luther King's "beloved community." They will serve with the faith of Jarena Lee, the fortitude of Ida B.

Wells and the fruitfulness of Mary McCleod Bethune. And along with William H. Pipes, the world will respond to their efforts with "amen, everybody."

Then Christian credibility and the bright horizons of newness of life in Christ will dawn on the world. The contrast between the hell of the inner city and the peace of the suburbs will be diminished, and the extremes of inordinate wealth and grinding poverty will be overcome. The chasm between rich and poor will be bridged, and this great obscenity within America will be stifled by the Word of truth.

People will no longer argue that religion is the opiate of the people. Instead, the communities of the world will open their doors to the eternal truths of God, who in Christ is reconciling us to himself, to others and to the universe.

PRAYER: THE TIE THAT BINDS

I found that prayer is essential to both Christian ministry and social change. My daily journey on the Jericho Road, where the unexpected occurs with unpredictability, is lived in communion with God. As the sixteenth-century monk Brother Lawrence practiced the presence of God even when he was washing the pots and pans in his kitchen, so do I live with a keen awareness of God's invisible presence as I move from one task to another.

A few years ago a number of my teachings on the subject of prayer were compiled into a book titled *Falling in Love with God*. In this work I gave the reader a glimpse into the life of prayer that has become so intrinsically a part of my walk on the Jericho Road.

I came to the conclusion a long time ago that we are helpless without God. Therefore I rely upon God. I cast myself upon his care. I call him from the dawn's first flash of light until the midnight dark covers the earth. What can I do without his leading?

There is a danger of oversimplifying my personal theology. However, I run this risk by saying that the prophet Micah says it for me in speaking of loving mercy, doing justly and walking humbly with God.

Prayer is the answer. Prayer works. When I look at the life of Vincent Short, one of our Allen Temple youth who grew up right here in the community, I see answered prayers. Vincent went to the naval academy at Annapolis and ascended to the rank of captain. One day he may become an admiral. It was our prayers that lifted him that far. He is just one of the many Allen Temple youth who have done so very well, due to the prayers of our people.

— 38 —

THE VALUE OF
FAMILY AND FRIENDS

—◈◈◯

As I take this time to reflect on my journey on the Jericho Road, I understand how sweet and rich true friends have made my life. As a young boy, my mother and grandmother taught me to appreciate my friends. My grandmother's dying wish was that God would send me friends to help me in my quest to spread the gospel. A minister inevitably finds it difficult to survive his or her personal Gethsemanes without confidantes. They are invaluable.

I have no closer friend than Kenneth Ray. If I were to impulsively fly to Kansas City and arrive at midnight tonight, Reverend Ray would be at the airport waiting to welcome me with his trademark grin. We grew up together. His father introduced me to the world of politics and I called him Dad. Ken and I went to elementary, junior and senior high school together. We both attended Pilgrim Rest Baptist Church. We also attended Western Baptist College together. We married and pastored small churches around the same time. The Lord blessed Ken as the pastor of the good-sized Highland Avenue Baptist Church, and then God blessed me as pastor of Allen Temple Baptist Church. We have been friends from boyhood to this very day.

Whenever I have a sickness or death in my family, Reverend Ray will jump on a plane and be out here in nothing flat. When Mama passed away, he presided over the home-going services. When my blood brother, Joseph Harold

Smith, died in 2002, Reverend Ray was by my side. I don't know how I would have survived those great losses without him.

God has blessed me with many, many friends, and not just black friends but friends from every shade of God's human rainbow, compatriots such as Reverend L. B. Jones, Reverend Charles Briscoe, Dr. Eldon Ernst, and the Reverend Drs. Amos Brown, W. A. (Bill) Jones and Gardner C. Taylor.

Since my early years at Allen Temple, I have forged strong ecumenical friendships with people like Bishop Hertzfield of the Evangelical Lutheran Church of America, Father Ed Haasel and Father Jay Matthews of the Roman Catholic Church, Rabbi Samuel Brodie, Imam Faheem Shuabe, Minister Keith X of the Nation of Islam, Pastor David Kitely and Bishop Bob Jackson, Pastor Frank Jackson, Dr. Earl Stuckey and my cousin the Reverend Dr. Joseph Gates. And I can't forget my Hebrew teacher, Pastor Bryan Woodson, or my dear friend Dean George Cummings.

I thank God for the corporate giants of the city who have worked with my church and me, people like Mr. Robert Shetterly of the Clorox Corporation, Mr. Cornell Meier of the Kaiser-Aluminum Corporation, Mr. Edgar Kaiser, the founder of Kaiser Corporation, and Mr. Stephen Bechtell of Bechtell Corporation. I'm also honored to have worked with Mayors Lionel Wilson, Elihu Harris and Jerry Brown.

God blessed me with the opportunity to pray at Governor Pete Wilson's inauguration. I served as an advisor to both President Jimmy Carter and Governor Gray Davis.

OUR CHILDREN ARE ALL GROWN UP

All my children have left home, but we remain quite close. I am proud of them all. My daughter Amy Smith Jones is a brilliant young lady who helps me care for my wife. She is a blessing to my life. I don't know what I would do without her. She was a music major at the University of Nevada and is an insurance professional.

Shari Smith-Rigmaiden graduated from the University of California, Berkeley, where she studied multiple languages, including Spanish, Portuguese, Latin and Yoruba. She majored in both Afro-American studies and humanities. Today she is a bilingual educator. She and her husband reside in California's central valley.

Ronald Craig Smith is a graduate of Antioch College. His degree is in urban planning and social policy analysis. He was a senior manager for the Tennessee Valley Authority and has served as a division director and senior policy adviser for the Michigan Public Service Commission. He is currently on the executive management team at the Snohomish Public District in Everett, Washington.

Anthony Gerard Smith is a graduate of the University of California, San Diego. He developed a successful career in the telecommunications industry. Currently he works for Qwest Communications in Seattle, Washington, where he provides technical support for Qwest's key business customers.

MY FORMER COPASTOR COMES INTO HIS OWN

My son J. Alfred Smith Jr. is a growing theologian, teacher and pastor. He taught African American religion at the University of California, San Francisco. Presently he serves on the doctoral faculty of the San Francisco Theological Seminary. He also coauthored a book on stewardship with me.

After he resigned as copastor of Allen Temple Baptist Church, J. Alfred Smith Jr. and his family went to Las Vegas, where he taught college classes and founded J. Alfred Smith Jr. Ministries. But then a phone call from California redirected his efforts. Antioch Baptist Church, the oldest African American Baptist church in the city of San Jose, was in search of a senior pastor. They asked James to come out for a visit. He preached a trial sermon at the church, and before too long the church said they felt God might be wedding the two of them together.

In April of 2003 more than one thousand members of the Allen Temple Baptist Church family made the trek to Santa Clara County for the installation service. Before the service began, all of my children, grandchildren and great-grandchildren joined me for brunch. Tears came to my eyes as we hugged and snapped pictures of one another. Among my family members was my niece Charlene Smith. She had lived with us while she attended the University of California, Berkeley and helps care for my wife. My late brother's family also came up from the Los Angeles region to share that important day with us.

The message that I preached that afternoon was "It's Time to Move Onward and Upward." I related the story of the day when Sir Edmund Hillary was at the base of Mount Everest, ready to climb its snowy peaks. He was surrounded by the news media. They watched him make his ascent. Eventually a cloud covered him from sight. The news media reported, "When he was last seen, he was moving on up toward the top." Like Hillary, my son was moving onward and upward. But his was a more important quest—ministry at the Antioch Baptist Church.

It was time of great elation and satisfaction and a time to be grateful to God for what he had done for a faithful young man. My son had put his own advancement on hold to help me build an institution. He was willing to be number two. Now God had elevated him to the role of number one in his own church. His life is a testimony to young men. Don't be in too big of a hurry. If you are faithful in a few things, God will reward you.

EPILOGUE
My Favorite Part of Ministry

I have served the Allen Temple Baptist Church family for more than thirty years. I stress that we are a family. We worship together, we pray together, we laugh together and, yes, we sometimes cry together. These wonderful people give my family far more than we could give them. They uphold our arms as we struggle. They provide caregiver support for my wife, JoAnna. They have consoled me when death snatched loved ones from my family circle. They have sent me around the world to preach the gospel.

When Reverend Amos Brown of the Third Baptist Church of San Francisco flew back to Washington, D.C., with my wife and me to consult with President Bill Clinton, it was because I was a part of the Allen Temple Baptist Church.

The Allen Temple family has not sent me to serve alone on the Jericho Road. They too are serving as healers to the battered, beaten and broken on that same road. Hundreds of them serve in places like Jamaica, Haiti, Kenya, Liberia, Zimbabwe and Sierra Leone.

I derive joy from walking shoulder to shoulder with Christians like Dr. Robert Scott, a noted physician who joined Allen Temple and became enraptured with the vision of the Jericho Road ministry. His heart for those stricken with HIV has led him to forge a cutting-edge ministry to our neighbors in need of both medicine and ministry. Each year he leads a team to the Mother of Peace orphanage for children in Zimbabwe who have lost their parents.

We also have a large number of volunteer staff persons who breathe life into Allen Temple's social service and community outreach ministries. Serving with these loving people brings me joy as I travel the Jericho Road. Here is just a partial list of Allen Temple's ministries:

- a community outreach center

- an emergency food program for the needy

- a free clothing pantry

- a community health fair

- case management services for people living with AIDS

- the Allen Temple/Haight Ashbury Recovery Center, a clinical program to assist people recovering from substance abuse

- six alcohol and drug recovery support groups

- anger management and domestic violence prevention classes, with over 350 current enrollees

- a senior citizens activity program

- a youth sports and recreation program

- a tutorial program for youth and children

- an adult literacy program

- a federal credit union (Kaiperm FCU – Allen Temple Branch)

- a job information center

- three senior citizens' complexes, totaling 175 apartment units

- Allen Temple Manor, with 24 units of housing for AIDS patients

- a family life center, including 22 classrooms, a gymnasium, a dance studio, a library, a computer literacy center, a children's center and administrative offices.

- the Dr. J. Alfred Smith Sr. Training Academy, offering job training and placement to ex-offenders and the urban poor

My favorite part of ministry occurs at the conclusion of each Sunday morning service. Between the end of my message and the benediction, I lead the members of the clergy down the dais and out to the foyer. Then I give the benediction and wait as the parishioners stream through the doors.

There is only one exit door opened in the rear of the church. I have it fixed that way on purpose. This way, no one gets away before I can get my hug or handshake. I love to touch the people. I thank God for the chance to touch and be touched by so many lives on the Jericho Road.

AFTERWORD

By Harry Louis Williams II

Reverend J. Alfred Smith Sr. is famous. It is a rare thing to find him traveling through the streets of his own Galilee without an entourage. That is why I coveted my first opportunity to interview him in the summer of 2001. As I sat in his pastor's study, I couldn't believe that dozens of people were not lined up at the door pounding for an audience. I remember thinking that perhaps Nicodemus was being more prudent than secretive in seeking out the Savior after the fanfare had ceased for the evening. Earlier in the day, a meeting such as this one would have been close to impossible.

Though the church was closed and dusk was falling, several knocks did come to the door. One of them belonged to three young Chicana women, former neighbors of the church who had left East Oakland and returned that day begging only a few moments with the pastor. And when I packed up to leave Reverend Smith's office, I noticed another lady waiting patiently at the door to take my seat.

Unlike many preachers that I have met, Reverend Smith has a love that exudes from every pore of his skin. It showers innocent bystanders with warmth and dignity.

On the day of our first interview, Dr. Smith sported a tasteful brown suit, which was neatly pressed down to the cuffs of his pants; his shoes were shiny black. He wore a colorful kente cloth kufi, which he raked from his head as he entered the room. His study was adorned with pictures from his illustrious career. There were numerous plaques and awards. Two walls were filled with books; everything from the *Annotated Shakespeare* to *The Life and Legacy of Frederick Douglass*. A robed Dr. Smith filled the cover of an *Image* magazine that rested in a glass case; the headline read "A Man for Oakland's Mean Seasons." To his left a plaque read "Life Is Fragile—Handle with Prayer." There were black and white pictures of the pastor shaking hands with Jimmy Carter and Andrew Young.

On the day that we began chapter one, I said to Reverend Smith: "About five years ago, I had the opportunity to visit West Africa. There are so many images that hang in my imagination like twinkling stars across a desert sky. On our way to the Gambia, we traveled through the countryside. In village after village, beside the broad trunk of the baobab tree, sat the elders. I still remember those clusters of black men, their long robes twirling in the wind. They were revered for their years of life, approached for their counsel, respected for their wisdom.

"This afternoon I have come to visit with one of the grand elders of not only our community but our faith tradition here on the shores of North America. I want you to know that I count these moments as sacred and this opportunity as an honor. I do not come to you as a fellow elder but as one of the younger men of the village seeking the counsel of one who has lived many lifetimes. The questions that I will ask will not come in a straight line. We will discuss ideas like two men seated around a fire."

During the course of the interview, Reverend Smith's eyes would squeeze tight as he recited some painful episode. His voice would halt and then rise in odd places. At times he would gesticulate as though assisting his mind in the shattering of stereotypes and presuppositions. At one point he stood up and strode around the office. I tried to follow him with my tape recorder without breaking his train of thought.

As I left his office, I saw Reverend Smith's fingerprints all over 85th Street and International Avenue: on the other side of Ms. Tee's Louisiana Playhouse a sign read "Allen Temple Community Outreach Center." The Allen Arms I jutted up from the sidewalk down the street.

At the time, I was serving as the associate pastor of a small Baptist church in Modesto, California. I had no inkling that God was in the process of steering my life in another direction. A few months later, I found employment as a professor at a small Christian college located about seven minutes from Allen Temple Baptist Church. I relocated and joined the church. Today I work with ex-offenders as a case manager for the Dr. J. Alfred Smith Training Academy.

When this book was in its embryonic stages, Reverend Smith was a mentor, but as time went on he became my pastor and, I would even presume to say, my friend. I sit next to him in the pulpit; on the street I walk at his side. On Sundays I have dinner with Reverend Smith, and his friends and family. There I observe him, listen to him and jot down his recollections over banana bread pudding and Earl Grey tea.

And through these times I have come to know Reverend Smith. I know when he's joyous and when he's troubled. I've visited the sick with Dr. Smith, and I've bowed my head in prayer in the pastor's study as Reverend Jesse Jackson laid hands on JoAnna Goodwin Smith, who had been stricken with Alzheimer's disease. I've sat with the pastor as he talked church politics and theology with the greatest African American preachers of our time.

Everybody in Oakland has a J. Alfred Smith story. I met a couple sipping from a paper bag at the bus stop one day. As we waited beneath the California sun, I mentioned that I was a member of Allen Temple. The man spoke, his breath betraying Wild Irish Rose fumes, "I know Reverend J. Alfred Smith. When my brother died, he and that church helped me to get back to Monroe, Louisiana."

As the killing epidemic rages in East Oakland, we live in a time where people are hungry for heroes. I'm sure you'll agree with me that the Reverend Dr. J. Alfred Smith is such a hero.

Appendix
Church Members Reflect

When we first began working on this book, I (Harry Williams) gathered some of Pastor Smith's longtime church members into his office one Sunday afternoon and asked them for their thoughts on his life and ministry.

A DEACON LEARNS FROM HIS PASTOR

John Harrison, a noted attorney, is a church deacon and chairman of the Allen Temple Housing and Economic Development board.

"When we were building the Allen Temple Family Life Center, we used municipal bonds. This is what my firm does. But the people at the church who were setting up the financing did not come to me. They just went on and did it. Then they were bringing in third parties. I started thinking, *Wait a minute. This is what I do!* It came to a point when I said, 'Am I going to participate?' They said, 'Oh yes, you are going to participate, but we don't want you to take any fees.' Well, this is how I support myself.

"We were sitting in a big meeting, and Pastor Smith said, 'Johnny, do you believe that the Lord will take care of you?' I said, 'Yeah, yeah.' That is all he said on the matter. But that really ministered to me because it put into real terms the meaning of faith on a personal basis: to acknowledge that God is the one who is going to take care of you.

"That little exchange has gone a long way in helping me as a businessman. Ultimately, you have to put your faith in God."

THOUGHTS FROM A LONG-TIME MEMBER

Marie Beth Johnson has been a member of Allen Temple for forty-five years. She has served under the guidance of four pastors there and served as Pastor Smith's secretary for a number of years.

"When Reverend Smith first came, I was a church secretary. He would say, 'Call these people and tell them such-and-such a thing.' And I would call these pastors, and they would ask, 'Who is this calling?' So I would tell them who I was and what I wanted. When I finished they would say, 'I don't talk to anybody but the pastor.'

"Finally, they carried on so that I told Pastor Smith, 'Pastor Smith, the gentlemen don't wish to talk to me. They want to talk to you directly.' So Pastor Smith got on the phone and *he* talked to them. After that I could talk to anybody I wanted to. I guess they got the word. He told them, *'You must respect women!'*

"A lot of churches in Oakland changed their policies about women in the pulpit because of Reverend Smith. Sometimes at the Good Friday services in our church, the men sing and the women preach the seven last words of Christ.

"Pastor Smith is not one to get favors. He will not be bought. I remember him standing in city hall and telling the powers that be, 'You do not pay my salary. My church pays my salary, and they let me speak, and I speak for them.' He told his congregation to stand up in city hall that night, and half of everybody in that room was from Allen Temple.

"To this day he's not one who has sold out. And I don't care what the rest of these people do, he won't trade us in. If Pastor decides to back a political candidate, he won't tell the church to do it. He says, 'I, J. Alfred Smith, support them.' He doesn't use his church to support any one position. Democrats, Republicans, Green Leaves, whatever—he'll bring them all up on stage and introduce them."

TAKING NAMES AT THE STATE PRISON

Deacon Mondy is a retired military officer and public school teacher.

"The warden at San Quentin State Prison came down to our church and said, 'I need some help.' He wanted to form an advisory committee with members of the community because the prison was experiencing a high rate of recidivism. So I figured this is God's work, and I felt good about it. I went to work and soon discovered that the program they had was not going to help the black boys.

"They had vocational training that was available if you wanted it. If you could get in, you could learn computer programming, dry cleaning, plumbing, electrical work, etc. However, there was a prerequisite that you had to have an eighth-grade education. Just a small percentage of blacks could get in.

"The entire board was white, except two Mexican guys and myself. The board thought that I was going soft on the inmates because I wanted to make the vocational programs easier to enroll in. I came back and told Pastor Smith about what happened. So he took Barbara Lee, who was a state assemblyperson at the time, and went directly to the warden. When I went up to San Quentin the next month, the warden was uptight. He wanted to know, 'What did you tell your pastor?' However, we got that program changed, and they broadened the scope of the courses available."

IN THE HALLS OF HIGHER EDUCATION

Reverend Martha Taylor is Reverend Smith's personal assistant.

"Recently I was in Washington, D.C., accepting an award on behalf of Dr. Smith from the Preaching Women of Shiloh Baptist Church. They honored Pastor Smith with an Agape Award for his support for the ministry of women.

"On a personal note, I am really in awe of the hand of God on my life for guiding me to come in contact with someone of the stature of Dr. Smith. He is so knowledgeable yet humble. Western society has yet to come up with a term to describe him. He is a prophet. And the love that he shows for our first lady, his wife Mrs. JoAnna Smith, makes him a role model not just for men but for all human beings.

"Because I work closely with Dr. Smith, I get to see a very gregarious personality that perhaps others don't get a chance to see. He is full of jokes. He will keep you laughing and then bounds right back into the serious side of life. And he loves books. If you ever say 'Dr. Smith, let's go to a bookstore,' he'll drop everything and say, 'Let's go.'

"Dr. Smith is the resident guru of the East Bay theological community. He is the professor of preaching at the eight seminaries of the Graduate Theological Union in Berkeley. Before the ink can dry on a new school catalog, students will be sending him notes asking for entrance into his class, which is limited to twelve students due to the constraints of personalized attention.

"The year before last, I told Dr. Smith, 'I think that they forgot to put a limit of twelve on your preaching class. I predict that there's going to be so many people taking your class . . .' He interrupted, 'Oh, no, no.' Well, the day that

class started, we had sixty-two people. People were flowing out into the hallway trying to get a seat in the lecture hall.

"Dr. Smith turned no one away. He got some sharp classroom aides to help
him. That semester he heard every single person preach. He gave them one-
on-one feedback and nurturing."

For more information on the ministries of Rev. Dr. J. Alfred Smith Sr. and the Allen Temple Baptist Church, contact:

Allen Temple Baptist Church
8501 International Boulevard
Oakland, CA 94621
Phone: (510) 544-8910
Fax: (510) 544-8918
www.allen-temple.org
www.jalfredsmithsr-ministries.org